The Changing Nature of Instructional Leadership in the 21st Century

A volume in
International Research on School Leadership
Alan R. Shoho, Bruce G. Barnett, and Autumn Tooms Cyprès, *Series Editors*

The Changing Nature of Instructional Leadership in the 21st Century

edited by

Bruce G. Barnett
University of Texas at San Antonio

Alan R. Shoho
University of Texas at San Antonio

Autumn Tooms Cyprès
University of Tennessee

INFORMATION AGE PUBLISHING, INC.
Charlotte, NC • www.infoagepub.com

Library of Congress Cataloging-in-Publication Data

The changing nature of instructional leadership in the 21st century / edited
by Bruce G. Barnett, Alan R. Shoho, Autumn Tooms.
    p. cm.
Includes bibliographical references.
ISBN 978-1-61735-938-5 (pbk.) – ISBN 978-1-61735-939-2 (hardcover) –
ISBN 978-1-61735-940-8 (ebook) 1. School management and organization. 2.
School supervision. 3. Educational leadership. I. Barnett, Bruce G. II.
Shoho, Alan R. III. Tooms, Autumn K., 1965-
LB2805.C472 2012
371.2–dc23

                                                          2012023959

DEDICATION

This book is dedicated to the principals, headteachers, headmasters, and other school leaders around the world who work tirelessly to improve the lives of students in their schools. Despite diminishing resources and mounting political pressure for reform, these school leaders persist in improving teachers' instructional and assessment practices. While these leaders are rarely acknowledged, the future generations of our societies are indebted to their devotion to teacher improvement and student learning. Through this book, their contributions and value to society are acknowledged. We also recognize the important roles teachers and system leaders play in supporting the instructional leadership efforts of school leaders.

CONTENTS

SECTION I

THE CONTEXT FOR INSTRUCTIONAL LEADERSHIP
AND SCHOOL IMPROVEMENT

SECTION II

INTERNATIONAL PERSPECTIVES OF INSTRUCTIONAL LEADERSHIP DEVELOPMENT

SECTION III

OBSTACLES AND CONSTRAINTS CONFRONTING INSTRUCTIONAL LEADERS

ACKNOWLEDGMENTS

Peer-reviewed publications exist because of the contributions of many people beyond the authors, editors, and publisher. As co-editors, we want to acknowledge the thoughtful guidance and commentary our peer reviewers provided. Their feedback to the authors allowed them to re-examine their assumptions, refine their ideas, and strengthen their knowledge base about 21st century instructional leadership.

Therefore, we thank the following individuals for serving as peer reviewers:

Alex Bowers, University of Texas at San Antonio
Sharon Brown-Welty, California State University, Fresno
Bradley Carpenter, University of Louisville
Casey Cobb, University of Connecticut
Gary Crow, Indiana University
John Daresh, University of Texas at El Paso
Lance Fusarelli, North Carolina State University
Helen Gunter, University of Manchester
Gene Hall, University of Nevada, Las Vegas
Pam Hallam, Brigham Young University
Jim Henderson, Duquesne University
Liz Hollingsworth, University of Iowa
Carol Karpinski, Farleigh Dickinson University
Sean Kearney, Texas A&M University, San Antonio
Kenneth Leithwood, Ontario Institute for Studies in Education
Carlos McCray, Fordham University
Peter Miller, University of Wisconsin, Madison

The Changing Nature of Instructional Leadership in the 21st Century, pages ix–x
Copyright © 2012 by Information Age Publishing

Ashley Oleszewski, University of Texas at San Antonio
Karen Osterman, Hofstra University
Cindy Reed, Auburn University
William Ruff, Montana State University
Martin Scanlan, Marquette University
Michael Silver, Seattle University
Amanda Taggart, Mississippi State University
Cynthia Uline, San Diego State University

CHAPTER 1

INTRODUCTION

**Bruce G. Barnett, Alan R. Shoho,
and Autumn Tooms Cyprès**

The volumes in the Information Age book series *International Research on School Leadership* examine the current-day challenges that affect instructional leadership. This third book in the series focuses on the changing nature of instructional leadership in the 21st century. Given the varying ways that instructional leadership has been conceived, studied, and practiced, the editors felt it would be valuable to explore the instructional leadership experiences of school-level and system-level leaders in supporting classroom instruction and student learning. From the effective schools research of the 1980s to today's relentless calls for improved student performance, attention has focused on the instructional leadership roles and responsibilities of school principals, headteachers, and educational system leaders. The emphasis on student performance has gone global as evidenced by highly-publicized international studies, such as the Trends in International Math and Science Studies (TIMSS) and the Program for International Student Assessment (PISA), comparing student achievement in different countries. As a result, school reform efforts aimed at improving students' learning outcomes have emerged around the globe.

These developments have had substantial effects on school leaders, especially building-level principals and headteachers. Rather than being the

The Changing Nature of Instructional Leadership in the 21st Century, pages 1–10
Copyright © 2012 by Information Age Publishing
All rights of reproduction in any form reserved.

only ones overseeing school improvement aimed at increasing student learning, many school administrators are distributing leadership responsibilities to other administrators and teachers on their campuses. To fully understand instructional leadership in the 21st century, the particular societal and organizational contexts in which school leaders find themselves must be taken into account. These shifts in leadership roles and responsibilities are occurring in a demanding policy environment where schools are being held accountable to show progress in serving increasingly diverse student populations.

Our goal in developing this edited book was to examine instructional leadership from multiple educational and international perspectives. Unlike many leadership books that focus on conceptualizations and personal narratives, the chapters in this book provide empirical evidence of how instructional leadership is evolving in the 21st century. In addressing these multiple perspectives, the seven chapters are organized into three sections. The first section (Chapters 2, 3, and 4) describes the current context for instructional leadership and school improvement by examining how school leaders strive to turn around low-performing schools, increase teacher effectiveness, and provide equitable outcomes for all students. In the second section (Chapters 5 and 6), attention is devoted to international perspectives of instructional leadership development, particularly the value of teacher coaching and leadership development for aspiring and practicing school leaders in a developing country. Finally, the obstacles instructional leaders confront as they deal with fiscal constraints, political pressure, diverse student populations, and high-stakes standards-based reforms are examined in the third section (Chapters 7 and 8).

In Chapter 2, The Judgment of Principals: A Key to Understanding Tough Calls and Instructional Leadership, Daniel Duke argues that a leader's judgment is both a skill set and an art form rarely examined within the field of leadership preparation. The chapter begins with a discussion of why researchers should devote greater attention to the judgments of instructional leaders, what the nature of judgment is, and why there is such a challenge to studying this area. Duke investigates through in-depth case study the judgment practices of 14 newly-appointed school turnaround principals. The term "turnaround principal" refers to school leaders who are charged with achieving quick and dramatic improvements in schools faced with sanctions under the No Child Left Behind Act and/or a state accountability system. Duke and his colleagues have been involved in studying turnaround principals since the University of Virginia launched its unique School Turnaround Specialist Program (STSP) in 2004. A collaboration between the Curry School of Education and the Darden Graduate School of Business Administration, the STSP grew out of Governor Mark Warner's belief that specially trained principals could effect quick and dramatic improvements in student achievement.

Findings of this research effort suggest that instructional leadership entails considerable reasoning and a variety of tough judgments. These judgments concern such matters as planning, staffing, operations, programs, leadership, and the distribution of one's time. Some of the judgment calls associated with school turnaround involved harder choices than others, but even seemingly obvious choices entailed opportunity costs. Because principals do not have access to unlimited resources, deciding to undertake one course of action may preclude a second, equally worthy course of action. The case studies demonstrate that turnaround principals live in a world where tradeoffs often are the rule, not the exception. Principals spent a great deal of effort considering whether they should seek assistance from the central office. For example, while principals desired support in removing or reassigning a teacher, they debated at length as to whether or not the request would be perceived by the central office as a sign of weakness or a lack of leadership. Understanding more about these variations and the reasoning behind them may yield clues to the differential effectiveness of principals. Is there a connection between judgment and effectiveness? Are principals able to recognize when they make bad judgments? Are bad judgments repeated? All of these questions speak to the huge need to study this line of inquiry with vigor.

Implications for those involved in preparing principals point directly to a need to increase the judgments of principals, as this knowledge could perhaps lead to more balanced instruction. Too heavy an emphasis on skills and competencies can suggest to prospective principals that judgment and reasoning are relatively unimportant attributes of leadership. While skill and competence are important, Duke maintains they are unlikely to compensate for bad judgment.

Chapter 3, Instructional Practice, Teacher Effectiveness, and Growth in Student Learning in Math: Implications for School Leadership, by Ronald Heck complements recent research that supports the view that school leadership facilitates growth in student learning (Leithwood, Day, Sammons, Harris, & Hopkins, 2006). The chapter extends the discussion of the role of school leadership by integrating two studies focused on the interplay among school leadership, teacher effectiveness, and student growth in math. Both studies employed a quantitative approach to data gathering and analysis. The first study examined the movement of 2,894 third and fourth grade students in 60 elementary schools over the course of two years. The study focused on the relationship between school leadership and its impact on teacher effectiveness at the classroom level. The second study examined 9,363 students in 154 elementary schools over four years, measuring teacher effectiveness in the middle of students' growth trajectories. Results from the first study demonstrated three findings relative to a school's instructional practices:

1. Teacher effectiveness influences students' ending math achievement at the classroom level.
2. Schools with a stronger focus on instruction had less variability in teacher effectiveness.
3. In schools with less variability in teacher effectiveness, ending math levels were higher.

Thus, Heck contends that instructionally related activity at a higher organizational level can influence the quality of individual activity at a lower level. This work is significant because it bridges the gap between what we think works in schools to authentic research that demonstrates what we know works in schools. The implications of this study speak to the importance of school leadership in terms of setting and maintaining a culture of teacher accountability centered on consistent instructional delivery.

The same arguments can be made for the implications of the results of the second study, which focused more heavily on teacher effectiveness and long-term student growth. Here again, schools with stronger, more consistent teacher effectiveness experienced more growth in math over time than schools with less consistently effective teachers. Considered in tandem, the results of these studies show that instructional practices, together with consistent teacher effectiveness, affect school growth in math. In other words, there is an overall positive effect on student success in schools where aggregate teacher effectiveness is consistent across grade levels. Because students experienced consistent teacher effectiveness as they matriculated, the chances for success were greater because the school faculty was consistent in its effectiveness and commitment to delivering quality instruction. And the one person most responsible for holding teachers accountable for the effective and consistent delivery is the principal. Overall, this study reveals the importance of principals knowing effective instructional practices, hiring and retaining quality teachers, and providing an instructional environment that values teacher collaboration and commitment. Heck concludes by noting that what remains is the challenge of configuring the puzzle of leadership in such a way that recognizes and honors teacher practice, student grouping, and instructional leadership.

Chapter 4, Leadership for Equity: Distributed Leadership in Linked Learning Schools, by Erica Hamilton and Jenifer Crawford-Lima examines the instructional leadership practices of principals in secondary schools in California using the Linked Learning (LL) model. The vision of LL schools is to provide an equitable approach to schooling by providing students with: a) college and career preparatory curricula, b) field-based learning opportunities, and c) individualized support. In their investigation, the authors report on four case studies of LL secondary schools to better understand how leadership is shared by revealing the similarities and differences across schools and the contextual factors affecting their shared instructional leadership practices.

Using interviews, observations, and document analysis over a two-year period, Hamilton and Crawford-Lima discovered several important elements regarding the instructional leadership practices in LL schools. First, these schools had clear visions for student success that were shared by teachers and administrators. Decisions about scheduling, hiring, personnel, budget, and professional development were guided by the shared vision. Similarly, the vision influenced teachers' collaborative cycle of planning and implementing thematic curriculum integration. Second, important resources, particularly key personnel and time, were essential for providing students with field-based learning opportunities and for leadership team members to meet to make operational decisions. Schools that did not provide these resources struggled in attempting to collaboratively plan and implement an integrated curriculum. Finally, teachers were provided a great deal of autonomy to develop and implement the curricula within the guidelines of the school vision. Teacher leadership emerged as small teams of teachers collaboratively planned their cross-curricular and career-thematic projects and mentored new teachers.

In summary, this study demonstrated that LL school principals were more likely to forego the traditional hierarchical, top-down model of leadership typically found in most secondary schools. Rather than taking sole responsibility for instructional decision making, these leaders employed a distributed approach to leadership by collaborating with teacher leadership teams to support the school's shared vision. The shared vision for student learning was largely the teachers' responsibility, especially grade-level teacher teams who shared the same students. Future research on these types of schools will be important to better understand the contextual factors that influence a more bottom-up, distributed style of leadership in secondary school settings.

Chapter 5, The Numeracy Coaching Program: An Examination of the Program Impact from the Training Room into School Classrooms, by Gary O'Mahony focuses on the design, structure, and impact of a math-centric program (The Bastow Institute's Numeracy Coaching Program) in Australian school classrooms. Guskey's (2000) professional development evaluation framework was used to examine the effects of the program. A mixed method (survey analysis and interviews) lens was used to analyze numeracy coaches' responses to two instruments: The Success Works Program Logic Survey and the Royal Melbourne Institute of Technology (RMIT) Numeracy Coaching Training Program Evaluation Report. The levels of Guskey's

(2000) framework were employed to examine the impact of the Numeracy Coaching Program based on: a) coaches' perceptions of the program, b) what coaches learned about coaching from the program, c) how various organizational structures affected their coaching roles, and d) how coaches used new skills in working with classroom teachers.

Responses to survey questions were analyzed using the constant comparative method (Glaser, 1965). The emerging patterns were discussed with RMIT staff to compare themes across the two sets of evaluation documents. Findings demonstrated that in order for change to occur through school-based coaching, an organizational infrastructure must be in place that values this model of instructional practice. Findings also illustrated that there is no better substitute for the primacy of making time for coaching within the school day. The emphasis on helping teachers enact small-scale classroom changes in teaching and learning with the support of a peer coach was an effective strategy for impacting consistent teacher growth. This harkens to Heck's chapter on the importance of school leaders setting and maintaining a consistent and clearly understood culture of effective teaching practices. Significant change in student achievement occurred when coaches were able to access specific support from school administration in terms of their roles as relationship builders, change agents, data coaches, and instructional models.

The findings of this study further suggest that coaches best develop via layers of learning that include storytelling, modeling, feedback, and reflection about experiences. Engaging in these activities within a support network of mentors, coaches, and peers is vital, and this work suggests that these conditions need to permeate coaching programs if they are to thrive. O'Mahony closes by recommending that future studies in this arena focus on extending the perspective of numeracy coaching efficacy by seeking insights from other school stakeholders, such as principals, teachers, students, and support staff. Finally, he reminds us that there is need to couple such inquiries with control groups of school coaches who have not been trained as numeracy coaches. While these kinds of designs are rare, Strong, Barrett, and Bloom's (2003) study of coaching for first- and second-year leaders is a good example of how to incorporate control groups for comparative purposes.

In Chapter 6, Responding to a Changing World: Challenges and Early Findings in Orchestrating a Principal Professional Development Program in Indonesian Schools, Khairan Indriani, Luana Zellner, and Steven Rose describe a developing country's attempt to create a principal preparation and development strategy. Recent legislation in Indonesia not only requires principals to practice transformational and instructional leadership competencies, but also to raise student outcomes by working collaboratively with multiple stakeholders. To assist aspiring and practicing principals in developing these competencies and achieving these outcomes, the Indonesian government has created regulations for the professional development of teachers, principals, and school supervisors. Two pilot programs have been launched to help aspirants and practicing administrators develop and refine their instructional leadership skills: a) the Principal Professional Program (PPP) for teachers who aspire to become principals and b) the Continuing Professional Development Program (CDP) for practicing principals. Both of these programs are part of the government's focus on improving educational outcomes for all Indonesian children.

The authors examine the initial implementation of the PPP and CPD to determine the effectiveness of the programs' procedures, training techniques, and training materials. For the PPP, the evaluation focused on the recruitment, selection, and training processes; several training modules in the CPD were examined to determine their effectiveness in developing transformational and instructional leadership competencies. Initial findings indicated that the PPP helped participants gain confidence and needed skills in preparing for school leadership roles. Similar results were found for the principals who participated in the CPD training. Program participants acknowledged the importance of creating tight linkages between what they learned and their "on the job" experiences. Despite these positive reactions, several challenges were identified, including how to sustain the programs over time, ensure program alignment across the country, develop an effective communication infrastructure for program coordination, and address potential delays in supervisor regulations and principal certification. The authors also suggest Indonesia will need to resolve the tensions of offering a national one-size-fits-all program against the backdrop of local control and uniqueness of a diverse country.

In Chapter 7, Leading with Less: Principal Leadership in Austere Times, Chad Lochmiller presents a two-year case study of how an urban K–7 school principal in the United States worked with her staff to implement district-imposed budget reductions. Given the declining resources facing most districts and schools, this study provides important insights about how principals can manage resources while maintaining the schools' instructional focus. As this principal demonstrated, astute instructional leaders can actively educate and engage staff in important resource-based decisions without sacrificing the instructional programs in their schools. When principals openly share budget reductions with staff, teachers not only become part of the decision-making process, but also determine viable ways of maintaining school improvement efforts aimed at sustaining student learning outcomes.

Lochmiller's case study illustrates specific instructional leadership strategies and actions principals can employ when dealing with severe budget cuts. On one hand, rather than acting alone, this principal actively sought to educate teachers about budget allocations by sharing the district's funding reductions with them. This collaborative process clearly demonstrated the principal's trust in her staff to examine possible options and make the best decisions possible for moving the school forward. One particularly effective strategy was to summarize two possible scenarios for staff to consider, one that maintained the school's focus on literacy and the other that addressed their growing ESL population. From these discussions, the staff realized the key differences between these options, particularly the implications for continuing to support a full-time literacy coach versus a full-time bilingual teacher. Their deliberations resulted in several staffing changes that focused their attention on the growing need to support programs for their language minority students.

On the other hand, the principal made it clear that certain staffing allocations were non-negotiable based on contractual obligations and previous commitments the staff had made. Besides acknowledging their need to comply with district and state policies, she maintained the importance of protecting several staff roles, including a full-time assistant principal and a half-time counselor. These positions were essential for her to be able to visit classrooms and work with teachers and for the school to serve their increasingly diverse student population and families. Declaring these non-negotiables at the beginning of the process was an effective way of alerting staff about what was in their control versus what was beyond their influence. Overall, this case study clearly shows the important instructional leadership role principals play when they are forced to reduce resources and still maintain instructional quality and school improvement.

Chapter 8, School-Based Instructional Leadership in Demanding Environments: New Challenges, New Practices, by Michael Knapp, Simangele Mkhwanazi, and Brad Portin provides a conceptual analysis of the changing landscape of instructional leadership. They challenge the traditional view of instructional leadership residing in a singular person like the principal. Instead, they suggest four interrelated dimensions of instructional leadership, each with theoretical as well as empirical roots that have come into prominence in the past decade. Each of these dimensions of instructional leadership is explored based on three questions: 1) what is the nature of the leadership work and who carries it out? 2) in what senses is it "new" work that departs from and adds to the work that instructional leaders might have done, or thought they needed to do, in prior years? and 3) in what ways does the new work reflect and respond to the conditions of schooling set by a high-stakes, standards-based reform environment?

The "new" work of instructional leadership suggested by Knapp and colleagues are: 1) orienting instructional improvement to the growing diversity of the classroom; 2) grounding instructional conversations in data, evidence, and inquiry; 3) working within and through instructional leadership teams; and 4) engaging demanding environments as a resource for instructional improvement. Using a three-level framework (i.e., professional learning, student learning, and system learning) to guide this "new" work of instructional leaders, Knapp and his colleagues provide a perspective that is more distributed, team oriented, and less dependent on the principal. In their view, instructional leadership occurs at multiple levels by formal and informal school leaders. Incorporating a perspective that views challenges as opportunities rather than obstacles, the authors provide the field with a rich, fresh way to examine and conceive instructional leadership. Their perspective also takes the weight off of principals to be the sole instructional leader and lends credence to the power of distributing the instructional expertise among educators with the most knowledge and skills.

Using empirical evidence and conceptual analyses, these chapters provide a portrait of the complexity of instructional leadership in the 21st century. One theme running through several chapters is the importance of understanding the nature of the decisions and issues today's instructional leaders are encountering. As leaders today are confronted by difficult judgments when attempting to quickly implement improvements, contentious budgetary cuts to staff and programs, massive educational reforms, and increasingly diverse student populations, these authors demonstrate that instructional leaders are still able to maintain their focus on quality teaching and learning. A second, and related, theme is how effective instructional leaders must enable teachers to contribute to the entire school's success, not just those students in their individual classrooms. By implementing consistent teaching practices over time, supporting teacher coaches, allowing teams of teachers to plan and deliver the curriculum, and involving the school staff in making important budgetary decisions, today's instructional leaders are being more publicly accountable for and transparent about school improvement, a practice Fullan (1998) advocated over a decade ago.

Although this volume will not be the last word on 21st century instructional leadership, the authors provide insightful glimpses of the realities of schools where principals are committed to instructional improvement and student learning for all children. We are indebted to the authors for sharing their work and insights and believe educators around the world can benefit from their messages.

REFERENCES

Fullan, M. (1998). Leadership for the 21st century: Breaking the bonds of dependency. *Educational Leadership, 55*(7), 6–10.

Glaser, B. G. (1965). The constant comparative method of qualitative analysis. *Social Problems, 12,* 436–445.

Guskey, T. R. (2000). *Evaluating professional development.* Thousand Oaks, CA: Corwin Press.

Leithwood, K., Day, C., Sammons, P., Harris, A., & Hopkins, D. (2006). *Seven strong claims about successful school leadership*. Nottingham, England: National College of School Leadership.

Strong, M., Barrett, A., & Bloom, G. (2003, April). *Supporting the new principal: Managerial and instructional leadership in a principal induction program*. Paper presented at the annual meeting of the American Educational Research Association, Chicago, IL.

SECTION I

THE CONTEXT FOR INSTRUCTIONAL LEADERSHIP
AND SCHOOL IMPROVEMENT

CHAPTER 2

THE JUDGMENT
OF PRINCIPALS

A Key to Understanding Tough Calls and Instructional Leadership

Daniel L. Duke

Wilma Williams faced a tough choice. As the newly appointed principal of Keswick Elementary School, she was charged with raising student achievement and "turning the school around." Williams understood that the School Board, the superintendent, and the community expected quick results. Unable to replace faculty members, she would need to gain the trust of teachers who had been at Keswick during its decline. These teachers had spent several years implementing Montessori teaching methods and curriculum units. Several teachers had received advanced graduate training in Montessori pedagogy. They believed that this approach to instruction was a good fit for Keswick students, most of whom were from poor families. Wilma Williams did not share this opinion. When she looked at student performance on state reading tests, she felt that a more structured approach to teaching literacy was required.

The Changing Nature of Instructional Leadership in the 21st Century, pages 13–32
Copyright © 2012 by Information Age Publishing
All rights of reproduction in any form reserved.

Should Williams replace the Montessori approach with a more structured literacy program? Doing so would threaten to incur faculty resentment before she had a chance to gain teachers' trust. Or should she defer making a decision about Montessori instruction and run the risk of another year of sub-par achievement on state reading tests? Perhaps Keswick teachers needed another year to perfect Montessori practices. But what if the Montessori methods really were ill-suited to the needs of Keswick students?

Clearly there were possible negative consequences associated with either choice. Since Williams was new to the school, there also might have been additional information that could have helped her make a decision. Time, however, did not allow her to gather more information. It was late August, and Williams needed to abandon Montessori or allow it to continue for another year.

Wilma Williams, like hundreds of her fellow "turnaround principals" in post-No Child Left Behind public schools, was expected to be an instructional leader.[1] Facing the effects of sustained low student achievement, these principals must effect "quick and dramatic" improvements in instruction, instructional interventions, curriculum alignment, and data-driven decision making. To do so necessitates dozens, if not hundreds, of tough calls like the one Williams had to make. This paper takes the position that instructional leadership cannot be fully understood until we know about the hard judgments instructional leaders are compelled to make and why they make them.

The chapter begins with a discussion of why researchers should devote greater attention to the judgments of instructional leaders. The following section examines the nature of judgment and the challenges of studying them. The main portion of the paper is devoted to an investigation of judgments made by 14 newly appointed school turnaround principals. The paper concludes with a call for more focused research on the judgments of principals.

WHY FOCUS ON INSTRUCTIONAL LEADERS' JUDGMENT?

Recognition of the importance of instructional leadership dates back to the earliest school effectiveness studies (Duke, 1987), but relatively little attention has been paid to the tough decisions, or judgment calls, that instructional leaders may have to make in order to raise student achievement. In their study of improving and declining elementary schools, Brookover and Lezotte (1979), for example, found that principals of the improving schools were more likely to function as instructional leaders, assuming responsibility for evaluating the achievement of instructional objectives and ensuring that classrooms were orderly and productive learning environments.

The researchers focused on what principals did, not the reasoning behind their actions. Efforts to conceptualize instructional leadership followed in the wake of the initial school effectiveness studies (Duke, 1987). What distinguished the conceptions of instructional leadership was the emphasis on the behaviors and functions of principals. Decisions and judgment calls received little attention. Instructional leadership came to represent "those actions that a principal takes, or delegates to others, to promote growth in student learning" (DeBevoise, 1984, p. 15).

The most widely researched conception of instructional leadership to date has been Hallinger's (2011) Principal Instructional Management framework. Three overarching functions—defining the school mission, managing the instructional program, and developing the school learning climate program—make up Hallinger's framework, and each function consists of several specific behaviors. Drawing on the work of Hallinger and others, Duke (1987) developed a model of instructional leadership involving seven "situations": teacher supervision and development, teacher evaluation, instructional management and support, resource management, quality control, coordination, and troubleshooting. The term "situations" was employed because this author maintained that instructional leadership entailed more than behaviors or functions:

> Handling each of these situations well requires far more than a particular skill or set of competencies. The situations constitute complex configurations of intentions, activities, people, and interrelationships. They call for a variety of technical skills and professional judgments, adapted to the particular needs of the moment. Since these needs are ever-changing, no single prescription for dealing with a given situation will suffice. (Duke, 1987, pp. 81–82)

The study of instructional leadership has continued since early efforts to conceptualize it, but investigations have tended to focus on the behaviors associated with instructional leadership (Leithwood & Duke, 1999). Relatively little attention has been devoted to the judgments made in the course of exercising instructional leadership. The lack of attention to judgment is somewhat surprising given the growing interest in the cognitive dimensions of educational leadership and the moral and ethical challenges facing school leaders (Begley, 1996). More will be said of these developments in the next section.

The reality of school leadership is that judgment is unavoidable. Simply deciding how to spend one's time as a principal can be a judgment of critical importance, given the fact that most principals cannot accomplish everything that could be done to promote teaching and learning. Each day in a principal's life becomes an exercise in temporal triage. Then there are the issues involving personnel, the allocation of scarce resources, and how to deal with discipline. All of which is to make the case that instructional leadership is more than a matter of "how"—it also involves matters of what, when, where, with whom, and whether or not. Instructional leadership, in other words, is a matter of judgment.

THINKING ABOUT LEADERS' JUDGMENT

Philosophers were among the first scholars to seek an understanding of judgment, and their efforts often focused on moral reasoning and its resulting judgments. Dewey (1910) took a more scientific approach in *How We Think*, linking judgment to phases of the problem-solving process. Interest in the judgment of leaders burgeoned among social scientists after World War II and led to various efforts to measure the phenomenon and develop a "general theory of executive judgment" (Forehand & Guetzkow, 1962). Judgment tended to be equated with decision making in much of this work (March & Simon, 1959; Simon, 1976). In one well-know study, researchers collected ratings of executives' decision-making from their superiors and co-workers (Forehand & Guetzkow, 1962). The decision categories for which ratings were gathered ranged from routine to complex decisions.

As the study of judgment expanded, efforts were made to distinguish judgment from routine decision making. In his investigation of the relationship between executive judgment and organizational performance, Priem (1994) regarded judgment as a "strategic choice." Mowen (1993) identified a variety of "judgment calls" that CEOs were likely to face at some point. A judgment call occurs, according to Mowen (1993), "when a decision maker must make a tough choice between two or more options based upon ambiguous information and conflicting goals" (p. 9). Examples of judgment calls for Mowen included choosing between present and future needs, risk and security, and staying the course or quitting.

Tichy and Bennis (2007) added another layer of complexity to the study of executive judgment by conceptualizing judgment as a multi-phased process involving preparation, the moment of decision, and execution of the decision. A judgment that is not successfully executed, they contended, "is a failed judgment no matter how smart the strategy" (Tichy & Bennis, 2007, p. 96).

While few studies of education leaders have employed "judgment" as a construct, there has been growing interest among researchers in the cognitive dimensions of school and district leadership. Hallinger and McCary (1990), for example, argued persuasively that "the research on instructional leadership must address the thinking that underlies the exercise of leadership, not simply describe discrete behaviors of effective leaders" (p. 89). Spillane and his colleagues (Spillane, Halverson, & Diamond, 2001) made the case that the thinking of school leaders is situated and cannot be understood without taking into account the context within which it takes place. This position is important because many of the studies of decision making by school and district leaders have been based on simulations, not job-embedded situations (Leithwood & Steinbach, 1995). How well these contrived exercises represent how leaders actually think is unclear.

Despite relying on hypothetical situations, Leithwood and Steinbach (1995) offered valuable insights into the problem-solving behavior of principals and superintendents. The researchers presented leaders with a variety of practical problems, some of which were routine and "structured" and others of which were ill-defined and "unstructured." In one study, principals identified as "experts" differed from principals identified as "typical" in the way they approached various aspects of problem solving, including problem definition and the development of solutions. Leithwood and Steinbach concluded that problem solving is best understood as a complex construct consisting of six key elements: interpretation, goals, principles and values, constraints, solution process, and effect.

There is little doubt that decision making and problem solving provide many opportunities for judgment calls. It is important, however, to bear in mind Mowen's (1993) conception of a judgment call as a "tough choice between two or more options based upon ambiguous information and conflicting goals" (p. 9). The point to be made is that some decisions and problems, as Leithwood recognized, are relatively routine (Leithwood & Steinbach, 1995). They do not involve, in other words, "tough choices." Judgment calls represent that sub-set of decisions for which trade-offs and compromises must be considered. Making such decisions compels the decision maker to acknowledge the possibility of undesirable consequences and unexpected outcomes.

One of the most substantial bodies of scholarship on the "tough choices" confronting principals and superintendents concerns moral and ethical dilemmas (Beckner, 2004; Strike, Haller, & Soltis, 1988). This work focuses on decisions involving conflicting principles and values. One reason these decisions can be so challenging, according to Strike, Haller, and Soltis (1988), is the fact that scientific inquiry may offer little help:

> It is not clear that any amount of scientific inquiry can tell us whether an evaluation is fair, whether a decision is democratic, or whether some allocation of resources is equitable. Indeed, sometimes we can know what the consequences of our actions will be but not know if the action itself is right ... We need to make moral as well as management judgments. (p. 15)

The scholarship addressing moral and ethical dilemmas raises a number of troubling questions related to leader judgment. Should a principal, for example, risk an undesirable outcome for the sake of a principle? As a professional, a principal may recognize the importance of treating every student as an individual. But such actions can create problems. What an educator intends to be personalized attention can be perceived as favoritism and discriminatory practice. Another troubling question concerns utilitarian choices. Should a leader make decisions based on the greatest good for the greatest number? Such decisions can place various minorities in a vulnerable position.

The final word on leader judgment is far from being written, but a cursory review of the literature provides some guidance for more focused investigation of the judgment of principals. Judgment, first of all, involves thinking as well as action. It should be distinguished from routine decision making and problem solving. Judgment calls necessitate "tough choices" between conflicting values, opposing intentions, or uncertain outcomes. To understand the judgment calls leaders are compelled to make, it is best to look at actual leaders as they go about the real work of guiding their organizations, rather than relying on responses to hypothetical situations.

EXPLORING THE JUDGMENT CALLS
OF TURNAROUND PRINCIPALS

Principals charged with turning around low-performing schools are likely to confront a variety of situations requiring tough choices to be made. So much needs to be done in these schools, but everything cannot be undertaken at once. Where should the turnaround process begin? What initiatives are best deferred? Should efforts focus on students most likely to pass tests or students who are furthest behind their peers? What should be done if resistance is encountered? Such questions reflect some of the judgment calls that may need to be made.

The author and various colleagues have been involved in studying turnaround principals since the University of Virginia launched its unique School Turnaround Specialist Program (STSP) in 2004. A collaboration between the Curry School of Education and the Darden Graduate School of Business Administration, the STSP grew out of Governor Mark Warner's belief that specially trained principals could effect quick and dramatic improvements in student achievement.

Between 2005 and 2011, 14 studies of turnaround principals participating in the STSP were undertaken. Two are in-depth case studies of Virginia elementary principals and their efforts over several years to achieve school turnarounds (Duke & Landahl, 2011; Duke & Salmonowicz, 2010). The other 12 studies are less detailed accounts of the challenges of leading the first year of the turnaround process. Ten accounts describe the work of Virginia principals (six elementary and four middle school principals) in the first STSP cohort (Duke et al., 2005). The other pair of accounts involve two Texas high school principals who were chosen to participate in the STSP in 2010 (Duke & Jacobson, 2011). It must be acknowledged that only two of the studies (Duke & Landahl, 2011; Duke & Salmonowicz, 2010) were designed specifically as investigations of a principal's judgment calls, but all the studies offer examples of and insights into the kinds of judgments turnaround principals are called upon to make. Every study was based on extensive interviews with the turnaround principal and on-site observations.

The present investigation entailed a careful review of each study along with the interview transcripts and notes upon which the study was based. The reviews focused on identifying "tough choices" made by the principals in their efforts to raise student achievement. Routine decisions and choices that did not involve ambiguous information and conflicting goals were omitted. No claim is made that the 14 studies captured all of the judgment calls that principals had to make in order to implement the school turnaround process. Nor is there sufficient evidence to link particular judgment calls with any outcomes. The findings that appear in the next section are simply suggestive of the kinds of judgment calls that principals may have to make in order to improve student achievement. The author believes that these judgment calls also reflect the kinds of decision-making challenges associated with instructional leadership.

Once all 14 studies were reviewed and judgment calls were identified, a system for classifying them based on their primary focus was developed. Most of the judgment calls fell into one of five categories: 1) planning, 2) staffing, 3) operations, 4) programs, and 5) approach to leadership. The next section looks at examples from each of these categories.

NO SHORTAGE OF TOUGH CHOICES

The purpose of this section is to provide concrete examples of the range of judgment calls that may be occasioned by efforts to turn around low-performing schools. None of the examples that surfaced in the studies should be regarded, however, as inevitable. A tough choice in one setting may be a straightforward decision in another. Every judgment is situated in a physical, cultural, temporal, and political context.

Planning for School Turnaround

All of the principals engaged in extensive planning for the first year of the turnaround process. Indeed, they were required to do so by state authorities and the STSP at the University of Virginia. Planning occasioned many judgment calls, and they can be sorted into four clusters: 1) setting priorities, 2) establishing measurable targets, 3) determining "first steps," and 4) considering mid-course corrections. Examples are presented below to illustrate each type of judgment call.

Setting priorities. The literature on instructional leadership underscores what each of the turnaround principals soon came to realize. There is more to be done to improve a low-performing school than can be accomplished in the first year of the turnaround process. Energies and resources must be focused on critical goals, leaving other goals to be tackled at a later time. Most of the principals initially were inclined to focus on too many priorities. They did so for obvious reasons. It is hard to decide to concentrate on two or three goals, knowing that other important concerns must be set aside or given less attention. Still, all principals eventually recognized that working on too many priorities risked undermining the entire turnaround process.

When it came to student achievement, the judgment calls regarding what to focus on in year one of school turnaround were relatively obvious for most of the principals. Each one understood that they had to raise student achievement for certain sub-groups of students in certain subjects in order to meet state and/or federal requirements. Achievement in reading/language arts and English was a focus for every principal. Nonetheless, there still were some tough choices for several principals. Matt Landahl had to choose between improving reading instruction for Greer Elementary School's upper elementary students or rebuilding reading instruction from the ground (kindergarten) up. He opted for the former, fearing that doing otherwise would mean sending students to middle school who still struggled with reading.

Landahl made another decision regarding the priorities for his first year at Greer. Worried that too singular a focus on raising test scores could backfire and foster an environment in which students became mere numbers, he developed a second goal to improve the climate at Greer. Strategies for achieving this goal included creating a variety of student clubs and engaging parents and students in sharing their cultures (Greer enrolled students from many countries and ethnic backgrounds).

Melissa Marshall, principal of Perrymont Middle School, knew that reading and mathematics had to be the focus of improvement efforts at her school. Knowing her resources would be stretched to the limit, she made a judgment call regarding what not to do. She tendered a request with the Virginia Department of Education to drop science and social studies as separate subjects until students demonstrated greater success with reading, writing, and mathematics. Such a choice entailed obvious risks, but she reasoned that improving the basics would pay dividends eventually. State authorities agreed and granted her waiver.

Besides raising student achievement, the turnaround plans developed by each principal typically involved several additional goals. These goals tended to be context-sensitive. They included changing school culture, developing interventions for struggling students, and promoting data-driven decision making. At Addison Magnet Middle School, Sharon Richardson decided that one of the first orders of business had to be establishing order and discipline. She determined that there could be little sustained instructional success with over 2,000 annual disciplinary referrals in a school of 500 students. The judgment call for Richardson had less to do with the need to improve discipline than how to do it. Should she focus on tightening up rule enforcement and surveillance? Would behavior be more likely to improve if the quality of instruction were better? She chose the former course of action, but not without some misgivings.

Richardson's judgment call illustrates why deciding on priorities can be especially challenging. Deciding on how to address goals necessitates judgments about the relationships between the causes of problems and their symptoms. It is easy to confuse symptoms with causes. Is misbehavior the result of poor teaching or lax enforcement or both? Choosing to focus on correcting symptoms instead of getting to root causes can ensure that problems eventually resurface.

Establishing measurable targets. As part of the turnaround planning process, principals were required to set measurable targets for goals related to improvements in student achievement. Far from an inconsequential exercise, deciding on targets for improvement can have immediate and long-term impacts on a school. If targets are set too high, faculty may feel that success is impossible. Less ambitious targets, on the other hand, may not generate the sense of urgency and concerted effort necessary to achieve a true turnaround.

Some of the principals decided to choose targets based on state-determined benchmarks linked to the federal No Child Left Behind Act. These benchmarks entailed achieving a designated passing rate on state tests or making a minimum percentage gain in passing rate ("safe harbor"). Other principals elected to aim for targets well above state-designated benchmarks. One elementary principal, for example, chose an 80 percent passing rate on state reading and mathematics tests as her school's target. A 70 percent passing rate would have met state requirements. Her school failed to achieve an 80 percent passing rate, which resulted in faculty disappointment and community concern. Her school was closed the following year.

Determining first steps. Every school turnaround initiative has to begin somewhere—a first act or symbolic gesture to let stakeholders know that things are changing. Most of the principals were appointed during the summer, and they gave considerable attention to the signals they wanted to send when school began. Low-performing schools have been characterized as "demoralized" environments (Payne, 2008). The stakeholders in such settings often lack confidence that conditions can ever improve. Turnaround principals face the challenge of choosing a few "quick wins" to demonstrate their ability to get things done for the benefit of the school. Selecting the wrong first step, one that results in stumbling instead of forward strides, can serve only to re-confirm a sense of failure for teachers, students, and community members.

Most of the "quick wins" chosen by the turnaround principals did not entail especially tough choices. Some principals got central office support to clean up school yards and put a fresh coat of paint on facilities. Ten principals made adjustments in the master schedule that enabled teachers to plan together during the school day and provided opportunities for struggling students to receive special help.

J. Harrison-Coleman, however, had to make a genuine judgment call to launch her turnaround efforts at Clarke Elementary School. She wanted parents to visit the school, but she did not want them interfering with instruction. Her predecessor had allowed parents in the neighboring housing project to come to school with their children and share in the breakfast program. The problem was that the parents continued to hang around the school after classes started, resulting in student tardiness and occasional disruptions. Parents also had been allowed to go directly to classes in the afternoon when they wanted their children to leave school before the last bell. Harrison-Coleman decided to limit parent access to the breakfast program and require parents to sign in at the office if they wanted their children to leave school. Instead of achieving a "quick win," Harrison-Coleman found herself on local television explaining why angry parents were demonstrating in front of her school. Her actions, however, sent the message that the school had a new leader, one whose goal was to protect instructional time.

Mid-course corrections. Planning is best regarded as a process, not an event. The STSP at the University of Virginia warns principals not to allow annual turnaround plans to sit on shelves gathering dust. One way to ensure that members of a school community continue to be mindful of their turnaround plan is to schedule times during the year when progress on the plan is reviewed. These times can lead to a variety of judgment calls and mid-course corrections. Is a new program working as expected, or should it be replaced before the end of the school year? How is a teacher who has been reassigned faring? Should the re-assignment be reconsidered? Waiting until the end of the school year to make adjustments in a turnaround plan can jeopardize students' opportunities to improve.

When Nancy Weisskopf became principal of South Hills High School, she made certain that struggling students had opportunities after school when they could receive assistance from teachers. Had she not checked up on the status of extended learning time, she would not have discovered that few students availed themselves of help sessions. Weisskopf convened an advisory group of students and asked them why they were not taking advantage of extended learning time. They told her that they were too tired at the end of the school day to stay after school. Some students had after-school jobs and other commitments. The students recommended scheduling help sessions on Monday evenings from six to eight o'clock. Weisskopf followed their advice, and contributed free pizzas for students who showed up. "Monday Madness," as these sessions came to be known, turned out to be a big success and a key to South Hills' turnaround.

Staffing for School Turnaround

Principals frequently admit that their toughest decisions involve school personnel. The turnaround principals probably would concur. Judgment calls were required regarding whether or not to remove or re-assign staff members. There is no set of guidelines for determining if teachers are performing inadequately because they are mis-assigned or because they lack the capacity to get the job done regardless of the assignment. Principals also must decide whether targeted professional development is likely to result in instructional improvement or simply delay the inevitable decision to remove teachers.

Each of the 14 turnaround principals inherited schools in which the quality of teaching was questionable. In the case of Nancy Weisskopf, she was *required* by her school system to replace at least 60 percent of the existing faculty. Her judgment calls focused on deciding which teachers should be retained because they had the potential to contribute to a turnaround at South Hills and which should be let go.

Other principals zeroed in on a few teachers who either were openly resistant to changes or who clearly lacked the competence to work with struggling students. Isabel Garza decided to replace the guidance counselors at Reagan High School after seeing that they had failed to ensure that dozens of students were accumulating the credits they needed to graduate. Deciding to document and remove staff members is almost always a risky decision, since it can result in a backlash from teachers, promote paranoia, and lead to time-consuming grievances from the teachers' union. There also is no guarantee the central office will be supportive. Failing to take action against unproductive and uncooperative staff members, of course, also involves risks. With several exceptions, the turnaround principals decided the latter risks were greater, and they followed through with decisions to remove teachers. One exception was a principal in a rural school who doubted that he could find better teachers to replace those about which he was concerned. He instead initiated a professional development program in the hopes of improving instruction.

Wayne Scott chose a different course of action at George Mason Elementary School. He detected significant disparities in the abilities of teachers to handle different content areas. Despite the potential for disruptions to the school day and possible curriculum coordination problems, he decided to implement departmentalization on a school-wide basis. He picked teachers who were effective at teaching mathematics to handle all mathematics instruction. Other teachers focused on language arts. His judgment call paid off and scores on state tests rose across the board.

When Wilma Williams found out that the central office refused to support her request to transfer several unsupportive teachers, she decided to re-assign them to jobs she knew they would not like. Williams hoped that the teachers would opt to resign rather than move to a different grade-level. She understood that her judgment call might backfire if the teachers decided to stay, but her hopes were realized when they chose to leave Keswick Elementary School.

Another kind of judgment involving school personnel concerned whom to trust and whom to count on to exercise leadership. Most of the turnaround principals were new to their schools, and, as a result, they were uncertain about which individuals to take into their confidence. Nor did they know with any certainty which teachers were prepared to function as peer leaders. Matt Landahl purposely held off for a year convening his predecessor's leadership council, made up of grade-level leaders, until he had an opportunity to judge the capabilities and commitments of individuals.

Operational Judgment Calls

During the first year of the turnaround process each of the principals had to make some challenging decisions related to school operations. The most common judgment calls involved the daily schedule, structures for teacher collaboration, and provisions for professional development.

Schedule changes. As indicated earlier, most principals decided to launch their turnaround efforts with a new daily schedule, one that provided opportunities for common planning time and assistance for struggling students. At the elementary level, common planning time typically was set aside when students participated in electives. Several principals decided that students who needed extra help in core subjects should receive assistance while their classmates attended electives. Some teachers of electives felt marginalized by these decisions, but principals reasoned that it was more important to address students' problems in reading and mathematics. Matt Landahl chose to increase instructional time in reading for all students, not just those experiencing difficulties. He boosted instructional time for reading to 150 minutes a day. To get the extra minutes for reading, he reduced mathematics instruction from 120 to 90 minutes a day, reasoning that the math scores for Greer students had risen sufficiently to no longer be a focus of concern. The risk, of course, was that reducing math time might result in slippage.

The middle and high school principals opted to create daily schedules that enabled struggling students to be double blocked in language arts/ English and mathematics. Requiring these students to spend twice as much time in core courses reduced the time available to take elective courses. Once again, principals recognized the problem but decided that some students were more in need of work on core content.

Structures for collaboration. Principals know that they cannot single-handedly turn around a school. Teamwork is an essential ingredient in successful turnarounds. Teamwork, though, does not just happen spontaneously. Each of the 14 turnaround principals had to lay the groundwork to support teacher collaboration because their predecessors had failed to do so.

Judgment calls were required regarding how much groundwork to lay and how soon to lay it. All of the principals believed that teachers needed to be engaged in analyzing data. They decided early on to introduce short-cycle (interim) tests in core content areas so that teachers would know which students were progressing and which students were lagging behind. Structures were needed, however, to ensure that teachers at the same grade-level or from the same content area conducted productive discussions of test data, discussions that would lead to targeted interventions for struggling students. Elementary principals relied primarily on grade-level teams to track student progress, while secondary principals relied on both grade-level teams and content-based teams.

To ensure that the curriculum was aligned across grade-levels, most of the principals also decided to establish vertical teams of teachers. Sometimes the vertical teams accomplished their work during the summer. In other cases, they met during the school year. Principals charged the vertical teams with ensuring that teachers at each grade-level covered content mandated by the state.

Wayne Scott initiated cross-grade-level homogeneous grouping in reading and mathematics. Teachers at George Mason Elementary School met on a regular basis to adjust groups in accordance with student performance. Grouping students by performance rather than age and grade-level can be very challenging when teachers are unused to cooperation across grade-levels. The arrangement worked at Mason, but it did not work at Greer. Matt Landahl believed that the success of his efforts to promote grouping across classrooms at the same grade-level justified the move to grouping across grade-levels. He discovered, however, that he mis-judged the capacity of his teachers to implement this arrangement, and he decided to revert to within-grade-level grouping.

Nancy Weisskopf opted to convene data analysis sessions with each academic department at South Hills High School at the end of the first semester. The progress of every student was reviewed at these sessions. Weiss-kopf asked teachers to predict which students were likely to pass particular courses and which students were likely to fail. An assistance program had to be developed for each of the latter group.

The most radical effort to promote teacher collaboration took place at Greer Elementary School, but not until the third year of Matt Landahl's tenure as principal. By this time he had hired over half the faculty, and he felt confident that most teachers bought into his vision for the school. He initiated a committee structure that devolved considerable responsibility for school operations to teacher-led groups. Committees took charge of improving achievement in reading and writing, promoting technology, revising the daily schedule, improving within-school and school-home communications, and enhancing school culture. Landahl understood that he was taking a calculated risk. If the committees failed to deliver, he would be blamed. The committees might siphon off teacher time and energy needed to meet instructional responsibilities. Landahl believed, however, in the potential of teacher leadership to improve the quality of education at Greer.

Professional development. Providing teachers with on-the-job training, in and of itself, is no panacea. Most of the principals' predecessors had offered occasional opportunities for teachers to work on professional development, but they had failed to produce significant improvements in teaching and learning. The turnaround principals understood that professional development, in order to be effective, needed to be aligned with specific school improvement goals. They also realized that what teachers learned in workshops and training sessions had to be reinforced and monitored.

All 14 turnaround principals targeted data analysis as a focus for professional development. This decision was not an especially difficult one. What was more challenging was determining how to gather performance data on a regular basis so teachers could analyze it. Principals grappled with using commercially available benchmark tests versus teacher-made interim assessments. They considered how frequently to monitor student progress. Some principals opted for nine-week assessments, while others decided to implement more frequent check-ups. The principals weighed the benefits of regular assessments against fears that teaching might be displaced by testing. When interim assessments every four-and-a-half weeks in all four core subjects became too much of a burden for teachers at Keswick Elementary, Wilma Williams made a mid-course correction, requiring short-cycle assessments only in reading and mathematics.

Another frequently chosen focus for professional development was literacy and language arts. Principals realized that many of their teachers had received little or no training in how to teach reading and writing. Deciding on the best way to make up for fundamental training deficits posed various challenges, however. Should training take place during the school day, after school, on released days, or over the summer? Should training be led by district specialists, outside consultants, or staff members at the school? What should be the principal's role in the process? Should principals reinforce training through the supervision and evaluation processes?

Anabel Garza faced a different kind of judgment call at Reagan High School. She debated whether or not to continue a district-supported professional development program. Her predecessor had initiated the expensive program, but Garza doubted that it fit Reagan's immediate needs. The training was heavily process-oriented and entailed lots of pair-and-shares and round robins. Teachers questioned the value of these activities. Though she knew that some of her superiors were committed to the training, Garza believed that her faculty was more in need of work on curriculum alignment and pacing. Risking the displeasure of the central office, she scrapped the training and initiated focused training tied to the curriculum.

Program Judgment Calls

Because schools facing turnarounds have struggled with student achievement for years, they are likely to have experimented with a variety of programs intended to raise achievement. Each of the 14 turnaround principals in the present cases needed to examine existing programs and determine if they should be continued, modified, or abandoned. Judgment calls had to be made regarding whether these programs had been in place a sufficient amount of time to have worked or if they needed additional time. Principals needed to decide if lack of program success was due to flaws in program design or problems with program implementation. Was more training required for a program to succeed? Were the wrong staff members assigned to implement the program? Was the program a poor fit for student needs?

The opening vignette described Wilma Williams' judgment call about Keswick Elementary School's Montessori program. She decided that the self-pacing nature of Montessori learning was ill-suited to the needs of Keswick students and that a more highly structured reading program would stand a better chance of raising reading achievement. Matt Landahl had similar misgivings about the district-mandated "guided reading" program, but he decided that dropping it at the same time he was asking teachers to initiate cross-grade-level reading groups would over-tax the faculty. He opted instead to *encourage* teachers working with struggling readers to use more direct instruction.

Both Landahl and Anabel Garza took a hard look at the after-school tutorial programs in their schools. Under the No Child Left Behind Act, they were required to offer parents after-school tutoring at no cost. Tutoring was provided by private vendors. The two principals observed tutoring sessions and concluded that they were generally unproductive. Landahl and Garza discontinued arrangements with some tutorial outfits, and Garza hired Sylvan Learning to train Reagan High School's remaining tutors.

Besides making decisions about what to do with existing programs, principals made judgment calls concerning new programs. If they determined that a new program was needed to address a turnaround goal, they next had to decide whether it was best to create the program or adopt or adapt a commercially available program. Considerations involved weighing the cost of purchasing programs against their likelihood of success. Some principals believed that teachers were more apt to embrace new programs when they had a hand in designing them. Others cared more that programs already had a track record of success in schools like their own.

Melva Belcher decided to adopt a commercial mathematics program because she was displeased with the existing program and she had seen the new one work in her previous school. After encountering a variety of technical problems with a purchased short-cycle testing program, however, she decided to have members of her faculty spend the summer developing a new set of assessments keyed to state curriculum objectives. At Berkeley Elementary School, Catherine Thomas chose to conduct evaluations of every program before determining which ones should be retained and which ones needed to be replaced. Six principals decided to move to an inclusion model for most special education students despite encountering resistance from some teachers and parents. They believed that most disabled students stood a better chance of learning required content in regular education classrooms than in self-contained special education classrooms. J. Harrison-Coleman instituted uniforms at Clarke Elementary School because she felt that they would reduce discipline problems related to student attire and promote a sense of community. When parents complained about the cost of uniforms, she found community donors to underwrite the initiative.

The high school turnaround principals were involved in two of the most controversial judgment calls regarding school programs. Nancy Weisskopf decided that students needing to repeat a failed course at South Hills High School should not be allowed to sit in class with first-timers. Repeaters were required to retake coursework online in the Plato Lab. She understood that this decision might be unpopular with some individuals, but she feared repeaters would be negative role models for first timers.

Anabel Garza insisted that English language learners (ELLs) at Reagan High School work on English tests in their academic courses. This decision created challenges for teachers of academic subjects and required ELL teachers to develop new ways of handling content-based instruction. Based on her own experience as an English language learner, however, Garza was convinced that failure to expose ELLs to English in academic subjects ensured they would continue to lag behind their English-speaking peers.

Deciding to introduce new programs in order to turn around a low-performing school requires careful consideration of costs as well as benefits. There are limits to how many new programs a school can effectively implement at one time. Choosing particular programs can preclude the adoption of other worthy programs. Programs, in order to stand a chance of succeeding, must be managed and nurtured. Professional development for teachers often is needed. The community must be "sold" on the value of new programs. All of this requires time, and time is a principal's most precious commodity. Part of the process of making judgment calls about new programs concerns determining whether the time needed to support a new program is a good use of the principal's time.

Judgment Calls about School Leadership

Evidence was provided in some of the cases that the principals made judgment calls regarding how they were going to lead the turnaround effort. Four principals, for instance, decided to implement shared decision making as a way to increase faculty commitment to the turnaround process. The vehicle for shared decision making in three of these cases was a leadership team consisting of teacher representatives. Melissa Marshall, though, chose to have all of her teachers participate in determining how to achieve the school improvement goals for Perrymont Middle School. Her alternative school, however, was relatively small.

In three other cases, principals made a conscious decision not to involve teachers in decision making during the first year of the turnaround process. Wilma Williams and Melva Belcher reasoned that there was insufficient time to build consensus. Improvements were needed quickly, and they both had definite ideas about how to achieve them. Matt Landahl opted for top-down leadership in his first year because he did not know his teachers and was uncertain about which teachers he could count on for support. By the third year of the turnaround process, however, he felt comfortable turning over many decisions to teacher committees.

Another type of judgment call involved how principals spent their time. Several principals desired to spend more time in classrooms monitoring instruction, but they felt compelled to focus on other matters during the early days of school turnaround. Other principals decided that getting into classrooms from the outset was their highest priority. J. Harrison-Coleman, Deloris Crews, and Catherine Thomas took instructional leadership one step further and taught demonstration lessons for faculty members.

Three cases indicated that principals gave serious consideration to whether or not they should seek assistance from the central office. Each desired support in removing or re-assigning teachers. The principals debated whether asking for assistance might be interpreted by superiors as a sign of weakness or lack of leadership. In a fourth case, the principal decided to ask for less help from the central office! Matt Landahl concluded that teachers at Greer Elementary School were getting mixed messages from all the district resource people sent to facilitate the school turnaround process, and he requested fewer specialists be assigned to his school.

CONCLUSION

The purpose of this study was to learn more about the kinds of judgments facing principals charged with turning around low-performing schools. Turnaround principals are expected to focus on improving instruction and achieving quick and dramatic increases in student achievement. Such expectations reflect the priorities typically associated with instructional leadership. Much of the literature on instructional leadership, however, has focused on its behavioral rather than its cognitive dimensions. The present study suggests that instructional leadership entails considerable reasoning and a variety of tough judgments. These judgments concern such matters as planning, staffing, operations, programs, and leadership.

Some of the judgment calls associated with school turnaround involved harder choices than others, but even seemingly obvious choices entailed opportunity costs. Principals do not have access to unlimited resources. Deciding to undertake one course of action may preclude a second, equally worthy course of action. The cases demonstrate that turnaround principals live in a world where trade-offs often are the rule, not the exception.

There is a clear need for greater understanding of the judgments associated with instructional leadership. The present study reveals that variations exist in the choices principals make. Understanding more about these variations and the reasoning behind them may yield clues to the differential effectiveness of principals. Is there a connection between judgment and effectiveness? Are principals able to recognize when they make bad judgments? Are bad judgments repeated?

For those involved in preparing principals, greater understanding of the judgments of principals perhaps can lead to more balanced instruction. Too heavy an emphasis on skills and competencies can suggest to prospective principals that judgment and reasoning are relatively unimportant attributes of leadership. Skill and competence, however, are unlikely to compensate for bad judgment.

NOTES

1. For the purposes of this chapter, the term "turnaround principal" refers to principals who are charged with achieving "quick and dramatic" improve-

ments in schools faced with sanctions under the No Child Left Behind Act and/or a state accountability system.

REFERENCES

Beckner, W. (2004). *Ethics for Educational Leaders*. Boston, MA: Pearson.

Begley, P. T. (1996). Cognitive perspectives on the nature and function of values in educational administration. In K. Leithwood, J. Chapman, D. Corson, P. Hallinger, & A. Hart (Eds.), *International handbook of educational leadership and administration* (pp. 551–588). Dordrecht, The Netherlands: Kluwer,.

Brookover, W. B. & Lezotte, L. W. (1979). *Changes in school characteristics coincident with changes in student achievement*. East Lansing, MI: Institute for Research on Teaching, Michigan State University.

DeBevoise, W. (1984). Synthesis of research on the principal as instructional leader. *Educational Leadership, 41*(5), 14–20.

Dewey, J. (1910). *How We Think*. Boston, MA: Heath.

Duke, D. L. (1987). *School leadership and instructional improvement*. New York, NY: Random House.

Duke, D. L. & Jacobson, M. (2011). Tackling the toughest turnaround—low-performing high schools. *Phi Delta Kappan, 92*(5), 34–38.

Duke, D. L. & Landahl, M. (2011). Raising test scores was the easy part: A case study of the third year of school turnaround. *International Studies in Education Administration, 39*(3), 91–114.

Duke, D. L. & Salmonowicz, M. (2010). Key decisions of a first-year "turnaround principal." *Educational Management, Administration & Leadership, 38*(1), 33–58.

Duke, D. L., Tucker, P. D., Belcher, M., Crews, D., Harrison-Coleman, J., Higgins, J. et al. (2005). *Lift-off: launching the school turnaround process in 10 Virginia schools*. Charlottesville, VA: Partnership for Leaders in Education, University of Virginia.

Forehand, G. A. & Guetzkow, H. (1962). Judgment and decision making activities of government executives as described by superiors and co-workers. *Management Science, 8*(3), 359–370.

Hallinger, P. (2011). A review of three decades of doctoral studies using the Principal Instructional Management Rating Scale: A lens on methodological progress in educational leadership. *Educational Administration Quarterly, 47*(2), 271–306.

Hallinger, P. & McCary, C. E. (1990). Developing the strategic thinking of instructional leaders. *The Elementary School Journal, 91*(2), 89–108.

Leithwood, K. & Duke, D. L. (1999). A century's quest to understand school leadership. In J. Murphy & K. S. Louis (Eds.), *Handbook of research on educational administration* (2nd ed. pp. 45–72). San Francisco, CA: Jossey-Bass.

Leithwood, K. & Steinbach, R. (1995). *Expert problem solving*. Albany, NY: State University of New York Press.

March, J. G. & Simon, H. (1959). *Organizations*. New York, NY: Wiley.

Mowen, J. C. (1993). *Judgment Calls*. New York, NY: Simon & Schuster.

Payne, C. M. (2008). *So much reform, so little change.* Cambridge, MA: Harvard Education Press.

Priem, R. L. (1994). Executive judgment, organizational congruence, and firm performance. *Organization Science, 5*(3), 421–437.

Simon, H. (1976). *Administrative behavior.* New York, NY: The Free Press.

Spillane, J. P., Halverson, R., & Diamond, J. B. (2001). Investigating school leadership practice: A distributed perspective. *Educational Researcher, 30*(4), 23–28.

Strike, K. A., Haller, E. J., & Soltis, J. F. (1988). *The ethics of school administration.* New York, NY: Teachers College Press.

Tichy, N. M. & Bennis, W. G. (2007). Making judgment calls. *Harvard Business Review, 85*(10), 94–102.

CHAPTER 3

INSTRUCTIONAL PRACTICE, TEACHER EFFECTIVENESS, AND GROWTH IN STUDENT LEARNING IN MATH

Implications for School Leadership

Ronald H. Heck

A large body of international research accumulated over the past 30 years supports the view that the school leadership facilitates growth in student learning (Bossert, Dwyer, Rowan, & Lee, 1982; Leithwood, Day, Sammons, Harris, & Hopkins, 2006; Robinson, Lloyd, & Rowe, 2008; Witziers, Bosker, & Kruger, 2003). One primary pathway is by shaping conditions in the school that foster the school's capacity to provide effective teaching and learning such as facilitating the development of school values that support learning, establishing educational partnerships, increasing teacher collaboration regarding curriculum development and organization, enhancing professional development opportunities, and fostering more effective assessment practices (e.g., Hallinger, Bickman, & Davis, 1996; Leithwood,

The Changing Nature of Instructional Leadership in the 21st Century, pages 33–62
Copyright © 2012 by Information Age Publishing
All rights of reproduction in any form reserved.

Louis, Anderson, & Wahlstrom, 2004; Leithwood et al., 2006; Robinson et al., 2008; Supovitz, Sirinides, & May, 2010). Leadership, therefore, serves as a key *mediating* construct between the school's context (e.g., community values, support, involvement) and composition and its instructional practices, which directly influence student outcomes (Bossert et al., 1982; Heck & Hallinger, 2009; Heck & Moriyama, 2010). School leaders targeting instructional improvement, then, must facilitate school changes that are embraced and owned by the teachers, who are responsible for implementation in classrooms (Barth, 2001; Hall & Hord, 2001).

A second pathway to instructional improvement is by intervening directly with teachers in ways that are aimed at improving the quality of *teaching* (e.g., enhancing student opportunities to learn, managing the quantity of time teachers spend with students without disruptions, supervising marginal teachers) and by improving the school's *instructional environment* (e.g., increasing teacher collaboration, providing professional development opportunities, developing school values that support learning). Previous research has suggested that the classroom level is more significant than the school and system level—concluding that greater attention should be directed toward improving teachers' instructional practices and attitudes directly (Creemers & Kyriakides, 2008; McCaffrey, Lockwood, Koretz, Louis, & Hamilton, 2004). Van de Grift and Houtveen (2006), for example, found that underachieving schools improve with improved teaching processes (e.g., clear, well-organized teaching; learning connected to students' background knowledge; active involvement of students in the learning process) and enhanced opportunities to attain curricular objectives (e.g., using appropriate textbooks and educational materials). Teachers create an instructional environment in the classroom and provide instructional learning opportunities for students through strategies such as orientation, structuring, questioning, teaching-modeling, and application (Creemers & Kyriakides, 2008; Good & Brophy, 1986; Seidel & Shavelson, 2007).

Although the issue of how teachers directly impact student learning outcomes has been well studied (e.g., Good & Brophy, 1986; McCaffrey et al., 2004; Seidel & Shavelson, 2007), less attention has been directed toward how classrooms, as a structural level within the school, may mediate the effects of school-wide improvement activities on individual student progress. More specifically, little is known about whether individual teacher effects may accumulate within a particular school, whether there might be observable differences in schools' instructional effectiveness (e.g., academic press, instructional practices) that provide academic advantages for students separate from, or perhaps contingent upon, teacher effectiveness (Bressoux & Bianco, 2004; Creemers & Kyriakides, 2008; Leithwood et al., 2004), as well as how leadership might impact some of these key school and classroom processes aimed at improving instruction (Supovitz et al., 2010). Although school-level improvement is *assumed* to influence what teachers do in classrooms, there have been few empirical tests of this hypothesis that capture the complexity of classrooms nested within schools and students nested within classrooms. More typically, only school-level relations are examined; for example, a number of leadership studies have identified various mediators measured at the school level that influence school-level achievement. Leithwood, Patten, and Jantzi (2010) provide one such summary of pathways of school leadership influence on mediating processes that may affect student achievement.

Unfortunately, however, previous research on school effects has several shortcomings in producing knowledge that can be directly implemented to produce improved school outcomes. Criticisms include its lack of adequate theoretical underpinnings, its primary focus on single indicators of effectiveness and school outcomes, its lack of examining relationships between structural levels, and its largely cross-sectional nature (Opdenakker & Van Damme, 2007). Initial efforts to represent growth in student learning have mostly relied on *linear* growth models, which require the assumption that students' rates of growth are the same over each time interval studied. Further empirical work is therefore needed that examines student growth in more detail and that builds and tests a theory that can provide a more integrated explanation about how school actions directed toward improvement may intersect with teachers' classroom practices in ways that impact growth in student learning (Creemers & Kyriakides, 2008).

Building on this line of research, the purposes of this chapter are to extend the discussion of the role of school leadership in enhancing school improvement by integrating the results of two studies focused on 1) the interplay between school leadership and teacher effectiveness in the classroom and 2) the relationships among school leadership, school instructional practices, and the effectiveness of the school's teachers that influence student growth in learning over several years. The primary focus in this chapter, then, is on instructionally-oriented leadership and the improvement of the school's instructional processes—what Creemers and Kyriakides (2008) identify as one of the key aims of educational effectiveness research. With respect to teacher effectiveness, in addition to classroom effects, I examine an organizational level, or "school," effect, which provides additional evidence that both the school's overall instructional environment and the collective quality of its teachers matter (Creemers & Kyriakides, 2008; Preis, 2010).

BACKGROUND OF THE STUDY

Recent research on educational effectiveness has focused on identifying a more integrated set of school educational processes that can lead to stronger student outcomes. Opdenakker and Van Damme (2007) specified three types of school factors that influence student outcomes. These are the school's *context* (e.g., its structure, size, facilities), its *composition* (i.e., including students' backgrounds as well as the teaching and administrative staff), and its *instructional practice*. This latter set of factors includes the school's educational framework (e.g., mission, goals), academic and social organization, work environment and climate (e.g., teacher collaboration regarding curriculum, teaching and students), and school-community partnerships. They found that both school context and student composition influenced schools' instructional practice, but, importantly, instructional practices partially mediated the direct effects of context and composition on achievement. In one recent test of this proposed model, my colleague and I extended Opdenakker and Van Damme's conceptual model by identifying the importance of instructionally-focused school leadership as a mediating construct between the context of school and community factors (e.g., educational expectations, patterns of interacting with school personnel, resources) and its instructional practice (Heck & Moriyama, 2010). In our longitudinal specification of school improvement processes among a large sample of elementary schools, we found that leadership influenced subsequent instructional practices, which, in turn, influenced subsequent student learning.

Leadership focused on student learning improvement signals the importance of creating and sustaining a school-wide focus on learning (Hallinger, 2003; Hallinger & Murphy, 1986; Robinson et al., 2008). It further highlights the importance of learning, not only for students, but also for teachers and staff (Barth, 1990; Fullan, 2006; Leithwood & Jantzi, 1999; Leithwood et al., 2010; Marks & Printy, 2003; Mulford & Silins, 2003; Robinson et al., 2008; Supovitz et al., 2010). For example, Supovitz and his colleagues noted that principal leadership influenced student learning indirectly through teacher interactions surrounding instruction. They found that both principal leadership and teacher peer influence were significantly related to teachers' instructional practices and student outcomes in language arts. Most of the leadership influence on teachers' instructional practices seemed to occur through fostering collaboration and communication around instructional issues.

In addition to school factors that support effective classroom teaching, previous research dating back to the 1970s has described variation among teachers in producing student outcomes (e.g., Hanushek, 1971; Murnane, 1975). Studies have focused on collective differences in teacher preparation, credentialing, and experience between schools and their impact on student learning, as well as on classroom teaching performance and effectiveness (e.g., McCaffrey et al., 2004; Seidel & Shavelson, 2007).

Earlier classroom studies emphasized a "process-product" model, identifying relationships between various aspects of teaching (e.g., time allocated for various curricular areas, structured teaching, feedback, reinforcement, adaptive instruction) and student outcomes (e.g., Berliner, 1989; Good, 1979; Good & Brophy, 1986; Rosenshine, 1986; Scheerens & Bosker, 1997; Teddlie, Kirby, & Stringfield, 1989). Teddlie and his colleagues (1989), for example, described differences in teachers' classroom practices between high-producing and low-producing schools (e.g., curriculum content covered, student time on task, discipline procedures). More recently, researchers have also examined a variety of cognitively-related instructional models that are more student-learning centered and focus on teacher beliefs, thinking processes, disciplinary knowledge versus pedagogical knowledge, cooperative grouping strategies, and situated descriptions of teaching and learning, to name a few more varied types of models (Seidel & Shavelson, 2007).

LIMITATIONS OF PREVIOUS RESEARCH

Despite greater flexibility in how teacher instructional practices are conceptualized and studied, the size, consistency, and sustainability of teacher-related effects on student learning have not been fully substantiated (McCaffrey et al., 2004), nor have pathways though which school-level improvement processes might lead to growth in student learning been adequately explicated (Creemers & Kyriakides, 2008; Heck & Hallinger, 2009). A number of issues therefore remains in clarifying pathways to school improvement and estimating their impact on actual changes in student learning over time.

One reason for the dearth of studies that explicitly examine the effects of school-level processes on classroom activity is the difficulty in developing data sets that contain information about processes at the school level, the classroom level, and the student level. Longitudinal assessment of individual students' progress within a particular school is superior to comparing successive grade-level cohorts (e.g., percentages of students in a particular grade who attain proficiency each year) for the purpose of monitoring school improvement (Willms, 1992; Heck, 2006). The former approach focuses attention more squarely on students' experiences in attending a particular school over several years with multiple teachers and provides a way of recognizing that schools serve students who start at different educational places and progress at different rates (Seltzer, Choi, & Thum, 2003). It can be difficult, however, to obtain the data and to link individual students to their teachers. This problem is likely to be reduced in the future, as "Race to the Top" has made longitudinal assessment of student learning, as well as the linking of students to teachers, a priority for obtaining federal funds.

A second reason is the challenge of examining complex relationships comprising several levels of a data hierarchy simultaneously (McCaffrey et al., 2004). Added to this problem is the complexity of cross-classifying students within successive teachers over the duration of a study. Cross-classified models represent a particular type of multilevel data where individuals may be placed simultaneously in different grouping combinations at a particular level of the analysis (Raudenbush, Bryk, Cheong, & Congdon, 2004). Empirical examples of cross-classified data include Garner and Raudenbush's (1991) study of neighborhood and school effects on student attainment and Goldstein and Sammons' (1997) study of elementary and secondary school effects on student achievement. In the first study reported on in this chapter, over the two-year period, any two students in the sample could have the first- and second-year teacher in common, one teacher in common, or no teacher in common. This creates various data dependencies over time, which makes the teacher-level data more complex than in a typical cross-sectional multilevel study, where each student is nested in only one specific classroom within each school.

A number of substantive issues also remains in providing further understanding on how leadership, instructional practices, and teacher effectiveness may be related to enhanced student learning. One issue concerns whether school-level improvement activity may impact teacher effects on student learning and, if so, might we capture hints of how that interplay takes place between the school level and classroom level to facilitate growth in student learning over time? The assumption is that over time teacher effectiveness contributes to variability in student growth rates (Cohen & Hill, 2000; Creemers, 1994; Creemers & Kyriakides, 2008); however, these effects may be moderated (i.e., enhanced or diminished) by various school-level actions. Although it is believed that school-level actions may influence improvement in student learning, there have been few empirical tests of whether school leadership actions may actually enhance or diminish teacher effectiveness in the classroom (Heck & Hallinger, 2010). It is expected that activity at a higher organizational level can "coordinate," or filter, the range of individual activity at a lower level. This *coordinating* aspect of school leadership is likely a key component in efforts to change instructional practices in schools. The question remains, however, to what extent does instruction-focused school leadership actually *enhance* teachers' effectiveness in the classroom?

A second issue concerns whether differences in the quality of teaching effectiveness within a particular school may accumulate to provide any type of added academic advantage to students. Positive effects of varying sizes have been found between earlier teachers and later student academic success (e.g., Bressoux & Bianco, 2004; Mendro, Jordan, Gomez, Anderson, & Bembry, 1998; Rowan, Correnti, & Miller, 2002). Collectively, however, this body of research has been unable to substantiate the size, consistency, and sustainability of teacher-related effects on growth in student learning (McCaffrey et al., 2004). Most of the variability in teacher effects appears to differ within schools. For example, one recent study suggests that approximately 80% of this variance is at the classroom level within schools (Heck, 2009). Less is known about whether differences in teacher quality at the school level (e.g., the average level of effectiveness and its variability) might also contribute to student achievement outcomes (Heck, 2007).

The multilevel analyses presented in this chapter attempt to add to existing evidence about how school practices and teacher effectiveness may influence growth in student learning by examining a constellation of variables in a multilevel framework focusing on students' learning in math over an extended period of time. In examining school-level instructional improvement, the studies employ a conceptualization of school leadership that is oriented towards building the academic capacity of the school to provide high quality instruction aimed at increasing student learning. Increasing the school's instructional capacity, therefore, represents a key target of strategic leadership efforts designed to impact teacher classroom practices and student learning (Fullan, 2006; Hallinger et al., 1996; Marks & Printy, 2003; Leithwood et al., 2004, 2010; Robinson et al., 2008; Wiley, 2001).

METHOD

Sample and design. The final sample used in the first study consisted of 2,894 students cross-classified in 240 third and 163 fourth grade classrooms in 60 elementary schools. This represented a subset of the data in the larger study conducted on elementary schools in Hawaii (Heck, 2009). The first study, using a subset of the data, was able to examine individual teachers' perceptions of their classroom practices and school instructional leadership, which could then be aggregated to develop measures of each school's instructional practices that could be tested for their moderating effects on individual teachers' classroom effectiveness, which was measured separately from teachers' perceptions of instructional practices and school leadership. This study examines students' movement through two consecutive teachers representing a two-year period of math instruction within each school.

The second study made use of the full data set (i.e., 9,363 students in 154 elementary schools) studied over four years. In this study, the temporal relations were such that teachers' instructional processes and teacher effectiveness estimates were developed during the earlier repeated observations (i.e., years one and two) comprising students' math trajectories.

This should provide a reasonable, if not optimal, test of the model's key constructs and student growth trajectories in math. Although an optimal test of the potential impact of school processes on student growth trajectories would involve examining how *changing* school relationships over time influences student growth (e.g., Heck & Hallinger, 2009), unfortunately, the teacher-level data on instructional practices and classroom effectiveness were not available during the entire period studied.

VARIABLES IN THE MODELS

Controls. Controls included a range of student background factors (i.e., gender, socioeconomic status, race/ethnicity, language spoken at home), classroom composition (i.e., a weighted factor score consisting of the percentage of special education students, low SES students, and students receiving English language services), school composition (i.e., a weighted factor score consisting of the percentage of low SES students, students receiving English language services, and students receiving special education services), and school context variables (i.e., enrollment size, staff teaching experience, staff stability).

Teacher effectiveness. Measures of teacher effectiveness were developed in several steps. First, estimates of effectiveness over a two-year period (i.e., over 500 teachers each year) were generated at the classroom level from the previous year's student cohort. These scores described teacher effectiveness in producing math learning within their classrooms above the learning that would be expected given their students' previous learning and backgrounds (McCaffrey et al., 2004). After adjustment for previous learning and background, the teacher scores were standardized ($M = 0$, $SD = 1$). Positive scores indicate teachers who produce student outcomes above what would be expected, given the composition of their classrooms. Second, teacher scores were transferred to the current data set. Individual teacher scores were then used in the first study to examine their validity in explaining the math outcomes of a subsequent student cohort, as well as whether school-level actions focused on instruction might moderate individual teacher effects on student learning. Third, individual teacher effectiveness scores were aggregated to provide a measure of average teacher effectiveness in each school. Importantly, then, teacher effectiveness scores were developed independently from the student cohort in this sample. The model therefore provides a test of their validity in describing each teacher's contribution to student learning.

Variability in teacher effectiveness. In the first study, variability in effectiveness was defined as the standard deviation (SD) of teacher effectiveness at the school level. More specifically, this variable represents a measure of the extent to which participating teachers were more tightly clustered in terms of their effectiveness within each school. It is expected that tighter clustering (i.e., a lower SD), which has been found to describe more effective schools (e.g., Teddlie et al., 1989), will yield higher math scores after controlling for the average level of teacher effectiveness in each school.

School instructional practice. Teacher survey data were used to develop a weighted factor score comprised of four dimensions of the school's instructional practices and the environment surrounding it. Items used to describe school instructional practices were measured on five-point, Likert-type scales and expressed as the percentage of positive agreement with each statement. The items used to measure the dimensions were preliminarily developed using multilevel (teachers nested within schools) confirmatory factor analysis (CFA) and a sample of 4,056 teachers within the 60 schools comprising the first study. At the teacher level, the item loadings were all statistically significant and ranged from 0.35 to 0.99. At the school level, the item loadings were all above 0.93. The subscales comprising instructional practices included a) classroom instruction, b) school academic expectations for student achievement, c) school-wide monitoring of student progress, and d) school climate. Cronbach's alphas for all subscales were above 0.80.

Classroom instruction made use of previous process-product and cognitive approaches regarding teaching and research (e.g., Berliner, 1989; Good & Brophy, 1986; Seidel & Shavelson, 2007). The items included:

- Teachers use class time primarily for instruction,
- Teachers maximize students' instructional time on task,
- Teachers present academic work in varied ways,
- Teachers collaborate to develop and refine the academic curriculum,
- Teachers participate in professional development activities regarding improving instructional practices,
- Teachers continually assess their instruction to refine teaching, and
- Teachers use varied instructional methods such as cooperative learning, peer tutoring, and computer-assisted instruction to promote learning for all students.

Academic expectations included the following items:

- All students are expected to learn a full range of skills from knowledge and comprehension to complex problem solving,
- Teachers clearly inform students and parents about what students are expected to know and do by the end of the school year
- School standards are challenging but attainable,
- Teachers have high academic expectations for students,

- Teachers assume responsibility for student learning,
- Teachers foster the development of independent learning, and
- Effective support programs exist for students with special needs.

Monitoring of student progress included these items:

- Teachers often provide specific feedback to students on their progress,
- Teachers promptly evaluate and return homework,
- Teachers diagnose academic problems early,
- Teachers give clear expectations for assignments,
- Students are given an active role in assessing and evaluating their academic progress,
- Teachers use tests and other varied methods of evaluating student learning,
- Information about student progress is used to adapt instruction to meet each student's needs, and
- Assessments of student progress are used in planning subsequent instruction.

School climate included the following:

- Students feel safe on campus,
- Staff cares about the well being of students,
- Teacher–student interactions are positive,
- Discipline problems are handled fairly and emphasize behavior, not personality,
- Classroom environments stimulate learning without undue pressure,
- The school staff works cooperatively; Teachers enjoy teaching at the school, and
- Students at the school are engaged in learning.

School leadership. The measure of school leadership focused on the extent to which instructional improvement is a primary school focus and included this set of items:

- The principal makes student achievement the school's top goal,
- The principal takes the lead in resolving school instructional problems,
- School administrators work with teachers, students, and parents to develop the school's improvement plan,
- School administrators regularly observe classroom instruction,

- School administrators regularly provide feedback to teachers regarding their classroom instruction,
- Administrators and staff share leadership roles using individual and team strengths,
- The principal ensures that there are sufficient school resources allocated to support instruction, and
- The principal ensures that there is an effective, on-going system for evaluating the school's progress toward its goals.

In the first study, the instructional practice factor is aligned with students' ending achievement at year two. In the second study, instructional practice is also aligned with the level of achievement at year two of the study, which implies that the survey was implemented just ahead of the second wave of student outcome data. A limitation to keep in mind regarding the instructional practices measure is that because of this temporal sequence, school instructional practices should be optimally aligned with the level of student math scores at year two, but it is likely that the measure will also be positively related to subsequent change in scores during subsequent years of the study.

I also draw attention to a couple of limitations of these data in providing a complete test of the proposed multilevel model. Preliminary findings about the positive relationship between estimates of teacher effects and teacher perceptions of instructionally-focused leadership and instructional practice lend credibility to their validity in differentiating between classrooms in terms of student achievement results. It remains unclear from the present data, however, what the actual day-to-day mechanisms are that link differences in the quality of schools' leadership and their academic processes to the effectiveness of teachers in contributing to student learning over time. For example, as a classroom-level measure, teacher effectiveness defined as a residual estimate leaves various unanswered questions about how observed differences in effectiveness might result from variability in teachers' expectations, curriculum coverage, and domain-specific learning activities (Seidel & Shavelson, 2007). A related limitation is that only the teachers from the first two years of the four-year study were used to develop the aggregate teacher effectiveness scores, so that the process of representing teacher effectiveness is only partial for each school in the second study.

Similarly, questions remain about the definition and measurement of the leadership and instructional practice constructs as collective properties of schools. Although the constructs were found to be reliable, annual school-level questionnaires are admittedly an imperfect means of extracting information about organizational processes. For example, an individual's reported involvement in decision making about school improvement may, or may not, adequately capture a key aspect of collaborative leadership;

and even if it does, the way the individual's reply is coded into a score may bias its exact meaning. Each construct is likely a proxy for more thorough information that could be assembled about school-wide efforts to improve curriculum and teacher expertise, as well as their instructional behavior in classrooms (Cohen & Hill, 2000: Creemers, 1994). Readers should keep in mind that school-level aggregates about classroom practices can ignore wide variations in teaching and learning conditions that may be important at the classroom level (McCaffrey et al., 2004).

DEFINING STUDENT GROWTH OVER TIME

Multilevel modeling facilitates examining changes in student learning that take place over time. This is captured in two different ways in the two studies. In the first study, I specified a four-level, cross-classified model to examine students' ending achievement (i.e., Y represents achievement at the end of the second year). The subscript t identifies achievement at time t nested within individuals, the subscript i identifies students at the individual level; the subscripts j_1 and j_2 identify the crossed structure at the classroom level (previous and current teachers, respectively); and the subscript k identifies schools at the school level. The combined multilevel model with teacher effects can be specified as follows:

$$y_{ti(j1j2)k} = \gamma_{000} + \gamma_{100}time_t + \gamma_{010}teach1_{j1k} + \gamma_{020}teach2_{j2k} +$$
$$v_{0k} + v_{1k}time + u_{j1k} + u_{j2k} + e_{ti(j1j2)k}$$

where γ_{000} is the grand mean of ending math achievement for schools; γ_{100} represents the school-level change in students' math achievement between year one and year two, and *teach1* and *teach2* represent the two teacher effects on ending achievement. The residuals for each level, which are assumed to be normally and independently distributed in the population (with means = 0 and some variance), were represented as v, u, and e and are associated with schools, teachers, and students, respectively. After examining several preliminary models, the *time* variable was also specified as randomly varying by adding a another variance term ($v_{1k}time$) at the school level, and school variables that might explain variability in student gains from year one to year two were examined. The other covariates described previously were then added at their appropriate student, classroom, or school levels to explain random variation in ending math achievement levels across schools. Results are summarized in Table 3.1.

In the second study, I made the assumption that students' learning rates may vary across occasions, such that a linear model (i.e., one which suggests a constant rate of change) would not adequately capture the growth in math. For example, recent work on student gains across several standardized tests (Bloom, Hill, Black, & Lipsey, 2008) suggests that students make different learning gains during elementary school, with larger gains made during early elementary and smaller gains during middle and upper elementary years. This suggests taking into consideration possible nonlinear growth in students' math achievement over time. Polynomial curves[1] are often used to represent nonlinear change over time because they can be adapted to standard linear modeling techniques (such as multilevel regression). Because there are four periods of time ($t = 4$), they can be fit using a polynomial of degree $t - 1$ (or 3).

Of course, we might prefer the ease of interpreting a linear growth model, but it is more likely that a *quadratic* (i.e., the rate of change may accelerate or decelerate at a constant rate) or *cubic* (i.e., there is a changing rate of change over time) polynomial describes the change over time more accurately. For example, the rate of change may slow during one interval and then speed up over another interval. Cubic polynomials often do a good job of approximating nonlinear growth, but as Hox (2010) cautions, the parameters of the growth trajectory have no *direct* meaning in terms of the growth process being examined (i.e., how much growth per interval takes place). Instead, they must be interpreted by examining plots of the average, or some typical, growth curves. In estimating a polynomial function, it is important to note that the linear, quadratic, and cubic components comprising the growth trajectory are multicollinear (i.e., with correlations above 0.9). The presence of multicollinearity can lead to biased estimates of student change. They must first be transformed to be uncorrelated by recoding them, using available tables of orthogonal polynomials.

At level one, for student i in school j measured at time t, we can define growth in math as consisting of linear, quadratic, and cubic polynomial components:

$$Y_{tij} = \pi_{0ij} + \pi_{1ij}(linear)_{tij} + \pi_{2ij}(quadratic)_{tij} + \pi_{3ij}(cubic)_{tij} + \varepsilon_{tij}.$$

The errors in the trajectory equations are contained in a covariance matrix that specifies the relationship between subsequent test scores within individuals. In this case, I assumed an autoregressive structure, which is appropriate when there are correlations between successive measurements within individuals. The assumption is that the residual errors are correlated within individuals but are independent across individuals. Missing data (which was actually only about 1 to 2% in these data) on individuals at some occasions can easily be accommodated in this type of growth model.

Because the focus is on changes at the school level, at level two (between individuals) the growth trajectory coefficients were fixed (i.e., not specified as randomly varying). Covariates describing differences possible between individuals were subsequently added (e.g., SES, gender, language background). At level three, variability in students' growth trajectories across schools can be examined, controlling for context and composition variables, and adding the instructional practice and teacher effectiveness variables. The preliminary results for describing the trajectory (see Table 3.2) suggested building a model to explain variability in the levels of math outcomes between schools and a model to explain variability in the cubic polynomial describing school change in math over time. This is consistent with interaction models in analysis of variance (ANOVA), which are generally interpreted in terms of the highest order significant interaction (Marcoulides & Hershberger, 1997).[2] School effects on student growth trajectories were modeled as cross-level interactions between the highest component of the trajectory (i.e., cubic) and each school-level predictor.[3]

The final model with covariates added at each level is presented in Table 3.3. For this final model, an interaction term between teacher effectiveness and instructional processes was also specified to determine whether there might be any added effect on student growth associated with schools that have more effective teachers and more strongly rated instructional practices than those observed in typical schools.

RESULTS

Study One

Models in the first study were estimated with SPSS MIXED, which can be used to estimate a variety of longitudinal cross-classified models. The syntax for estimating the final model is provided in the Appendix. The first step in this type of multilevel study is often to partition the variance in math outcomes (not tabled). The variance in math across schools was 9%. At the teacher level, there are three variance components to consider. The first variance component considers the variance in achievement for students who had the first teacher in common but had a different second teacher (8%). The second considers students having the second teacher in common but a different first teacher. This was also about 8%. The final component is the variance accounted for by having both teachers in common (which is then 16%). This suggests considerable variability due to successive teacher combinations in accounting for ending student achievement.

The results of the final model with standardized estimates (which can be interpreted as effect sizes) are summarized in Table 3.1. As the table shows, teacher effectiveness influences students' ending math achievement at the classroom level (i.e., 0.256 for teacher two and a smaller effect of

TABLE 3.1   Standardized Estimates of Model Predictors on Ending Student Achievement

Variables	Estimate	SE	95%CI Lower	95%CI Upper
Between Schools				
Intercept	–0.026	0.134	–0.292	0.240
School composition	–0.115*	–0.023	–0.160	–0.070
Enrollment	0.037	0.038	–0.039	0.113
Staff stability	0.034	0.030	–0.025	0.093
Instructional practices	0.225*	0.097	0.033	0.417
Average teacher effectiveness	–0.080	0.058	–0.194	0.035
Variability in teacher effectiveness	–0.077*	0.036	–0.148	–0.005
Between Classrooms				
Teacher 2 effectiveness	0.256*	0.103	0.052	0.460
Effectiveness*Instructional practices	0.136*	0.059	0.020	0.254
Effectiveness*School composition	0.027	0.019	–0.011	0.065
Teacher 1 effectiveness	0.120*	0.019	0.081	0.159
Class composition	0.002	0.014	–0.026	0.030
Between Students				
Female	0.042*	0.019	0.004	0.081
Minority by race/ethnicity	–0.289*	0.023	–0.334	–0.245
ELL	–0.001	0.027	–0.054	0.052
Low SES	–0.236*	0.023	–0.281	–0.192
Growth	0.551*	0.010	0.527	0.575
Growth*Average effectiveness	0.102*	0.051	0.004	0.208
Growth*Student composition	–0.045*	0.022	–0.089	–0.002
Variance in Ending Achievement (R^2)				
School	0.89			
Classroom	0.72			
Student	0.47			

Note: *$p < .05$

0.120 for the first teacher). This suggests that having two successive teachers who were one SD above the average level of effectiveness of each respective sample of teachers would result in a 0.38 SD increase in ending achievement. As hypothesized, the cross-level interaction between school instructional leadership and teacher classroom effectiveness was statistically significant (0.136, $p < .05$). This can be interpreted that a one SD increase in teacher perceptions of the quality of their school's instructional practices would increase the average individual teacher effect on achievement by about 0.14 SD. Another way to interpret this would be that a one SD increase in instructionally-focused leadership above the grand mean for the sample would increase the size of the current teacher's effect by a bit more than 50% (0.26 + 0.14 = 0.40). Note that because instructional practice was aligned with year two, it should not influence the previous teacher effect. This "impossible" temporal effect was also tested and found to be not significant.

Table 3.1 also suggests that in schools where there was less variability in teacher effectiveness estimates, ending math levels were higher (–0.077, $p < .05$), after controlling for other variables including *average* teacher effectiveness. This result implies that a one SD increase in variability in average teacher effectiveness would result in an average *decrease* in ending math achievement of about 0.08 SD. Although this is a small effect size, the finding is consistent with the proposition advanced that in schools with stronger teaching effectiveness, there will be less variability in effectiveness across classrooms. As expected, the two variables were negatively correlated ($r = –0.23$, $p < .05$, not tabled). Moreover, average teacher effectiveness also positively moderated student gains in math between year one and year two (0.102, $p < .05$). This suggests that a one SD increase in average effectiveness would result in an expected 0.10 SD increase in student gains in math, holding other variables in the model constant. The table also indicates that school instructional practice was positively related to ending achievement (0.225, $p < .05$). At level one, several student background variables influenced ending math achievement (i.e., gender, socioeconomic status, race/ethnicity).

The results regarding school leadership are summarized visually in Figure 3.1. The figure suggests there was no direct effect of leadership on ending math achievement observed. Consistent with other studies, however, leadership indirectly affected math achievement through its direct effect on school instructional practices (0.54, $p < .05$) and the direct effect of instructional practice on math outcomes (0.225, $p < .05$). The size of the indirect effect was 0.122 (0.54 × 0.225 = 0.122, $p < .05$). I also tested whether the effect was fully mediated or partially mediated by including a direct path for leadership to math outcomes. The path was found to be small and not significant (.06, $p > .05$, not shown in Figure 3.1), and the resulting change in model deviance for one degree of freedom was also not statistically significant ($\Delta\chi^2 = 0.60$, $p > .05$). This suggests that the fully mediated relationship (i.e., with indirect leadership effects only) specified in the figure can be supported as a more parsimonious fit to the data (MacKinnon, 2008). This provides one result that has direct implications for strategies to improve student outcomes—leaders might focus efforts on facilitating changes in the school's instructional practices.

The results of this study provide preliminary evidence that instructionally-related activity at a higher organizational level can influence the quality of individual activity at a lower level. This *coordinating* aspect of school lead-

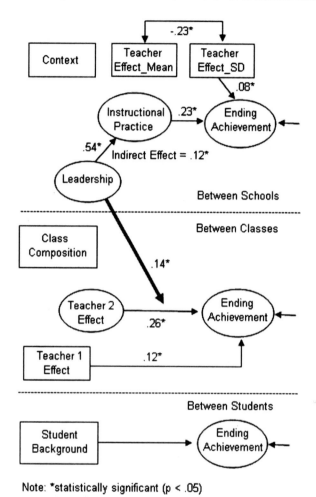

Note: *statistically significant (p < .05)

Figure 3.1 Standardized effects of variables explaining math outcomes.

ership is likely a key component in efforts to change instructional practices in schools. It provides evidence consistent with the theoretical premise that school leadership that is more strongly focused on instruction can *enhance* individual teacher effects on student learning. For theory building, this provides another viable avenue of school leadership influence that is empirically derived. The exact mechanisms for enhancing teacher effectiveness, however, remain unknown from these data. Because data on individual teachers' classroom practices were positively correlated with their perceptions of leadership within each school through preliminary confirmatory factor analysis ($r = 0.51$, $p < .01$), however, the educated *guess* is that more effective teachers have stronger classroom instruction, academic expectations, and monitoring of student progress than their less effective peers.

Study Two

Preliminary analyses. Analyses in the second study were estimated using Mplus 6.1, which is well suited to examining multilevel growth models with random slopes and path models with direct and indirect effects. The syntax for the final model is also provided in the Appendix. The preliminary model summarized in Table 3.2 was useful in identifying the shape of individuals' growth trajectories. As the table suggests, the linear, quadratic, and cubic polynomials were all significant in explaining the shape of students' math trajectories over the four-year period ($p < .001$). Each was therefore retained in subsequent analyses.

It is important to note that with higher order polynomial models, the separate components cannot be added and subtracted together to determine how much change is made during each interval (Hox, 2010). This is because growth between intervals is changing over the temporal period of the study. When the cubic component is included in the model, it implies that the focus should be on the entire trend under consideration as opposed to a particular interval. The significant cubic polynomial in Table 3.2 implies that students have differing rates of growth in math over time, as shown by the overall trajectory shape in Figure 3.2. The figure implies that student growth was not simply linear (a constant rate) or quadratic (accelerating or decelerating at a constant rate) over time. The results (not tabled) also suggested that both the intercepts and cubic growth slopes varied *randomly* across schools ($p < .05$), which lends credibility to building the explanatory model for growth on the cubic component of the student math trajectory.

TABLE 3.2 Initial Estimates of Student Growth in Math Over Time

	Estimate	SE	Significance
Intercept	646.70	1.11	.000
Linear	13.29	0.15	.000
Quadratic	–7.40	0.17	.000
Cubic	3.01	0.10	.000

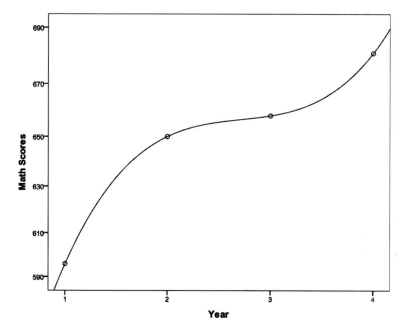

Figure 3.2   Examining the shape of average student achievement in math.

EXAMINING TEACHER EFFECTS AND INSTRUCTIONAL PRACTICES

After ensuring that the student growth in math was properly described, we can proceed to investigate school variables that might influence growth in student math outcomes. As noted previously, because the model includes higher order polynomial contrasts, the unstandardized effects are reported, and the focus is on the overall meaning of the growth trend over time, rather than trying to estimate effects at any particular interval. Because of the variable coding, the intercept describes the grand mean for math achievement, which is centered just after the second interval of the trend (i.e., in terms of the four observed mean estimates for each time interval). At the school level, the results in Table 3.3 suggest that average teacher effectiveness was unrelated to math intercepts (0.840, $p > .05$). Second, school instructional practice was positively related to math intercepts (1.583, $p < .05$). Third, staff average teaching experience was positively related to math intercepts (1.767, $p < .05$). Fourth, school composition was negatively related math intercepts (−5.098, $p < .05$). In this latter instance, this indicates that schools with greater percentages of low SES students, students requiring English

TABLE 3.3 Unstandardized Estimates of Predictors on Student Achievement and Growth

Variables	Estimate	SE	95%CI Lower	95%CI Upper
School Level				
Intercept	653.140*	0.888	651.138	654.890
School composition	–5.098*	0.782	–6.644	–3.552
Enrollment	–1.813	1.027	–3.843	0.217
Teaching staff experience	1.767*	0.687	0.408	3.126
Instructional practice	1.583*	0.766	0.171	3.001
Average teacher effectiveness	0.840	0.848	–0.838	2.518
Student Level				
Female	5.113*	0.330	4.466	5.761
Minority by race/ethnicity	–10.096*	0.363	–10.808	–9.385
ELL	0.187	0.498	–0.788	1.162
Low SES	–12.687*	0.371	–13.413	–11.960
Linear growth	13.285*	0.150	12.989	13.581
Quadratic growth	–7.396*	0.168	–7.726	–7.066
Cubic growth	3.076*	0.097	2.883	3.268
Growth*School composition	0.473*	0.103	0.270	0.677
Growth*Instructional practice	–0.051	0.101	–0.252	0.150
Growth*Average effectiveness	0.155*	0.065	0.024	0.286
Growth*Average effectiveness* Instructional practice	0.166*	0.075	0.016	0.315
School achievement R^2	0.67			
Individual achievement R^2	0.44			
School growth slope R^2	0.71			

Note: $*p < .05$

language services, and students receiving special education services had lower levels of math achievement. Regarding student background variables, the results were consistent with the previous study.

Turning to student growth over the four-year period, there were also some findings that were consistent with initial propositions. First, schools with stronger teacher effectiveness experienced greater growth in math over time (0.155, $p < .05$). Although in this model school instructional practice was not directly related to growth in math (–0.051, $p > .05$), the interaction between teacher effectiveness and instructional practice was found to be positive and significant in explaining growth (0.166, $p < .05$), after controlling for the context variables in the model. This result implies that the effect of instructional practice was contingent on levels of average teacher effectiveness.

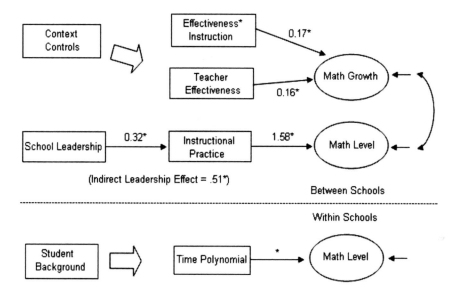

Note: *statistically significant ($p < .05$)

Figure 3.3 Unstandardized effects of school leadership, instructional practices, and aggregate teacher effectiveness on math outcomes.

Figure 3.3 illustrates several additional school leadership relationships tested in the model. Consistent with the first study, this suggests that instructional practice was a mediator between school leadership and math outcomes. Once again, leadership was not directly related to outcomes ($p > .05$), but the indirect unstandardized effect of leadership on achievement was significant (0.51, $p < .05$). This finding also lends support to the view that schools' instructional practices are a statistically significant pathway of indirect leadership influence on academic outcomes.

The finding that instructional practices and teacher effectiveness together affect school growth in math is viewed as one of the key findings of the study because it suggests that the school's instructional practices were perceived as stronger in settings where aggregate teacher effectiveness was stronger. Because these variables were defined very differently (i.e., instructional practice was defined from teacher surveys and aggregate teacher effectiveness from the residual estimate of individual teachers' observed versus expected student outcomes), this result lends credibility to the validity of both measures as a means of differentiating schools in terms of their instructional processes. It suggests teacher effects do accumulate within schools to provide a measurable academic advantage to students attending schools with stronger teacher effectiveness. Figure 3.4 illustrates the differ-

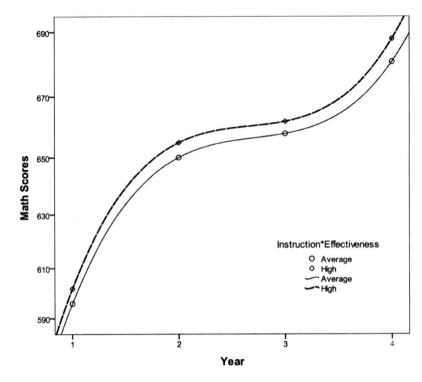

Figure 3.4 Differences in school trajectories due to instruction and effectiveness.

ence in math achievement between schools at the grand mean in terms of teacher effectiveness and instructional practices versus those schools where instructional practices and effectiveness were considerably stronger (i.e., defined as one SD above the grand mean).

DISCUSSION AND IMPLICATIONS

Currently, there is a strong expectation that school leaders can improve the quality of teaching and learning environments in ways that lead to higher student outcomes (Barth, 1990; Cohen & Hill, 2000; Creemers & Kyriakides, 2008). In contrast with even a decade ago, the image of school leadership focused on increasing organizational learning has gained global acceptance. This imagery directs attention to the role that leadership plays in improving the school's instructional practices based on increasing collaboration, commitment, and shared responsibility for results. Drawing inspiration from a body of work on instructional (Hallinger & Murphy, 1986), transformational (Leithwood & Jantzi, 1999), and distributed leadership

(Gronn, 2002), leadership aimed at instructional improvement signals the importance of creating and sustaining a school-wide focus on learning, not only for students, but also for teachers and staff (Barth, 1990; Fullan, 2006; Marks & Printy, 2003; Mulford & Silins, 2003; Robinson et al., 2008). The results of these studies begin to address questions about the importance of associations among school actions, teacher effectiveness, and changes in student outcomes over time. This has been a limitation of previous cross-sectional research on school leadership and teacher effects.

This chapter addressed several propositions about school-level improvement actions. One proposition was that school-level leadership actions might positively influence improvement in learning through enhancing teacher effectiveness in the classroom (Heck & Hallinger, 2009). The results provided considerable support for this hypothesis. More specifically, in the first study, in schools with a stronger perceived focus on instructional leadership (i.e., as defined by student achievement being a top priority, a focus on developing a school improvement plan that addresses instructional needs at the school, resource allocation to support instruction, effective ongoing evaluation of instruction, and the school's progress toward meeting goals), individual teacher effects on student classroom learning were considerably larger than in schools where these processes were rated as more average. This provides support for the view that improvement activity at a higher organizational level can "coordinate," or filter, the range of individual teacher activity at a lower level. This *coordinating* aspect of school leadership is likely a key component in efforts to change instructional practices in schools (Leithwood et al., 2006). Moreover, after controlling for other variables in the model including average teacher effectiveness, less variability in effectiveness was associated with significantly stronger ending school achievement.

A second proposition was that differences in the average quality of teaching effectiveness between schools might provide an academic advantage or disadvantage to students over time (Heck, 2009). It is known that differences between teachers exist within schools. For example, a considerable academic advantage accrues to a student having two successive highly-effective teachers compared with her peer having consecutive teachers of average effectiveness. Less is known, however, about whether differences in teacher effectiveness at the school level may also contribute to student growth in math. Taken together, the results of the two studies suggested teacher effectiveness seems to a) compound across levels of the data hierarchy (i.e., from classrooms to the school level) and b) affect growth in math over time. In addition, the evidence also suggested that in schools with stronger instructional practices, teacher effects on student growth in math were enhanced. More specifically, teacher effectiveness exerted a main effect on school growth in math, which was compounded in high-effectiveness settings through the additional positive interaction with instructional practices. The size of the combined teacher effect is hard to ascertain, how-ever, because of the nonlinear nature of the growth process (Hox, 2010).

A third proposition was that a leadership focus on instructional practices at the school level would have positive benefits in terms of achievement levels in math (Supovitz et al., 2010). In both studies, school leadership indirectly affected math outcomes through instructional practices. These results pro-vide support for the view that the overall learning environment of the school matters in affecting school improvement (Kyriakides, Creemers, Antoniou, & Demetriou, 2009; Preis, 2010). Moreover, school leadership processes appear to be more positively perceived in schools with stronger instructional prac-tices (Leithwood et al., 2010; Robinson et al., 2008; Supovitz et al., 2010) and, as the first study indicated, instructionally-focused leadership appears to play a coordinating role in facilitating *stronger effectiveness* of individual teachers.

The results should be considered in light of a couple of limitations. First, although it would be ideal to study individual teacher effects over a longer period, it can be challenging to specify such models owing to a number of technical problems (e.g., accommodating several cross-classified teacher/ student settings and resulting complex temporal relationships). The results therefore suggest adopting a more modest view of differences in student achievement that are due to teachers and schools than is often advanced in the literature. Second, although teachers' responses were used to develop school measures of instructional practices, it was not possible to link data on students directly to teachers and to teacher (and student) perceptions of classroom practices over the full period of this study. It must be assumed, therefore, that in schools with stronger instructional processes (i.e., chal-lenging educational activities, close monitoring of student progress, high learning expectations), this environment positively affects teachers' class-room effectiveness. One way this might occur suggested from the first study is through greater coordination and consistency in teacher effectiveness. Some evidence of correlations between teachers' perceptions of their own classroom practices also partially corroborates this assertion.

These studies begin to address the "black box" among various school factors directed at improving teacher effects and the learning environment within the school. They imply some promising avenues for school leaders to pursue in focusing on school improvement (Barth, 1990; Leithwood et al., 2010; Robinson et al., 2008). These might include hiring quality teachers, retaining them over time, and providing a focus on building the school's instructional environment, for example, through developing a strategic im-provement plan, emphasizing teacher collaboration and commitment in building a strong instructional environment and set of achievement expec-tations, and providing targeted professional development to change the effectiveness of teacher classroom practices.

NOTES

1. Polynomial regression designs are often used to fit various curvilinear or non-linear trends. For data that have one curve, such as slowing down or speeding up over time, a quadratic term can be added. If the curve trends up or down again at the end, a cubic term can be added.

2. The addition of the cubic term puts the focus on the entire trend rather than a particular interval. More specifically, the cubic term contributes to the overall effect of going from low to high values of the independent variable, so that one cannot interpret the linear trend of going from low to high on the independent variable for each interval.

3. Polynomial designs do not have to contain all effects up to the same degree for every predictor variable. Preliminary models were also tested for linear cross-level effects, but these tended to be redundant with the cross-level cubic effects so they were not included for sake of parsimony. This is consistent with interpreting differences over the entire course of the trend as opposed to a particular interval.

APPENDIX

SPSS Syntax for First Model

```
MIXED
 zscoremath by time with studcomp zenroll zperteach5yr zinstlead
zinpractice
 zeffect_mean zeffect_sd classcomp zteffect1 zteffect2
 female minor lowses otherlang
 /fixed =  studcomp zenroll zperteach5yr zinpractice zeffect_mean
zeffect_sd
 classcomp zteffect1 zteffect2 zinstlead*zteffect2
studcomp*zteffect2
 female minor lowses otherlang
 time time*zteffect2_mean  time*studcomp
 /Random = intercept  time | Subject(schcode) COVTYPE(UN)
 /Random = intercept | Subject(teach4id) COVTYPE(ID)
 /Random = intercept | Subject(teach3id) COVTYPE(ID)
 /Repeated = time | Subject(person*teach3id*teach4id*schcode)
COVTYPE(AR1)
 /missing = include
 /METHOD =ML
 /PRINT = G  SOLUTION  TESTCOV.
```

Mplus Input Statements for Model 2

```
TITLE:     Growth Model for Chapter;
DATA:      FILE IS C:\program files\mplus\shoho2.dat;
           Format is 6f8.0,2f8.2,3f8.0,6f8.0;
VARIABLE: Names are schcode female lowses Ell minor math schcont
           instprac lincon quadcon cubcon enroll_y tch_exp teacheff
           instteff zmath prinlead;

           usevariables are female lowses Ell minor math schcont
           instprac lincon quadcon cubcon enroll_y tch_exp teacheff
           instteff prinlead;

           Cluster = schcode;

           within = female lowses Ell minor lincon quadcon cubcon;
           between = schcont enroll_y tch_exp teacheff instprac
              instteff
           prinlead;
```

```
ANALYSIS: TYPE = twolevel random; (to specify models with random
                parameters)
          Estimator is MLR;
          Iterations = 1000;

Model:
          %Between%
          math on schcont enroll_y tch_exp
          teacheff instprac;                 (intercept model)
          S on schcont teacheff instprac
          instteff;                          (random slope model)
          instprac on prinlead;              (leadership effect)
          teacheff with prinlead;

       %Within%
          math on quadcon lincon female lowses Ell minor;
          S|math on cubcon;        (used to specify the random slope)

OUTPUT:   SAMPSTAT;
```

REFERENCES

Barth, R. (1990). *Improving schools from within.* San Francisco, CA: Jossey-Bass.

Barth, R. (2001). Teacher leader. *Phi Delta Kappan, 82*(6), 443–449.

Berliner, D. C. (1989). The place of process-product research in developing the agenda for research on teacher thinking. *Educational Psychologist, 24,* 325–344.

Bloom, H. S., Hill, C. J., Black, A. R., & Lipsey, M. W. (2008). Performance trajectories and performance gaps as achievement effect-size benchmarks for educational interventions. *Journal of Research on Educational Effectiveness, 1,* 289–328.

Bossert, S., Dwyer, D., Rowan, B., & Lee, G. (1982). The instructional management role of the principal. *Educational Administration Quarterly, 18*(3), 34–64.

Bressoux, P., & Bianco, M. (2004). Long-term teacher effects on pupils' learning gains. *Oxford Review of Education, 30*(3), 327–345.

Cohen, D., & Hill, H. (2000). Instructional policy and classroom performance: The mathematics reform in California. *Teachers College Record, 102*(2), 294–343.

Creemers, B. P. M. (1994). *The effective classroom.* London: Cassell.

Creemers, B. P. M., & Kyriakides, L. (2008). *The dynamics of educational effectiveness: A contribution to policy, practice and theory in contemporary schools.* London: Routledge.

Fullan, M. (2006). *The development of transformational leaders for educational decentralization.* Toronto, Canada: Author.

Garner, C., & Raudenbush, S. (1991). Neighborhood effects on educational attainment: A multi-level analysis of the influence of pupil ability, family, school, and neighborhood. *Sociology of Education, 64*(4), 251–262.

Goldstein, H., & Sammons, P. (1997). The influence of secondary and junior schools on sixteen year examination performance: a cross-classified multilevel analysis. *School Effectiveness and School Improvement, 8,* 219–230.

Good, T. L. (1979). Teacher effectiveness in the elementary school. *Journal of Teacher Education, 30,* 52–64.

Good, T. L., & Brophy, J. E. (1986). Teacher behavior and student achievement. In M. C. Whittrock (Ed.), *Handbook of research on teaching* (3rd ed. pp. 570–602). New York, NY: McMillan.

Gronn, P. (2002). Distributed leadership as a unit of analysis. *Leadership Quarterly, 13,* 423–451.

Hall, G., & Hord, S. (2001). *Implementing change: Patterns, principles, and potholes.* Boston, MA: Allyn & Bacon.

Hallinger, P. (2003). Leading educational change: Reflections on the practice of instructional and transformational leadership. *Cambridge Journal of Education, 33*(3), 329–351.

Hallinger, P., Bickman, L., & Davis, K. (1996). School context, principal leadership and student achievement. *Elementary School Journal, 96*(5), 498–518.

Hallinger, P., & Murphy, J. (1986). The social context of effective schools. *American Journal of Education, 94*(3), 328–355.

Hanushek, E. (1971). Teacher characteristics and gains in student achievement: estimation using micro data. *American Economic Review, 61*(2), 280–288.

Heck, R. H. (2006). Assessing school achievement progress: Comparing alternative approaches. *Educational Administration Quarterly, 42*(5), 667–699.

Heck, R. H. (2007). Examining the relationship between teacher quality as an organizational property of schools and students' achievement and growth rates. *Educational Administration Quarterly, 43*(4), 399–432.

Heck, R. H. (2009). Teacher effectiveness and student achievement: Investigating a multilevel cross-classified model. *Journal of Educational Administration, 47*(2), 227–249.

Heck, R. H., & Hallinger, P. (2009). Assessing the contribution of distributed leadership to school improvement and growth in math achievement. *American Educational Research Journal, 46*(3), 626–658.

Heck, R. H., & Hallinger, P. (2010, May). *Examining the effects of school leadership on the instructional learning environment, teacher effectiveness, and student math achievement.* Paper presented at the annual meeting of the American Educational Research Association, Denver, CO.

Heck, R. H., & Moriyama, K. (2010). Examining the association between elementary schools' instructional capacity and student achievement: A regression discontinuity approach. *School Effectiveness and School Improvement, 21*(4), 377–408.

Hox, J. (2010). *Multilevel analysis: Techniques and applications.* New York, NY: Routledge.

Kyriakides, L., Creemers, B., Antoniou, P., & Demetriou, D. (2009). A synthesis of studies searching for school factors: Implications for theory and research. *British Research Journal, 36*(1), 1–24.

Leithwood, K., Day, C., Sammons, P., Harris, A., & Hopkins, D. (2006). *Seven strong claims about successful school leadership.* Nottingham, England: National College of School Leadership.

Leithwood, K., & Jantzi, D. (1999). The relative effects of principal and teacher leadership on student engagement in school. *Educational Administration Quarterly, 35*(Supplement), 679–706.

Leithwood, K., Louis, K., Anderson, S., & Wahlstrom, K. (2004). *Review of research: How leadership influences student learning.* New York, NY: The Wallace Foundation.

Leithwood, K., Patten, S., & Jantzi, D. (2010). Testing a conception of how school leadership influences student learning. *Educational Administration Quarterly, 46*(5), 671–706.

MacKinnon, D. P. (2008). *Introduction to statistical mediation analysis.* New York, NY: Taylor and Francis.

Marcoulides, G., & Hershberger, S. (1997). *Multivariate statistical methods.* Mahwah, NJ: Lawrence Erlbaum.

Marks, H., & Printy, S. (2003). Principal leadership and school performance: An integration of transformational and instructional leadership. *Educational Administration Quarterly, 39*(3), 370–397.

McCaffrey, D. F., Lockwood, J. R., Koretz, D., Louis, T. A., & Hamilton, L. (2004). Models for value-added modeling of teacher effects. *Journal of Educational and Behavioral Statistics, 29*(1), 67–101.

Mendro, R., Jordan, H., Gomez, E., Anderson, M., & Bembry, K. (1998, April). Longitudinal teacher effects on student achievement and their relation to school and project evaluation. Paper presented at the annual meeting of the American Educational Research Association, San Diego, CA.

Mulford, B., & Silins, H. (2003). Leadership for organisational learning and improved student outcomes: What do we know? *Cambridge Journal of Education, 33*(2), 175–195.

Murnane, R. (1975). *The impact of school resources on the learning of inner city children.* Cambridge, MA: Ballinger.

Opdenakker, M. C., & Van Damme, J. (2007). Do school context, student composition, ands school leadership affect school practice and outcomes in secondary education? *British Educational Research Journal, 33*(2), 179–206.

Preis, S. (2010). *Teacher effectiveness and teacher compensation.* Report prepared for the Joint Committee on Education. Downloaded on Feb. 20, 2011, from http://www.senate.mo.gov/jced/Teacher%20Effectiveness%20and%20Teacher%20Compensation%20Report%209.14.10.pdf

Raudenbush, S., Bryk, A., Cheong, Y. F., & Congdon, R. (2004). *HLM 6: Hierarchical linear and nonlinear modeling.* Lincolnwood, IL: Scientific Software.

Robinson, V., Lloyd, C., & Rowe, K. (2008). The impact of leadership on student outcomes: An analysis of the differential effects of leadership types. *Educational Administration Quarterly, 44*(5), 564–588.

Rosenshine, B. V. (1986). Synthesis of research on explicit teaching. *Educational Leadership, 43*, 60–69.

Rowan, B., Correnti, R., & Miller, R. J. (2002). What large-scale survey research tells us about teacher effects on student achievement: Insights from the Prospects Study of elementary schools. *Teachers College Record, 104*, 1525–1567.

Scheerens, J., & Bosker, R. J. (1997), *The foundations of educational effectiveness.* Oxford, UK: Pergamon.

Seidel, T., & Shavelson, R. J. (2007). Teaching effectiveness research in the past decade: The role of theory and research design in disentangling meta-analysis results. *Review of Educational Research, 77*(4), 454–499.

Seltzer, M., Choi, K., & Thum, Y. M. (2003). Examining relationships between where students start and how rapidly they progress. Using new developments in growth modeling to gain insight into the distribution of achievement within schools. *Educational Evaluation and Policy Analysis, 25*(3), 263–286.

Supovitz, J., Sirinides, P., & May, H. (2010). How principals and peers influence teaching and learning. *Educational Administration Quarterly, 46*(1), 31–56.

Teddlie, C., Kirby, P. C., & Stringfield, S. (1989). Effective versus ineffective schools: Observable differences in the classroom. *American Journal of Education, 97*(3), 221–236.

Van de Grift, W., & Houtveen, A. (2006). Underperformance in primary schools. *School Effectiveness and School Improvement, 17*(3), 255–273.

Wiley, S. (2001). Contextual effects on student achievement: School leadership and professional community. *Journal of Educational Change, 2*(1), 1–33.

Willms, J. (1992). *Monitoring school performance. A guide for educators.* London: Falmer Press.

Witziers, B., Bosker, R., & Kruger, M. (2003). Educational leadership and student achievement: The elusive search for an association. *Educational Administration Quarterly, 39*(3), 398–423.

CHAPTER 4

LEADERSHIP FOR EQUITY

Distributed Leadership in Linked Learning Schools

Erica Hamilton and Jenifer Crawford-Lima

For over a hundred years high school classrooms in the United States have looked much the same: students sitting in rows with the teacher in the front of the room lecturing (Tyack, 1974; Oakes & Saunders, 2008). Similarly, the organization of schools has changed very little, with the principal as the leader, the teachers organized by subject area and teaching in isolated classrooms, and the students sorted onto academic or vocational tracks based on their perceived ability and potential (Graham, 2005). This efficient, but inequitable approach to schooling has been challenged over the course of the 20th century through reforms such as career-thematic coursework, college prep for all, and differentiated instruction.

In the past twenty years an equity-focused school transformation effort has brought many of these reforms together with the goal of creating an equitable approach to schooling that integrates *both* college and career preparation for *all* students. This approach, first called "multiple pathways" and now "linked learning," integrates previously isolated content and responsi-

The Changing Nature of Instructional Leadership in the 21st Century, pages 63–87
Copyright © 2012 by Information Age Publishing

63

bilities, and requires changes in the operations of the school, particularly the leadership practices. The study discussed in this chapter explores the leadership practices at four high schools implementing linked learning. This study was part of a more comprehensive study of ten high schools conducted by a team at the Institute for Democracy, Education, and Action (IDEA) at the University of California, Los Angeles. The larger study described key conditions that support the implementation of linked learning with a particular focus on vision development, the integration of instruction, personalization, collaboration, and assessment practices (Saunders, Fanelli, Hamilton, Cain, & Moya, 2012). The present study examined the leadership that occurs within linked learning schools, asking specifically: 1) How is leadership organized at each linked learning school? 2) What are the similarities and differences across multiple linked learning schools regarding how leadership is organized? And 3) What contextual elements influence and/or are influenced by leadership practices at linked learning schools? In this chapter, we introduce linked learning as an important equity-based approach to schooling, review the findings of our study on the leadership that takes place within linked learning schools, and discuss the implications of these findings.

WHAT IS LINKED LEARNING?

Linked learning is not a program or specific model, and thus each school implementing it may look very different. However, there are four key components that exist in some way at all linked learning schools (California Center for College and Career, 2010a).

The first two components of linked learning include a *college preparatory curriculum and career preparatory curriculum for all students.* College preparatory coursework teaches for the minimum entrance requirements for a four-year college or university, including the core curricula such as English, math, science and social studies as well as the arts and foreign language requirements. Career preparatory coursework typically engages students in a particular field such as forensics or computer networking through projects, class offerings, and internships. For some schools career preparation does not focus on a specific career but embeds professional 21st century themes such as communication, collaboration, problem solving, and technological literacy within a particular thematic elective or throughout the curriculum (California Center for College and Career, 2010b).

The third component is *field-based learning opportunities* that expose students to real-world environments through connections with local businesses, organizations, and community members to provide internships, mentoring, job-shadowing, virtual apprenticeships, and school-based enterprises or projects (California Center for College and Career, 2010c).

The last component of linked learning includes *individualized supports* such as differentiated instruction, academic intervention, and individualized attention and counseling for students experiencing academic and socio-emotional difficulties that may threaten their success at school. This component is critical to ensure that all students can access a challenging curriculum and learn the skills and content necessary to succeed in college and career (Oakes & Saunders, 2008).

Linked Learning Today

Linked learning is still a relatively small movement. Career academies are the most common form of linked learning, and there are approximately 6,275 career academies in schools nationwide, and 467 in California (Dayton, Hester, & Stern, 2011). In California the "going small" movement in the early 2000s contributed greatly to the development of career-themed small schools, academies, and small learning communities (Darling-Hammond, Ross, & Milliken, 2006). Research on these schools has demonstrated that linking academics and career education is improving student attendance, credits earned, graduation rates, and college attendance (Stern, Dayton, & Raby, 2010), with greater improvements for students at risk of dropping out of school (Dayton et al., 2011).

Linked Learning and Leadership

Research on academic and vocational integration in the 1990s and current research on linked learning briefly touch on what school-site leaders need to *do*. This research indicates the importance of a school-site leader having a vision of integration, and the ability to communicate and persuade others to act on that vision (Grubb, Davis, Lum, Plihal, & Morgaine, 1991). More recent research identifies the "skills and competencies" necessary for leaders of linked learning schools, focusing on the importance of building community, business, institutional and civic partnerships, the value of understanding how to "bridge the divide that traditionally exists between career and technical content and academic content," and the necessity for school-site leaders to facilitate collaboration within the school and between the school and outside partners (California Department of Education, 2010, p. 140).

This chapter builds on these studies and explores *how* leadership is manifested at the school site, and in particular how it exists across multiple individuals and not just in the position of principal.

Why is Leadership Important?

A multitude of qualitative and quantitative studies have demonstrated the direct and (primarily) indirect impact that leadership has on student performance (Dinham, 2004; Jacobson, Brooks, Johnson, Ylimaki, 2007; Marks & Printy, 2003; Robinson, 2007; Verona & Young, 2001; Witziers, Bosker, & Kruger, 2003). Additionally, leadership-focused educational researchers have found that distributing school-site leadership among teachers has a positive impact on student engagement, student outcomes, and teacher self-efficacy and morale (Leithwood, Louis, Anderson, & Wahlstrom, 2004; Louis, Leithwood, Wahlstrom, & Anderson, 2010; Marks & Louis, 1997). Research on school change has revealed that to successfully implement any new strategies, programs, or policies, school-site leaders have to take the local context into consideration, which typically entails engaging all stakeholders (particularly teachers) in the implementation process (Datnow & Stringfield, 2000). Other leadership experts advocate for shared leadership structures that "have many leaders at all levels" (Fullan, 2001, p. 134) and comment that "given the complexity of school-based reform, ideas from the entire school community are essential" (Goodman, Baron, & Myers, 2004, p. 310). These studies have illustrated the impact of leadership on student performance, teacher experiences, and reform implementation. In 2006 James Spillane built on this body of leadership research to look more deeply at *how* leadership is distributed across multiple individuals at a school site.

Spillane (2006) describes the distributed leadership practices he discovered as "co-performance" (individuals performing the same leadership function in a collaborative fashion), "division of labor" (individuals separately performing different leadership functions), and "parallel performance" (individuals separately performing the same leadership functions without coordination among them). He also points out that this distribution is not limited to formal distribution among positional leaders such as administrators, but frequently includes informal distribution among both formal and informal leaders. Spillane's findings show that the distribution of leadership is dependent on multiple factors: the function of the leadership (e.g., resource procurement or teacher development), subject matter (e.g., language arts or science), school type (e.g., charter, private or public), school size, and development stage (years since the school or program has been implemented).

Another relevant leadership study explored the extent to which leadership is distributed in relation to contextual issues regarding "what is to be accomplished" (Leithwood et al., 2004). For example, the leadership is more distributed with leadership functions such as "managing instruction," and "developing people" than it is with "structuring the workplace" and "setting directions." This inclusion of context is of particular importance when considering the variations in context that the components of linked learning may create, and thus the potential for a variation in the distribution of leadership.

The literature on leadership lays an important foundation for the present study. It tells us that leadership (and distributed leadership in particular) positively impacts students, teachers and the implementation of reforms. It establishes a typology for the examination of distributed leadership practices, and introduces the role of context in the variation of distributed practices. Finally, it establishes the role of both formal and informal leaders within the distribution of leadership at the school site. In our study, we sought to describe how leadership is organized at linked learning schools as well as identify the contextual elements that influence and/or are influenced by leadership practices at linked learning schools.

METHODS

This study drew on a subset of data drawn from a larger 10-school study with over 125 teachers, administrators, and community partners, as well as school-level data and documents, over 300 interviews, and 4,000 surveys all conducted by the Institute for Democracy, Education and Access (IDEA) at UCLA. The purpose of the larger study was to examine the overall implementation of the linked learning approach to schooling (Saunders et al., 2012). As part of the larger three-year study, there was a brief analysis of the leadership present at the school sites. However, given the breadth of the study, the leadership analysis was minimal and focused primarily on the challenges faced by the positional school-site leader (principal) in the implementation of the linked learning components.

Sites and Participants

The sites for the larger study were selected as part of an intensive process that started with 115 school sites across California implementing some form of linked learning. From this list, we eliminated 49 schools for poor performance and/or lack of fidelity to the linked learning components. Of the 66 remaining schools, 27 agreed to participate in the study, and our research teams visited and created brief reports on these schools during the fall semester of the 2008–2009 school year. Finally, we created lists of the 27 sites visited, grouping them according to diversity criteria (governance, geographic and demographic) and held extensive discussions regarding the other criteria (implementation of linked learning components, student success, and equity). From those discussions, we arrived at 10 school sites.

Data sources were drawn from this larger study focusing on four linked learning high schools across California where there was ample leadership data, similar number of years implementing linked learning, and geographic representation of four major cities across California. Three of the schools in this sample are small autonomous schools (131 to 469 students) and one is a half-day program with approximately 700 students per session (morning and afternoon). All of the schools opened within a range of four to 10 years. It is important to note the relative consistency of school size and developmental stage, as Spillane (2006) indicates the relationship between these contextual elements and the distribution of leadership.

Data Collection

The first round of site visits took place during the spring semester of the 2008–2009 school year. Each visit spanned three days and involved two to three researchers from the IDEA team. During each visit, the researchers conducted approximately three to five interviews with school administrators (principal, assistant principals, deans, counselors and support staff) and eight to 16 interviews with teachers (depending on the size of the school). The second round of site visits took place during the spring semester of the 2009–2010 school year. These visits were typically two days and primarily involved follow-up interviews with the individuals we interviewed during our first round of visits. See sample questions from our interview protocols in Tables 4.1 and 4.2 in the Appendix.

Data for this project include 61 interviews with administrators, teachers and support staff at four of the schools in the larger study. See Table 4.3 in the appendix for the counts of people interviewed, including their roles and number of interviews conducted at each site. Throughout the findings the four school sites will be referred to by pseudonyms used by the researchers throughout data collection and analysis. These pseudonyms include: Northern California Medical Academy (NCMA), Central High School (CHS), Southern Creative Academy (SCA), and Southern International School (SIS).

Data Analysis

Focusing primarily on interview data collected over the course of 2008–2010, this research employed typology-based mixed-methods data analysis (Miles & Huberman, 1994) that explored the presence of particular leadership practices at each and across linked learning schools, and illuminated the contextual elements that occurred at school sites in relation to the leadership practices and linked learning. One set of codes corresponded to the components of linked learning. These codes were based on the codes used for the larger study, which were created from the ConnectEd rubric (California Center for College and Career, 2010c) and the work of Jeannie Oakes and Marisa Saunders (2008). The other set of codes corresponded to the types of leadership practices. The leadership codes were based on Spillane's distributed leadership typology and also drew from Vroom and Yetton (1973). Spillane's framework breaks distributed leadership into three primary arrangements: co-performance, division of labor, and parallel performance. Throughout the rest of the paper we will use the emic term *collaboration* in reference to co-performance because it is the way that the teachers and administrators referred to this leadership arrangement. Spillane did not include a leadership practice description for a lack of distribution. To address this, we used Vroom and Yetton's (1973) characterization of autocratic decision-making as a contrast to "consultative" or "group-based" decision-making and expanded the concept of "manager" to include formal and informal leaders in any action that does not involve a participative (distributed) leadership practice. Since this type does not fall within the category of "distributed," when we refer to all leadership types considered in this study, we will use the more general term "leadership practices" instead of "distributed leadership" so as to be inclusive of the "autocratic" leadership practice.

An additional set of codes was created to facilitate a grounded approach and identify relevant contextual and other elements that occur in the data but were not identified in the typology (Strauss, 1987). During the intercoder reliability check meetings at the beginning of the coding process, we identified a pattern within this third set of codes and created a code for "structures" associated with linked learning and leadership. This code included references to time, personnel, schedule, and so on.

Throughout the coding process consistency in applying the codes was maintained through use of data reporting charts. Results were shared in ongoing analytic discussions and member checking was frequent and used for continual analysis.

Through the development of four qualitative case studies and a review of the prevalence of particular types of leadership in relation to components of linked learning, the following findings emerged. We arrange these findings by the research questions that guided our work: 1) How is leadership organized at each linked learning school? 2) What are the similarities and differences across multiple linked learning schools regarding how leadership is organized? And 3) What contextual elements influence and/or are influenced by leadership practices at linked learning schools?

LEADERSHIP PRACTICES AND LINKED LEARNING
AT FOUR CASE STUDY SITES

Each case study school offers a unique narrative that illustrates the relationships between leadership practices and linked learning components within
a particular context. In the first section, we present four brief case studies
that provide a snapshot of each school, an overview of the linked learning
components at the school, and a description of the leadership practices
present at the school.

Central High School

Central High School (CHS) is a unique half-day program that opened
in 2000. During our site visits, CHS served approximately 1400 11th and
12th grade students from 13 traditional high schools and four alternative
schools across two central California school districts. Students attended either a morning or afternoon session at CHS and spent the rest of their day at
the "home school" in their attendance area. The classes were arranged in 14
career-themed "labs" where teachers from different subject areas collaboratively planned and implemented complex projects that integrated the subjects and the theme of the lab (e.g., forensics, finance, bio-technology, etc.).

Since opening, the school had maintained its vision of immersing a diverse body of students in hands-on, project-based curricula that integrate
academic study and career/thematic coursework to prepare all students to
attend college or start a career after graduation. Some of the labs within
the school also provided field-based learning opportunities when possible.

The teachers at CHS had complete autonomy to plan the curricula, implement the projects, and assess student learning. One teacher who had
over 20 years of teaching experience and had been at the school since it
opened shared:

> We are able to pull together what we believe is necessary for the students to
> understand the concepts, and what we believe they need to understand by
> the time they get out of our classroom. So that's increasingly important. We
> pretty much have license to create the projects, with the understanding that
> we are professionals. We understand the standard, and we make sure that the
> students are learning what they need to know in order to be successful.

The role of the two administrators at CHS was to support the work of
the teachers through providing them with time to plan (during the summer, within the school day, and throughout the school year); the material
resources to conduct projects; and the training and continuous profession-

al development necessary to engage in highly collaborative project-based learning. The principal shared her philosophy:

> I really believe, if you're going to ask teachers to be creative, to come up with ways to get kids excited about school and motivated, then you've got to give them what they need to do it...My job is to give them what they need, so they can do what they do.

Additionally, there was an elected leadership team that worked closely with the administrators to maintain the vision through participating in the hiring process for new teachers and preparing them to teach in an integrated environment.

Southern International School (SIS)

The Southern International School (SIS) opened in 2006 as a small autonomous school located on the site of a learning complex in the center of a large metropolitan area of Southern California. During our visits, the student population averaged 370 students. SIS is a new tech school, a major component of which is the integration of core academic curricula, technology and 21st century skills. This approach is different from the other case study schools in that the theme of the school was not directly associated with a particular career track. Instead the theme (global studies) connected students to their community and the world while giving them the skills they needed to be successful in the workplace.

The integration initially took place through co-taught classes with English/social science and math/science pairings. During our first visit in 2008, SIS had seven co-taught classes. However, state budget cuts had a severe impact on SIS, and when we returned in 2010, the number of co-taught classes had been reduced to two, the school had lost four teachers (25% of the staff) to layoffs, and these teachers were replaced by displaced teachers from other schools. Despite this, many teachers attempted to collaboratively develop cross-curricular projects, but the lack of planning time during the summer and school year made it challenging. Beyond the budget cuts, the school district mandated assessments and pacing plans in addition to the state testing requirements. This created additional challenges for scheduling projects across multiple subjects.

In addition to the integrated curriculum, SIS attempted to start an internship program during our fist site visit. It was cancelled during the first semester due to lack of personnel to manage the program. During our second visit a non-profit organization was providing a part-time internship coordinator and had 24 students in internships or job shadowing placements.

The principal was in his first year at the school and as a principal during our first visit. He worked with the founding counselor and a core group of founding teachers to collaboratively make decisions regarding schedules, hiring, resource allocation and professional development. The decisions were typically discussed during a weekly meeting after school and implemented by the administration and participating teachers. While all teachers were invited to attend, the majority did not participate. The division between the informal leadership team and the other teachers at the school had two main sources. Some teachers cited the lack of time and compensation for participating in what they saw as additional work, and other teachers stated that they had philosophical differences with the leadership team. These teachers (a minority at the school) believed in tracking students by ability, and the administration and teacher leaders were adamantly opposed to it.

Southern Creative Academy

The Southern Creative Academy (SCA) is a small public high school (approximately 450 students) serving a large urban district in Southern California. In 2004 the large comprehensive high school in which many current SCA teachers taught was reconstituted in the form of four small autonomous schools. SCA became one of these schools and adopted a theme that exposed students to experiences and careers in website design, graphic design and video production through project-based learning that integrated academic and career/thematic coursework.

The integration of academic and career/thematic coursework was the key priority at SCA. To support this integration, the principal directed all of the schools resources to support grade-level teaming and project-based learning. This included scheduling teachers in grade-level teams and providing them with planning time during the summer and during the school day. Additionally, the principal used internal and external funding to provide two additional counselors, one literacy coach and one employment outreach specialist (EOS)—all of whom were directed by the principal to support the work of the grade-level teams.

The principal, a very dynamic individual, maintained a firm grasp over the operational elements (staffing, budgeting, and scheduling). Beyond that, the staff had a great deal of autonomy to develop and implement their cross-curricular projects and to conduct their classes as they saw fit, as long as they were keeping with the vision (participating in projects) and their students were performing well on standardized tests. The principal explained that she told the teachers each year:

You are responsible for every student in this grade level and their achievement, socially, emotionally and academically. However you do it, you are responsible. Do not come to me and say, 'Well, I didn't have this,' or, 'I didn't understand this.' Come ask. But don't tell me at the end when they're not proficient or something hasn't happened. You're totally responsible.

Northern California Medical Academy (NCMA)

In 2001, the Northern California Medical Academy (NCMA) changed from a non-autonomous academy in a comprehensive school into a small (averaging 250 students) autonomous medical-themed high school. Located in an urban area of Northern California, NCMA aimed to prepare all students for college while exposing them to careers within the medical field. This school was different from the other schools in the study in that the structure was divided into 9th and 10th grades, which prioritized medical-themed cross-curricular projects, and 11th and 12th grades, during which every student participated in internships or job shadowing in a medical field.

To support this, the lower grade teachers were scheduled into collaborative teams with shared conference periods, and the upper grade teachers and students had a schedule that was more conducive to providing internships (with core classes in the morning and electives with more flexibility in the afternoon). In addition, a full-time internship coordinator facilitated the development and maintenance of the internships and job shadowing opportunities. During both visits, the principal and leadership team were experimenting with the schedules, and many teachers complained about the lack of time they had to plan their cross-curricular projects.

Over the course of our visits, there was a change in principals. Both principals were teachers at the school since it became autonomous, and were self-declared "collaborative leaders." Similar to the Southern International School, NCMA had a leadership team comprised primarily of founding teachers who met frequently with the principal regarding scheduling, hiring, budgeting and professional development. These meetings took place after school hours and, like at SIS, were not compensated. During our second visit, the principal was attempting to formalize the leadership team meetings by arranging the schedule to provide time during the school day every Friday for the leadership team to meet.

LEADERSHIP PRACTICES AND LINKED LEARNING: SIMILARITIES AND DIFFERENCES ACROSS SITES

In this section we address each leadership practice and discuss the similarities across the sites and the differences between them. These findings answer the second research question: What are the similarities and differences across multiple linked learning schools regarding how leadership is organized?

Autocratic Leadership Practices

At each site the principal (typically in collaboration with a leadership team) made autocratic decisions related to operations (staffing, scheduling and budgeting). These decisions were guided by the vision of the school and correlated with a component of linked learning (curricular integration, community/work-based learning, and/or equity). We characterized these decisions as autocratic because although they were sometimes made by the principal with a leadership team, they did not include input from the teaching staff at large.

The differences between sites broke down into two basic categories: by whom the autocratic leadership practice was enacted and what the vision of the school was. Southern Creative Academy (SCA) was the only site in which the autocratic leadership practices were enacted solely by the principal. At Central High School (CHS), the principal managed the budget and non-staff-related resources, but the leadership team participated in the hiring and training of new teachers as well as all scheduling decisions. Both the Northern California Medical Academy (NCMA) and Southern International Academy (SIS) were in transition during our site visits and both were struggling with issues of time that impacted the leadership practices at the school. At these schools, the teacher leadership team (comprised of founding teachers) played a large role in the decision-making and implementation.

The other difference among the case study schools was the vision. While every case study site had a vision connected to linked learning, this connection varied by the type of component. CHS and SCA had visions primarily rooted in integration between academic and career/thematic curricula. The leadership of these schools directed the majority of the resources to support the grade-level teams to create cross-curricular projects. NCMA split its vision between the lower and upper grades, engaging students in cross-curricular medical-themed projects in the 9th and 10th grades through integrating and providing medical internships and job shadowing in the 11th and 12th grades. Thus, the lower grades were scheduled in grade-level teams and the teachers were provided with time during the school day to collaborate. The principal and leadership team at NCMA directed the resources for the upper grades towards providing support personnel in the form of an internship coordinator. While SIS also integrated curricula and provided some internships to students, the main focus of the leadership team decisions was equity. This vision is reflected in the decision of the principal and leadership team to not ability track students, and to schedule teachers in co-teaching pairs when possible. As we will discuss, the first year the internships were implemented, resources were not directed to support them, and the internship program failed. This was remedied in the second year.

Collaborative Leadership Practices

In every case study there was some form of collaborative planning to integrate academic and career/thematic curricula where teachers who share the same students spent some time (paid or unpaid) meeting face to face to plan a project that integrated their subject areas. The implementation of the planned curricula was conducted through co- or team teaching in some sites, or among separate classes but united through a project based on the theme of the school. Throughout the implementation of the project, the teachers met during the school day in common planning times and/or during paid or unpaid time before or after school to check in and reflect on the project implementation. All of the collaborative leadership practices were related to instructional leadership (e.g., curriculum development and implementation) rather than operational leadership (staffing, budgeting and scheduling) and were guided by the vision of the school.

The differences among the case study sites break down by the type of collaboration employed to implement the integrated curricula. This was influenced by the programming of teachers and students into co-teaching or individually-taught classroom structures. The two schools that had co-taught classes (CHS and SIS) collaboratively implemented the cross-curricular projects, although during the second year at SIS the number of co-taught classes was reduced substantially so they shifted to the model the other two schools were using. That model was the collaborative planning of projects with the implementation conducted in individual classes but coordinated among teachers during check-ins and reflection time.

Division of Labor Leadership Practices

While division of labor leadership practices were referenced less frequently than collaborative or autocratic leadership practices, these practices point to the important resource of personnel. Across every site in the case study, division of labor leadership practices were primarily related to personnel hired for a particular purpose or from a specific program (literacy specialist, employment outreach specialist, internship coordinator, etc.).

The primary difference among the case study sites were the number of these additional personnel available, and whether they were funded internally or through outside sources. CHS had four teachers hired and funded through the Regional Occupational Program. These teachers taught the specific career-focused elective within four labs and also managed the majority of the internships for students within those labs. At SCA, the principal was able to procure internal and external funding to support two additional counselors, one literacy coach and one employment outreach specialist. As discussed earlier, all four of these individuals were directed to support the integration work of the grade-level teams. However, they also engaged with individual students and student groups to provide academic supports and a small number of internships. The NCMA hired a full-time internship coordinator through a grant and provided one period out for a teacher to act as an internship supervisor to support the school's commitment to providing every student with access to a medical-themed internship. Finally, SIS provided important insight into attempting to implement internships without a division of labor practice that involved personnel dedicated to coordinating the internships. In the first year the teachers were solely responsible for implementing the internship program and it failed. During the second year, the school was slowly building a pilot program with a small number of students, but that was only with the assistance of an external partner who acted as the internship coordinator for those students and the internship sites.

Parallel Performance Leadership Practices

Parallel performance was also referenced much less frequently than autocratic or collaborative leadership practices. However, the existence of parallel leadership in the case studies provided insight into the context in which this leadership practice tended to occur. There appears to be a reverse relationship between the component in which the parallel leadership occurs and the vision of the school. At the SCA, for example, the parallel leadership occurred within the field-based learning component, and the vision focus was on integration (not field-based learning). Some teachers and staff complained that they were supporting internships separately from one another without any coordination. In converse, at NCMA, the vision focus in the 11th and 12th grades was on internships, and the parallel leadership occurred in the integration of academic and career/thematic coursework in the 11th and 12th grades. Teachers in these grades complained that they wanted to, but did not have the time they needed to create and implement cross-curricular projects.

LEADERSHIP PRACTICES AND LINKED LEARNING: CONTEXTUAL ELEMENTS ACROSS SITES

Three key elements continuously emerged in relation to linked learning and leadership practices across the four case studies:

- *Vision* played a critical role in providing a direction and guiding collaborative decisions.
- The *resources* of personnel and time impacted the capacity of schools to make collaborative decisions and implement the components of linked learning.
- *Instructional autonomy* is a fundamental paradigm shift that occurred to support the implementation of the curricular integration component of linked learning.

Vision

The literature is clear on the importance of the role of the vision as a guiding force in school leadership (Darling-Hammond & Orphanos, 2005; Fullan, 2001; Jacobson, Brooks, Johnson, & Ylimaki, 2007). The findings of this study reaffirm that literature. What is different is that previous studies tend to focus on the importance of the principal having a vision.

The four schools in this study expanded the role of the vision and placed it at the center of the work of the school, and throughout our research teachers and administrators often referred to their schools' vision statements during interviews.

The vision influenced the decisions made by the principal and the leadership team in structuring the school (scheduling and hiring), directing resources (personnel and budgeting), and providing instructional direction (professional development). The vision also guided the teachers in their collaborative cycle of planning, implementation and reflection by providing clear parameters for thematic curriculum integration.

Resources

Throughout the interviews, teachers and administrators commented on the importance of the resources of personnel and time. Personnel were primarily referenced in relation to providing field-based learning opportunities for students. Teachers and administrators at the schools with the full-time internship coordinators stated that providing internship opportunities to all students was a priority. The schools that did not have a dedicated internship coordinator only provided internships to a small number of students. See Table 4.4 in the Appendix.

Time was referenced at least once at every site in the study. At SIS and NCMA the principals and teachers shared a frustration with the lack of time to meet as a leadership team to make operational decisions. At all sites, time was referenced both positively and negatively in relation to collaboratively planning, implementing and reflecting on the integrated curriculum.

In order to develop a more quantitative analysis, coded interviews were re-analyzed with a focus on these references. See Table 4.5 in the Appendix for a counts summary of these findings.

The results of this analysis revealed that for two of the sites (CHS and SCA) there is a positive correlation between the number of positive references to time and references to integrating academic and career-themed curricula. However, the sites that did not follow this pattern also told an important story about the use of the critical resource of time at linked learning schools.

At SIS there were multiple positive references to creating cross-curricular projects, but very few positive references to time. The majority of the negative references were in relation to teachers using their own time during their lunch break, after school or during the summer to plan, discuss and reflect on integrated curricula. Teachers also expressed concern regarding the sustainability of this practice. At NCMA the vision outlined a divide between integrating curriculum in 9th and 10th grades and providing internships for students in the 11th and 12th grades; thus resources were focused on providing planning time for the 9th and 10th grade teams and providing personnel to support the internships in the upper grades. Despite this divide, the upper grade teachers saw value in making connections across the curriculum, and the majority of negative references to time for collaborative planning were from these teachers. At both sites, administrators and teachers on the leadership team referenced the lack of time to meet and make collaborative decisions to support the linked learning program at the school.

Instructional Autonomy

In the literature the term "instructional leadership" is generally in reference to the position of the principal (Leithwood et al., 2004; Robinson, 2007; Witziers et al., 2003). In contrast, all of the sites in the present study gave teachers a great deal of autonomy to develop and implement the curricula within the parameters of the vision. It is critical to acknowledge this as instructional leadership, especially given the increasing deprofessionalization of teaching through scripted curricula and top-down programs (Newkirk, 2009). At the schools in our study, this leadership typically manifested within the teaching teams as teachers collaboratively planned their cross-curricular and career-thematic projects, and as experienced teachers mentored new teachers in the collaborative process of planning, implementation, and reflection.

RESEARCH IMPLICATIONS: SHIFTING LEADERSHIP MODELS FOR EQUITY-BASED SCHOOLING

Traditional high schools typically have hierarchical leadership (see Figure 4.1). In such a structure the principal makes the operational decisions including staffing, budgeting and scheduling (which includes the calendar, the daily bell schedule and the programming of students and teachers). He or she is also responsible for the overall instructional decisions such as determining the courses offered, directing curricula, supervising instruction and providing professional development for teachers (Callahan, 1962; Cuban, 1988). In this model, teachers are responsible for following the prescribed curricula, developing lessons, and providing instruction to students within their individual content areas. Students are typically divided into separate tracks depending on their perceived abilities, and teachers are grouped based on their content area and the tracks they teach (Oakes, 1985).

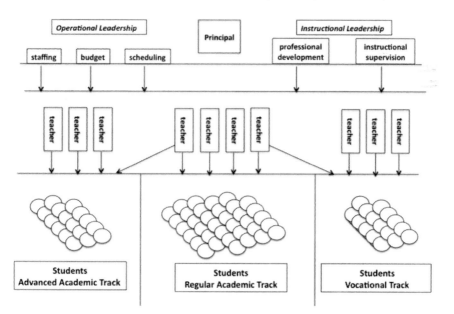

Figure 4.1 Leadership model for traditional schools. This figure illustrates the singular, top-down organization of operational and instructional leadership in a traditional high school.

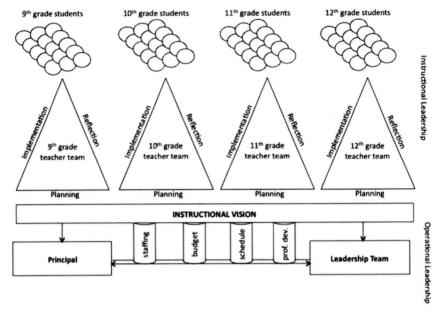

Figure 4.2 Leadership model for linked learning schools studied. This figure illustrates the multiple bottom-up organization of operational and instructional leadership in the four high schools studied implementing linked learning reform.

At the sites in our study, a different model emerged (see Figure 4.2). This model utilized a distributed approach to leadership in which the principal (frequently in collaboration with a teacher leadership team) directed the operational decisions to support a shared vision. Such decisions included budget, schedule, staff and professional development. This vision guided the instructional leadership, which is largely within the purview of the teachers, and took place within a continuous cycle of planning and implementation among grade-level teacher teams who shared the same students.

This model appears as if the traditional model is upside down. This is a critical shift that places the principal, the leadership team and the operationally-focused leadership practices at the bottom, providing the supports (staffing, budget, schedule and professional development) for the vision on which the collaborative cycle of instructional planning, implementation and reflection rests.

Limitations of the Study

This study utilized interviews with teachers and school-site administrators as the primary data set. This creates limitations regarding the unreliability of self-reporting, and contextual limitations. In self-reporting, it is possible that people described the linked learning components and leadership practices as they would like them to be rather than how they actually existed at the school. While we compared individual interviews with each other, with primary documents and with a limited number of direct observations, the primacy of interview data in this study is a limitation to be considered. Furthermore, the limitation of the interviews to the school-site did not permit a thorough examination of factors external to the school site that may have been impacting the implementation of the components at the school site and/or the use of specific leadership practices at the school site. Finally, this study was conducted as part of a larger study examining the implementation of linked learning. As such, the development of the interview protocols, the survey questions, and the observation guides included a substantial amount of questions not related to this study. Additionally, due to the differences in timing, none of the data collection instruments were created with the leadership typology used for this study.

These limitations could be addressed in future studies through a clearer alignment between the typology and the research instruments, the inclusion of additional stakeholders in the interviews/surveys/observations (e.g., students, external partners and district representatives), and the addition of more observations beyond the classroom, particularly leadership and planning meetings, and professional development sessions.

Given these limitations, however, this study provides a good foundation for deriving more specific studies on leadership practices and linked learning.

Further Research

This study reveals that in a distributed leadership model, if there is a clear instructional vision guiding the decisions and a teacher leadership team shares operational decision-making power with the principal, then there is an increased likelihood that the supports for the vision can maintain consistency even with shifts in the administration, as demonstrated by two sites in the study that had new principals during the course of the study. It is important, however, that teacher leadership teams (which in this study are primarily comprised of founding teachers) engage new teachers in understanding and supporting the vision so that the vision can live on after the founding teachers leave. At the time of this study, the schools were all within their first 10 years of implementation and still had many of the founding teachers in the staff. Within the next 10 years, many of those teachers will retire or leave the school for other reasons. There is great potential to return to these schools and conduct a study on how the vision is preserved, transformed or lost during this transition.

Another potential study to build off of this research could be an exploration of the role of professional development in the support and maintenance of the vision and the collaborative/collective work of the teachers. There were a few references to professional development within the interviews for this study, some of which connected the vision to professional development. These references pointed to potential links between professional development and instructional vision; however, there were not enough references to establish a clear connection, and no reference included enough detail to provide a useful description of the connection.

Finally, the findings for both division of labor and parallel-distributed leadership practices were thinly supported within the individual case studies and were referenced rarely across the four sites in the sample. This may be due to the fact that the leadership typology was developed as a means of analysis and was not constructed and used as part of the interview protocol development process. Nevertheless, the findings and lessons regarding these leadership practices may serve as an important foundation on which additional research can build.

CONCLUSION

This research paints a picture of how leadership is organized at four schools implementing an equity-focused approach to schooling. These schools illustrate a shift from traditional top-down leadership practices and demonstrate support-oriented leadership distributed among formal (administrator) and informal (teacher) roles. The operational supports of staffing, budget, schedule, and professional development are guided by a shared vision, as is the collaborative work of the grade-level teaching teams. Beyond this guidance, however, the teachers have autonomy to plan and implement their curricula as they see fit. This structure is not without its challenges, particularly in relation to finding the time to collaborate, but it provides a promising model for leadership in the 21st century.

REFERENCES

California Center for College and Career. (2010a). *California linked learning district initiative.* Retrieved from http://www.connectedcalifornia.org/services/initiative.php

California Center for College and Career. (2010b). *Linked learning: Core components.* Retrieved from http://www.connectedcalifornia.orbg/pathways/index.php

California Center for College and Career. (2010c). *Linked learning: Rubric.* Retrieved from http://www.connectedcalifornia.org/pathways/rubric.php

California Department of Education. (2010). *Multiple pathways to student success: Envisioning the new California high school. A report to the legislature and governor pursuant to Chapter 681, Statutes of 2008.* Retrieved from http://www.carocp. org/library/document/M2_adhoc_pathways_report.pdf

Callahan, R. E. (1962). *Education and the cult of efficiency: A study of the social forces that have shaped the administration of the public school.* Chicago, IL: The University of Chicago Press.

Cuban, L. (1988). *The Managerial Imperative and the Practice of Leadership in Schools.* Albany: State University of New York Press.

Dayton, C., Hester, H. C., & Stern, D. (2011). *Profile of the California Partnership Academies, 2009–2010.* Berkeley, CA: C. A. S. Network, California Department of Education, University of California, Berkeley.

Darling-Hammond, L., & Orphanos, S. (2005). *Leadership development in California.* Palo Alto, CA: Stanford University, Institute for Research on Education Policy and Practice.

Darling-Hammond, L., Ross, P., & Milliken, M. (2006). High school size, organization and content: What matters for student success? In T. Loveless & F. Hess (Eds.), *Brookings papers on education policy: 2006–2007* (pp. 163–203). Washington, DC: Brookings Institution Press.

Datnow, A., & Stringfield, S. (2000). Working together for reliable school reform. *Journal of Education for Students Placed at Risk* 5(1), 183–204.

Dinham, S. (2004). *The influence of leadership in producing outstanding outcomes in junior secondary education.* Paper presented at the British Educational Research Association (BERA), Manchester.

Fullan, M. (2001). *Leading in a culture of change.* San Francisco, CA: Jossey-Bass.

Goodman, J., Baron, D., & Myers, C. (2004). Constructing a democratic foundation for school-based reform. In A. Hargreaves (Ed.), *Sage handbook of educational leadership: Advances in theory research and practice.* Thousand Oaks, CA: SAGE Publications.

Graham, P. A. (2005). *Schooling America: How the public schools meet the nation's changing needs.* New York, NY: Oxford University Press.

Grubb, W. N., Davis, G., Lum, J., Plihal, J., & Morgaine, C. (1991). *"The cunning hand, the cultured mind": Models for integrating vocational and academic education.* Berkeley, CA: National Center for Research in Vocational Education.

Jacobson, S. L., Brooks, C. G., Johnson, L., & Ylimaki, R. (2007). Successful leadership in three high-poverty urban elementary schools. *Leadership and Policy in Schools, 6,* 291–317.

Leithwood, K., Louis, K. S., Anderson, S. E., & Wahlstrom, K. (2004). *How leadership influences student learning. The Learning from Leadership Project.* University of Minnesota: Center for Applied Research and Educational Improvement and University of Toronto: Ontario Institute for Studies in Education. Commissioned by: The Wallace Foundation.

Louis, K. S., Leithwood, K., Wahlstrom, K., & Anderson, S. E. (2010). *Investigating the links to improved student learning.* New York, NY: The Wallace Foundation.

Marks, H. M., & Louis, K. S. (1997). Does teacher empowerment affect the classroom? The implications of teacher empowerment for instructional practice and student academic performance. *Educational Evaluation and Policy Analysis, 19*(3), 245–275.

Marks, H. M., & Printy, S. M. (2003). Principal leadership and school performance: An integration of transformational and instructional leadership. *Educational Administration Quarterly, 39*(3), 370–397.

Maxwell, N. L. (2001). Step to college: moving from the high school career academy through the four-year university. *Evaluation Review 25*(6), 619–654.

Miles, M. B., & Huberman, A. M. (1994). *Qualitative data analysis* (2nd ed.). Thousand Oaks, CA: Sage.

Newkirk, T. (2009). Stress, control, and the deprofessionalizing of teaching. *Education Week, 9*(8), 24–25.

Oakes, J. (1985). *Keeping track: How schools structure inequality.* New Haven, CT: Yale University Press.

Oakes, J., & Saunders, M. (2008). *Beyond tracking: Multiple pathways to college, career, and civic engagement.* Cambridge, MA: Harvard Education Press.

Robinson, V. M. J. (2007). School leadership and student outcomes: Identifying what works and why. *ACEL Monograph Series, 41,* 1–28.

Saunders, M., Fanelli, S., Hamilton, E., Cain, E., & Moya, J. (2012). *Linked learning guidebook.* Los Angeles, CA: Institute for Democracy Education and Access (IDEA) at the University of California, Los Angeles.

Spillane, J. P. (2006). *Distributed leadership.* San Francisco, CA: Jossey Bass.

Stern, D., Dayton, C., & Raby, M. (2010). *Career academies: A proven strategy to prepare high school students for college and careers.* Berkeley, CA: Career Academy Support Network, University of California, Berkeley.

Strauss, A. (1987). *Qualitative analysis for social scientists.* Cambridge, England: Cambridge University Press.

Tyack, D. B. (1974). *The one best system.* Cambridge, MA: Harvard University Press.

Verona, G. S., & Young, J. (2001, April). *The influence of principal transformational leadership style on high school proficiency test results in New Jersey comprehensive and vocational-technical high schools.* Paper presented at the Annual Meeting of the American Education Research Association, Seattle, WA.

Vroom, V. H., & Yetton, P. W. (1973). *Leadership and decision-making.* Pittsburg, PA: University of Pittsburg Press.

Witziers, B., Bosker, R. J., & Kruger, M. L. (2003). Educational leadership and student achievement: The elusive search for an association. *Educational Administration Quarterly, 39*(3), 398–425.

APPENDIX

There are multiple questions within the protocols and surveys that are not related to the present study; however, a selection of the interview questions related to our two research questions are listed below. The interview protocols were intended to be very broad as we were still in the initial stages of understanding of how leadership manifested at Linked Learning school sites.

TABLE 4.1   Selection of First Round of Interview Questions

Topic	Research Instrument Question
General School Site Leadership	How would you describe the leadership model/organizational structure in this school? How is it different, if it is, from traditional schools?
	How are decisions made in this school?
	What structures are in place for student, teacher and parent feedback?
	Do you have structured time for communication within the administration, between the admin and teachers, between the teachers who share students, etc?
Linked Learning Component General	Describe what the four multiple pathways components look like at your school. (administrator interview)
	How do you integrate the multiple pathways components and principles in your classroom and curriculum? (teacher interview)
Linked Learning Component Integration of college preparatory and career preparatory coursework	How well does this school integrate A-G and career preparation? (administrator interview)
	In what ways do you integrate A-G requirements and career preparation? (administrator and teacher interview)
Linked Learning Component Work-based learning experiences	Does this school have work-based learning opportunities? (administrator and teacher interview)
Linked Learning Component Additional supports for struggling students	What supports exist for students who are struggling? (administrator and teacher interviews)
Linked Learning Component Equity	How does the socioeconomic composition of your student body affect the school? How does SES affect the choice of pathways? The racial composition? (e.g., student ability & effort; parent engagement; teachers' expectations and attitudes; practices). (administrator and teacher interviews)
	Where do students typically go after graduating? How many go to a four-year college? How many do you think should or could go to a four-year college? (administrator and teacher interviews)

These questions are not directly related to the forms of distributed leadership (division of labor, co-performance and parallel performance); however, these questions, like the earlier leadership questions, are open ended enough that teachers and administrators were able to give a robust picture of the formal and informal leadership structures in existence at the schools.

TABLE 4.2 Selection of Second Round of Interview Questions

Topic	Research Instrument Question
Issues of Equity	Do you feel that there is tension here in terms of beliefs as to whether "all kids should be prepared to go to college" and " not all kids are going to go to college so let's get them career ready"?
	Do all students have access to the same classes? Do you think struggling students get a different education than other students?
Leadership roles that teachers were taking on at the school sites.	What are the formal and informal responsibilities you (or your teachers) take on in addition to teaching? Are these additional responsibilities required or voluntary?
	What structures are in place for teachers to take part in the leadership at the school? Is there a leadership team? If so, who is on it and how are they selected? Do the teachers at this school feel represented by the leadership team?

Data were collected over two site visits that occurred during the 2008–2009 and 2009–2010 school years. The total interviews from these two sets of visits are combined below, along with the number of years in Linked Learning reform since 2000.

TABLE 4.3 Data Collected by School Site

School	Total Teacher Interviews	Total Administrator Interviews	Number of Years in LL	Location in California
NCMA	13	3	9	Northern
CHS	9	4	10	Central
SIS	17	2	4	Southern
SCA	10	3	6	Southern

The table below indicates the personnel responsible for internships at each site, whether or not the individual responsible for the internships also has other responsibilities, and whether or not the vision of the school prioritizes internships.

TABLE 4.4   Internship Personnel

School	Position	Only does internships	School focus on internships
NCMA	Internship coordinator (full time)	Yes	Yes
	Internship supervisor (part time)	No (also teaches)	
SIS	Internship coordinator (part time)	Yes	Yes
CHS	ROP teachers	No (also teach)	No
SCA	Employment Opportunity Specialist	No (also supports PBL)	No

Each reference was identified as positive when teachers or administrators referred to school-day or compensated time provided for teachers to collaborate, and identified as negative when teachers or administrators referred to a lack of time or uncompensated time (teachers using their own time). To derive the "total" positive references number for each site, the negative references are subtracted from the positive references.

TABLE 4.5   Time Reference Counts

School	R/pos	R/neg	Total	Collaboration for Integration
CHS	6	2	4	25
SCA	7	0	7	31
SIS	2	5	−3	28
NCMA	6	4	2	6

SECTION II

INTERNATIONAL PERSPECTIVES OF INSTRUCTIONAL LEADERSHIP DEVELOPMENT

CHAPTER 5

THE NUMERACY COACHING PROGRAM

An Examination of the Program Impact from the Training Room into School Classrooms

Gary R. O'Mahony

INTRODUCTION

The public perception of schooling in Australia is driven by a media resplendent with headlines reporting how the results of student assessment are becoming less competitive in comparison to the test performance of math students of other countries. This alarming perception is further supported by the Australian government's establishment of a website (http://www.myschool.edu.au) where parents can find the performance of their child's school in both numeracy and literacy. This also means parents can form favorable or odious perceptions/ comparisons with other schools, thus further opening the debate about the state of educational standards in mathematics in Australia. Like it or not, this is the level of public scrutiny that schools now receive, and they must continue to respond to the changing demands

The Changing Nature of Instructional Leadership in the 21st Century, pages 91–123
Copyright © 2012 by Information Age Publishing
All rights of reproduction in any form reserved.

in student performance in mathematics. In terms of this dynamic, two fundamental questions are: 1) What are the facts that underlie the present state about Australian mathematics education, beyond the hysteria created by the press and policy makers? and 2) Is there a need for a fundamental change in the teaching and learning of mathematics in Australia?

To address these questions, this chapter will examine the impact and structure of a numeracy coaching training program for teachers. First, it will examine the need for changes in the teaching and learning in the classroom of mathematics in Victoria and the emergence of numeracy coaching to support its improvement through the Bastow Institute of Educational Leadership Tender on Numeracy Coaching. Second, a focus is given to the design and delivery of Bastow Tender requirements through an examination of the components of the Bastow Numeracy Coaching Program (NCP) coaching capabilities elements and how they were configured to meet the development of numeracy coaches as instructional leaders. The third section will examine the research design features and data sources underpinning this examination using components of Guskey's evaluative framework (2000, 2005) and findings from the evaluation studies conducted by Success Works and the Royal Melbourne Institute of Technology (RMIT) in Victoria, Australia. Finally, key findings from the study are examined and recommendations for future research are made.

MATHEMATICS TEACHING AND LEARNING IN AUSTRALIA

The first section will examine the need for changes in the teaching and learning in the classrooms of mathematics in the state of Victoria, Australia. There has also been an emergence of numeracy coaching to support its improvement through the Bastow Tender NCP. Two fundamental questions that need to be asked are really as to whether there was a need for numeracy coaching: 1) What are the facts that underlie the present state of Australian mathematics education, beyond the hysteria created by the press and policy makers? and, 2) Is there a need for a fundamental change in the teaching and learning of mathematics in Australia?

THE FACTS ABOUT MATHEMATICS EDUCATION

If Australian students are to become and remain numerate in the present educational system, then something significant will have to change. The Programme for International Student Assessment (PISA, 2006) was developed by the Organisation for Economic Co-operation and Development (OECD, 1999) in order to study performance in basic education across various countries. The first survey took place in 2000, and the second in 2003 with 41 countries taking part. It assesses the abilities of 15 year olds to apply knowledge and skills to real-life problems and situations. In 2003, PISA results showed Australian 15 year olds performed well when compared with 41 OECD and other countries across both mathematics and science scores. Australia's average (mean) scores of 524 in mathematics literacy placed it above the OECD average of 500 for each skill area and in the top third of countries. Four countries performed significantly better than Australia in mathematics literacy—Finland, Hong Kong, Republic of (South) Korea and the Netherlands—while nine countries, including Canada and New Zealand, had similar scores.

The research about the mathematics performance of students in year four and year eight in the Trends International Maths Sciences Study (TIMSS; Martin, Mullins, & Chrostowski, 2003) assessment reveals some interesting results. For example, year four mathematics students at the advanced international benchmark were able to apply mathematical understanding and knowledge in a variety of relatively complex problem situations and were able to explain their reasoning, whereas those at the low international benchmark demonstrated some basic mathematical knowledge and were able to compute with whole numbers, recognize some geometric shapes, and read simple graphs and tables. At year eight, students at the advanced international benchmark were able to organize and draw conclusions from information, make generalizations, and solve non-routine problems involving numeric, algebraic, and geometric concepts and relationships. In comparison, those at the low international benchmark demonstrated some knowledge of whole numbers and decimals, operations, and basic graphs. With the release of each new international mathematics assessment, concern about Australian students' mathematics achievement has grown, with each result that slips back indicating that the teaching and learning of mathematics need drastic improvement. Thus, the country (once more) has begun to turn its worried attention to mathematics education and the search for panaceas to address this concern.

THE NEED FOR CHANGE IN MATHEMATICS

What is the present status of mathematic performance for Australia students, and why is there a need for reform? While past international comparative student performance results appear reasonable when compared with other countries, there appear to be some glaring inconsistencies about the way math is learned and taught, prompting demands for reform to improve it. Some significant ideas that have emerged in Australian athematics research are about how it is both learned and taught. The mathematics research on teaching and learning has been highly influential and a pivotal driving force for reform in the Australian context. Siemon (2005) notes that up to 25% of Australian years eight and nine students do not have the foundational knowledge and skills needed to participate effectively in further school mathematics, or to access a wide range of post-compulsory learning opportunities. This is supported by Siemon (2000) in her work with the Australian Council of Educational Research, which states that while Victorian and Australian students compare very well with students from other countries, there is a "long tail" needing drastic attention and remedy. So how does reform begin to address this concern? The first way is to identify the problems underlying the underperformance in math. In their final report on the Middle Years Numeracy Research Project in Victoria, Siemon, Virgona, and Corneille (2001) suggested the following considerations in incorporating changes in mathematics instruction:

- *There is as much difference within year levels as between year level spread in program and course coherence and subsequent delivery.* Program coherence is a measure of integration of the different elements in the school as an organization. Newman, King, and Youngs (2000) developed the concept of "program coherence" as a dimension of school capacity as the extent to which the school's programs for student and staff learning are focused on clear learning goals, sustained over time and have a guaranteed and viable structured curriculum to follow (Waters, Marzano, & McNulty, 2003).
- *There is considerable within school variation, which suggests that individual teachers can and do make a significant difference in student learning outcomes.* Hattie (1992) argues that we should focus on the greatest source of variance that can make a difference—the teacher—who is the greatest influence so that optimal ways must be found to build powerful learning and sensationally positive effects for students through encouraging student engagement, success, and building of self-esteem in mathematics education. Contemporary approaches indicated that in the TIMSS video study of year eight mathematics in classrooms in seven countries found that while the Australian lessons had the second highest proportion of real life contexts, they had the highest proportion of similar problems and problems of low procedural complexity known as the *shallow teaching syndrome* (Vincent & Stacey, 2008). Despite the multitude of past impact reform initiatives in Victorian training and substantial state curriculum change, it appears that there is no major change in the way middle school mathematics is taught (Siemon, 2009).
- *Teacher knowledge about what constitutes effective mathematics needs to improve.* Shulman (1986) proposed three categories of teacher subject matter knowledge. What is clear is that the professional knowledge

of teaching should include at least three distinctly different but related categories:

1. *Knowledge of the subject* is what to teach to students and its relationship to other content (both within and outside of mathematics). Content knowledge, according to Shulman (1986), includes both facts and concepts in a domain, but also why facts and concepts are true and how knowledge is generated and structured in the discipline (Bruner, 1960; Schwab, 1978).

2. *Pedagogical content knowledge* is a knowledge of pedagogy that includes an understanding of how students process, store, retain, and recall information and how teachers interact with students (Shulman, 1986).

3. Knowledge of how to manage a complex instructional setting to Shulman (1986) is the *curriculum knowledge*, which involves awareness of how topics are arranged both within a school year and over time and ways of using curriculum resources, such as textbooks, to organize a program of study for students. Until now, however, it has not been possible to link teachers' professionally usable knowledge of their subjects to student achievement.

Furthermore, Siemon (2001, 2005, 2009), a leading Australian researcher into mathematics, suggests failure in mathematics can be attributed to fragmentation, a lack of knowledge and understanding by teachers in integrating course content, assessment practices, and learning. She gives particular importance to a number of big ideas and strategies, without which student progress in mathematics will be seriously impacted. Numeracy (place value), meaning for operations (concepts), and mental strategies (number facts) are the basis for developing understanding and mastery (Booker, Bond, Briggs & Davey, 1997).

THE NUMERACY COACHING PROGRAM

Leadership Development in Victoria

In 2008, the *Blueprint for Education and Early Childhood Development,* was designed to create a culture of strong leadership and professional learning through the Bastow Institute of Educational Leadership. Within this framework is embedded a coach training process aimed at improving teaching and learning through numeracy, with one of the modules for development described as Numeracy Coach Training Program. In 2009, the Bastow Institute of Educational Leadership partnered with RMIT University to facilitate the training of primary and secondary school leaders and teacher numeracy coaching. Numeracy coach training was designed to facilitate and guide school-based professional learning programs, focusing on numeracy, with the goal of building a professional learning community that supports collective leadership, continuous improvement of teaching practice, and ultimately, improved student learning in numeracy. The program involved:

- Numeracy coaching workshops spread across the year,
- On line and face-to-face Facilitated Communities of Practice (FCOPs),
- Face-to-face site visits,
- Between session activities and a portfolio of reflective practice,
- A Coaching Learning Improvement Project (CLiP), and
- A presentation by participants and exposure to exemplar teaching and learning coaches

Figure 5.1 provides an overview of the required Bastow coaching capabilities for development, workshop outlines over the year, and support structures underpinning the numeracy coaching program (NCP).

Numeracy Coaching Capability Elements

The Bastow Tender emphasized the element of participants' self-development as coaches and leaders through the NCP by being able to strengthen their own capacity through reflecting upon their leadership practices. Overall, there is lack of research on the subject of how teacher coaches learn their role and build capacity (Galluci, Van Lare, Yoon, & Boatright, 2010). Insights gleaned from existing research provided some guidance about designing the NCP professional development of coaches that encourage developing understanding of self through reflective practice and strengthen their capacity as leaders. Previous research stressed that coach learning should be integrated over time with the study of math content instruction, observations of model teacher coaching, and opportunities for practice with feedback from experts (Joyce & Showers, 1982, 2002). These became prime motives for the NCP.

Unfortunately, too many professional learning activities involving coaching have reported that the process is disconnected from teachers' actual practices and school improvement goals (Cohen & Hill, 2000; Lave, 1993). Also, coaching practices are not designed with attention to the needs of adult learners (O'Mahony & Barnett, 2006, 2008). Joyce and Showers (2002) argued persuasively that coaching is a crucial determinant of improvement in performance; however, few research studies have focused on

Bastow Tender Coaching Capabilities Elements
Developing Purposeful Instruction
Professional Relationships
Substantive Conversation
School Improvement

Workshop Outline

Workshop 1 Numeracy: The Big Ideas—Scaffolding Numeracy in the middle years (SNMY) Topic 1: Trusting the Count	**Workshop 1:** The role of the Numeracy Coach in Building a Coaching Relationships
Workshop 2 Numeracy: The Big Ideas Topic 2: Place Value Numeracy Assessment—Using data to support numeracy improvement & differentiation	**Workshop 2:** Using Differentiated Coaching activities to work with individuals and teams
Workshop 3 Numeracy: The Big Ideas Developing On demand Testing data collection (Adaptive) Mathematics—Number. Topic 3: Multiplicative Thinking	**Workshop 3:** The Numeracy Coach as a Change Facilitator and a Leader in School Numeracy using data and evidence and managing coaching concerns through the CBAM
Workshop 4 Numeracy: The Big Ideas Maths online Collect data from 2–3 teachers prior to the workshop. Coaching with a focus on numeracy conversations. Collect school NAPLAN data and discuss the implications with the school administration Topic 4: Partitioning; Topic 5: Proportional Reasoning	**Workshop 4:** Conducting Coaching Learning Conversations around authentic coaching problems and challenges
Workshop 5 Leadership coaching in Math. Topic 6: e^5 and structuring inquiry and strengthening connections to facilitate substantive conversations about important mathematics in Years P–10. Topic 7: Making Connections: Mathematics Developmental Maps.	**Workshop 5:** Numeracy Coaches as Developing School Leaders using situational leadership styles and Studio workshops model to address problem based learning

Support Structures Underpinning the NCP

Pre Program Support
    Survey of needs and concerns
    Maths survey of capabilities

Program Support
    Workshops Spread Over the Year—6 days of BSA coursework demonstration and modeling workshops; applied case studies and scenarios
    Between Session Activities—To trial and get feedback on modeled structured numeracy and coaching tasks to be debriefed in follow-up workshops
    On-line Support Wiki—Coaches on-line; RMIT numeracy and mentor coaches; on-line data base; participant ideas on themes
    Communities of Practice—Regular regional group meetings at host schools with either NC mentors or Numeracy facilitators as mentors RMIT on issues and developmental workshops on CLIPs
    Visits to Schools by RMIT Numeracy Coaches
    School Visits by RMIT Faciltators—School based application of NC role; CLIP/Portfolio; visits by numeracy coaches; principal; meeting and initial school visit
    Sharing of Resources—Poster session sharing of artifacts
    Text—Resource required reading: Power of Coaching (O'Mahony, Barnett & Matthews, 2008) text and readings to underpin the course

Figure 5.1   The NCP components and support structures.

teacher coaching in math teacher programs (Marsh et al., 2008). Recent reports on coaching initiatives have described the need for phased learning and ongoing coach training over extended time periods for coaches' success and development (Brown, Stroh, Fouts, & Baker, 2005; Gallucci & Swanson, 2008; Knight, 2006; Marsh et al., 2008;). Galluci et al. (2010) suggested the need for targeted and customized professional development and organizational support in negotiating the coaching role (Smith, 2009). Some research outlined by Galluci et al. (2010) indicates care needs to be taken in supporting the development of teacher coaches because some practitioners can be ill-prepared for the facilitation skills that are associated with coaching (Coggins, Stoddard, & Cutler, 2003; Lowenhaupt & McKinney, 2007; Neufeld & Roper, 2003; Tung, Ouimette, & Feldman, 2004). Taken together, empirical studies are extremely limited and focus only peripherally on the learning of coaches or on structural supports for their work (Gibson, 2005). The literature tends to depict coaches as merely static entities who enter the position with some expertise and skill, when in fact, learning the role is one of an active participant in the developmental socialization process.

Recent reports have called for professional development for coaches that focuses on the support of adult learners (Marsh et al., 2008). The situated nature of instructional coaching makes the following particularly useful for NCP program development:

- *Self-directed learning.* Most adults prefer to be actively involved in their own learning process, rather than passive recipients (Knowles, 1978).
- *Prior experience and knowledge.* Adults come to most learning situations with a wide range of experiences, knowledge and skills, interests and competencies, and this was recognized in differentiating the NCP.
- *Relevancy.* Making self-directed learning and development relevant and focusing on the self learning for adults is best facilitated through conversation and social situations in which there is an open and meaningful exchange of ideas and information relevant to the learner.
- *Affiliation.* Adults' personal and social contexts shape their learning (Caffarella & Barnett, 1994; Merriam & Caffarella, 1999). Self–esteem and motivation are heightened when individuals are in situations where they feel accepted and valued. The affiliation needs of adult learners, namely the desire and need to be connected and supported by others, are the keys to collaborative learning that coaching offers.

Numeracy Coaches as Teacher Leaders

Leadership research indicates successful school leaders directly and indirectly affect student learning by influencing other people, the organization, and school processes (e.g., Darling-Hammond et al., 2005). Furthermore, teachers have been seen by Leithwood, Seashore-Louis, Anderson, and Walstrom (2004) to be the most influential in impacting student performance outcomes. Specific examples of how instructional coaches can influence student outcomes include:

- Influencing other people—supporting teachers (Waters, Marzano, & McNulty, 2003),
- Impacting school practices—redesigning the organization and instructional programs (Leithwood et al., 2004), and
- Altering school processes—restructuring the curriculum (Waters, Marzano, & McNulty, 2003).

Erkens (2008) reminds us that growing stronger teacher leadership requires building capacity by having the best teachers empower their peers to explore and master the art of learning and teaching. Building the depth and breadth within the capacity of teacher leadership becomes paramount to help create the conditions for a culture of successful learning for all.

Conceptually, the NCP was aimed at developing what Lieberman and Miller (1992) identify as three types of knowledge acquisition for improving practice: a) knowledge *for* practice, which is gained by reading existing research, discussion and exploration of best practices, exposure to exemplary classrooms exhibiting best practice numeracy practices; b) knowledge *in* practice, which occurs through reflecting on exemplary practice of others through modeling, sharing, guiding and collaboration about good practice models in reciprocal individual and team teaching practices; and c) knowledge *of* practice, which happens as leaders engage in and reflect on their own leadership through influencing others, focusing, probing, and reflecting upon what constitutes improved collegial numeracy teaching practices. The basis of the numeracy coaching role was embedded and situated in work that includes observations with classroom teaching; demonstrations of model practices; and cycles that include pre-reflection, observation and data collection, and post-reflective conversations with practitioners (Neufeld & Roper, 2002).

Descriptive literature about teacher coaches (Knight, 2006) suggests that instructional coaches are expected to be: a) relationship builders who engage and enroll teachers to be coached, b) change agents and data coaches able to identify appropriate interventions for teacher learning, c) instructional coaches to model teaching, d) gatherers of small-scale formative assessment data in classrooms for math improvement, and e) resource coaches to provide teachers with resources and engage teachers in dialogue about classroom and other math data (Knight, 2006). In addition, coaching requires skills in communication, relationship building, change management, and leadership for teacher professional development (Knight, 2006; O'Mahony & Barnett, 2008; O'Mahony, Matthews, & Barnett, 2009). These features were incorporated into the NCP, remembering though that these skills and activities add up to a tall order for professionals who are placed in what have been described as ambiguous and contextually dependent numeracy coaching roles (Poglinco et al., 2003). Research on the impact of mathematics coaching is limited to seven studies reported by Becker (2001). McGatha (2008) and Mangin and Stoelinga, (2008) reported on improving instructional practices through linking the "big ideas" with problem-solving and skill-based instruction when designing coaching programs. Mangin (2005) found that an effective component of successful mathematics coaching programs was broad communication about the role and responsibilities of the mathematics coach so that everyone (supervisors, principals, coaches, and teachers) worked from a common understanding. Nevertheless, direct links between coaching and improvement of student achievement have been hard to substantiate in these studies.

RESEARCH METHODOLOGY.

This section describes the guiding research questions, data collection methods, and data analysis strategies employed in the study coaches involved in the NCP. In particular, Guskey's (2000) professional development evaluation framework will be used to examine the effects of this coaching program.

Research Questions

1. How effective was the NCP in affecting coaches' knowledge, skills, and practices?
2. What organizational structures affected how well the coaches were able to perform their roles?

Participants

Tables 5.1–5.3 (see Appendix) indicate that almost half (46%) of the state employed respondents were teachers, with most being in the highest classification of leading teacher. Approximately two-fifths of respondents were coaches (38%), and one in ten were assistant principals. Under "other," one respondent noted a network-based position. Around two-fifths of respondents had been in their position less than two years, and four-fifths had been in their position less than five years. Nearly all respondents were between 35 and 59 years old, with over half 45 years or older. The majority of respondents (66%) were from primary schools; about one-third were from secondary schools. Return rates for the two questionnaires were quite high: 91% of the participants completed the RMIT evaluation and 65% returned the Success Works evaluation.

Data Collection Procedures and Instruments

Data collection sources were derived from two evaluation reports:

1. Success Works Program Logic Survey. The Program Logic instrument was designed to determine if respondents showed improved capabilities across the six elements of the *Coaching Teachers in Effective Instruction* framework: self development, substantive conversations, school improvement, professional relationships, data and evidence, and purposeful instruction.
2. RMIT University Numeracy Coaching Training Program Evaluation Report. The RMIT evaluation was the summation of the formative evaluations completed by participants at the conclusion of each of six workshops. Survey questions asked coaches use a six-point scale to rate the effectiveness of the program's content, process, delivery, learning, and components of the NCP (See Appendix).

Data Analyses

The data from these two instruments were analyzed to address each research question. Means and frequencies were collected from the Success Works and RMIT evaluation studies survey rating scales along with interview data. The levels in the Guskey (2000, 2002, 2003) framework were employed to examine the impact of the NCP on: a) coaches' perceptions of the program (level one), b) what coaches learned about coaching from the program (level two), c) how various organizational structures affected their coaching role (level three), and d) how coaches used new skills in working with classroom teachers (level four). Data were examined to determine patterns of responses across Guskey's levels using the constant comparative method (Glaser, 1965). The emerging patterns were discussed with RMIT staff to compare themes across the two sets of evaluation documents designed by Success Works and RMIT.

Limitations of the Study

The major limitation of this study was the short duration of the program evaluation, making it difficult to assess the full effects of coaching on classroom teaching practices and student learning. Also, because this was a small-scale case study, results are not generalizable beyond the NCP.

FINDINGS

Guskey's (2000, 2003, 2005) multi-level implementation framework was used to examine the effects of the NCP on coaches' knowledge, skills, and application with teachers. As little actual student performance data was in evidence to track changes in school improvement (level five in Guskey's framework), this level of analysis was removed from the study.

Research Question 1: Influence on Coaches' Knowledge, Skills, and Practices

Level 1—Numeracy Coaches' Reactions to NCP
    RMIT evaluation. As shown in Figure 5.2, the content of the NCP was well received by the participants, with all criteria rated 5 or above on a 6 point scale. Over 80% of the participants were satisfied with the program's objec-

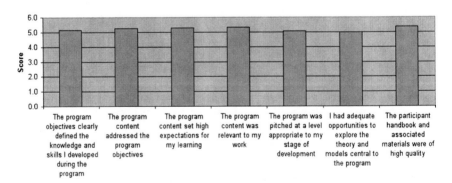

Figure 5.2   RMIT evaluation of NCP content. *Scale:* 1 = Not Applicable, 2 = Strongly Disagree, 3 = Disagree, 4 = Neither Agree nor Disagree, 5 = Agree, 6 = Strongly Agree

tives, content, expectations, relevancy, developmental stage, theories and models, and materials. The positive responses were particularly high from primary school teachers (95% or higher) and from participants on school leadership teams. In contrast, secondary teachers did not find the content to be as useful. Teachers in leadership positions were also more positive about the program than the less experienced teachers.

Success Works evaluation. The external reviewer, Success Works, collected data on the participants' reactions to the design and delivery of the program (see Appendix, Tables 5.4 to 5.9). Survey responses indicated high levels of satisfaction with the program. First, 46% of respondents agreed and 38% of respondents strongly agreed that they were satisfied with the *content* of the program (mean of 4.1 on a six point scale). Second, 46% of respondents agreed and 38% of respondents strongly agreed that they were satisfied with the program's *design* (mean of 4.1). Third, 54% of respondents agreed and 35% of respondents strongly agreed that they were satisfied with the *delivery* of the program (mean of 4.2). Finally, 50% of respondents agreed and 42% of respondents strongly agreed that they were satisfied with the *program overall* (mean of 4.3). Interviews with participants revealed their positive assessment of the program:

> I thought the training program was fabulous . . . you were treated as a real professional not just a teacher. There were very high expectations of participants, which made it all the more valuable.

Achievement of Expectations, the data shown in Table 5.9 (see Appendix) indicated that 85% of respondents felt they had achieved what they had expected from the program. Additional comments reflected they gained knowledge, skills, and confidence in regards to numeracy coaching.

> This course really helped develop my confidence and competence as a numeracy coach.

Level 2—Numeracy Coaches' Learning

RMIT evaluation. Data was collected on each session's effectiveness, which was used as a barometer of session needs and wants and requirements to adapt and modify the program. The respondents rated their development of new skills and knowledge at level five or above (see Figure 5.3). Participants reported that they had improved their capacity to assist teachers' understanding of effective numeracy teaching practices and were able to assist teachers to reflect on their practices. The two areas where responses were less positive were the ability to assist teachers with data analysis and the capacity to support and develop connected and distributed leadership.

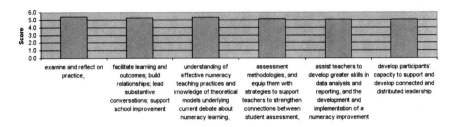

Figure 5.3 RMIT evaluation of new knowledge and skills. *Scale:* 1 = Not Applicable, 2 = Strongly Disagree, 3 = Disagree, 4 = Neither Agree nor Disagree, 5 = Agree, 6 = Strongly Agree

Success Works evaluation. As mentioned in the NCP overview, the workplace project in numeracy coach training was called the Coaching Learning Improvement Project (CLiP). Table 5.13 (see Appendix) indicates that this project provided a useful vehicle and a positive focus in supporting the school's endeavor to improve numeracy. On all of the statements related to the CliP, the average score was about four, corresponding to a response of "agree." The statement regarding the CLiP having a positive impact (mean of 4.5 on six point scale) on knowledge and skills received slightly higher ratings than the others. Comments reflected the positive impact of the CLiPs, with most explaining the impact it had had for their colleagues or the school.

> Working on my network project helped to focus staff on the bigger picture of numeracy improvement.

In terms of the six coaching capabilities (see Figure 5.4), most participants agreed that they increased their knowledge and understanding of these capabilities. Results indicated that the means for each capability area ranged from 4.0 to 4.5 (out of a possible 5). Areas of greatest impact were in self-development and substantial conversations. Tables 5.10–5.11 (see Appendix) indicate that the means for the purposeful instruction capability was the least effective area of development.

The comparison of pre- and post-program surveys (see Figure 5.5) revealed an increase in the familiarity with the coaching framework after the program. The difference in the responses between the two surveys indicates that both the upper and lower tail-ends of the cohort (represented by 95% confidence intervals) have increased their familiarity with the coaching framework. The lower tail-end of the cohort moved from knowing about it but not using it, to now using it but not yet confidently. The upper tail-end of the cohort moved from planning use of the coaching framework to now using it confidently. A statistical analysis comparing the responses from the two surveys confirms a statistically significant increase in familiarity with the coaching framework (.05 level of confidence).

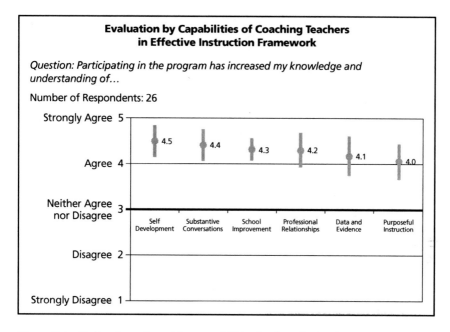

Figure 5.4 Evaluation of coaching capabilities in the effective instruction framework. *Source:* Draft Success Works Post Program Evaluation Report of the NCP, 2010, p. 10

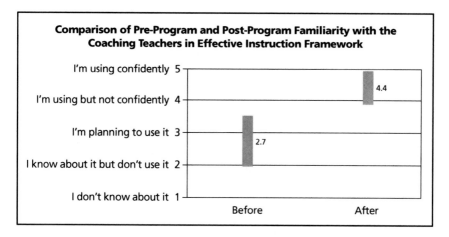

Figure 5.5 Comparison of pre and post program confidence. *Source:* Draft Success Works Post program Evaluation Report of the NCP, 2010, p. 11

As shown in Table 5.12 (see Appendix), respondents agreed that the program had a positive impact on their current and future leadership knowledge and skills, confidence, and motivation to lead. The average scores for the three statements were around four, corresponding to a response of "agree." Comments reflected respondents' increased knowledge, skills, confidence and motivation to lead improvements in numeracy instruction in their school or network. Some referenced the content knowledge as the driving force behind this improved leadership capacity:

> I now know I have the knowledge and skills to lead others.

Interestingly, most respondents (58%) indicated that they had changed their leadership aspirations as a result of the program by having been promoted, seeking promotion, or considering moving to a leadership role. This comment was echoed by many NCP coaches:

> I wish to pursue coaching as a future direction in my professional development.

Level 4—Numeracy Coaches' Use of New Knowledge and Skills

The question of how numeracy coaches applied their knowledge and skills is the litmus test of whether training room learning has been understood and applied in schools and classrooms. Many respondents were able to give specific examples of how they had applied the knowledge and skills gained from the program in their school or network. Some respondents focused on the benefits of having completed their portfolios as part of the program as a tool for self-reflection. Others noted their improved numeracy content knowledge as an indicator of improved self-confidence. Others talked about modeling their improved reflective practice to others through their coaching role. A typical response was provided by this coach:

> My belief in my coaching capacity strengthened and it really became about our staff and students and developing a culture of continuous improvement for all. I openly share my reflective practices through professional learning to model that we are all learning irrespective of our current capacity and that we can learn from each other.

Respondents also gave examples of how they applied the knowledge and skills they received from the program in the area of substantive conversations. The main theme from their comments was their increased skill in using listening and questioning techniques to guide coaching conversations, facilitate reflective practice, and set goals:

> I had always found it difficult to hold teachers to account, when they would say 'yes, yes, yes' and wouldn't change their teaching practice.

A number commented on specific materials used during the program:

> We were given a set of cards titled 'Skills Needed for Good Coaching' that suggested possible questions to ask teachers in order to assist them to reflect on their learning. I refer to these cards regularly.

Some respondents focused on how they developed rapport with coachees, allowing them to promote more accountability:

> [NCP] gave an insight into what roles and standards of teaching should be a given in schools and that leadership needs to back up the coaches in expecting that these are adhered to.

The main theme from the examples given by respondents on how they had applied their learning was around improved ability and confidence in working with the school's leadership. Respondents gave examples of improved ability to influence school improvement initiatives and staff development plans:

> The work we did improved my ability to work with the Year Maths team I coached and to work with the assistant principal at the school to ensure accountability and improved leadership of the maths domain leader.

Respondents provided examples of how data and evidence influenced their coaching strategies. The most common among respondents was their improved aptitude in collecting quality data and using it to assist coachees improve.

> I have introduced On Demand testing... Data is analyzed and teams using data to plan, monitor progress and cater for individual and cohort needs... and daily lessons are better informed with tracking student progress using evidence.

Some examples given by respondents on how they had applied their learning focused on their improved ability to support differentiation; however many reflected about their improved ability to extend teachers' content knowledge. This reflects the program's strength, outlined above, regarding the quality of the numeracy content.

> The numeracy sessions... really helped me understand some basic concepts that I did not know how to explain before.

Research Question 2: Organizational Factors Affecting Coaches' Roles

Level 3—Organizational Structures Affecting Numeracy Coaches' Role

Examining school policies and gathering input from participants about the organizational structures affecting their coaching experiences can reveal factors that facilitate or impede the practices being advocated in the professional development program (Guskey, 2000, 2003, 2005). Examples of organizational structures that can affect coaching include inadequate support from school leadership teams and the lack of understanding of the purposes of coaching programs (Barth, 1991).

RMIT evaluation. Figure 5.6 presents the findings on the effectiveness of the components of the NCP based on the RMIT evaluation. The components that reflect organizational support structures include the communities of practice and WIKI. As shown in Figure 5.6, communities of practice was rated at almost a 5 and the WIKI component at almost a 4 (on a 6 point scale), indicating fairly high agreement that these elements assisted participants in achieving the NCP's objectives.

Success Works evaluation. The Success Works evaluation provided insights on several organizational structures: online WIKI, mentors, communities of practice, and workplace support aspects of the NCP (see Tables 5.14–5.16 in the Appendix). Some respondents commented that the benefits of their FCOP centered on the online WIKI component (Table 5.15). However, the mean of 2.7 indicated that respondents were ambivalent or disagreed about the usefulness of this online component. The mentoring component was intended to be an important element to support the NCP; a mean rating of 4.1 suggests mentoring was useful (see Table 5.14). It should be noted,

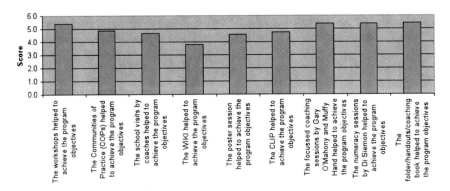

Figure 5.6 RMIT evaluation of components underpinning the NCP. *Scale:* 1 = Not Applicable, 2 = Strongly Disagree, 3 = Disagree, 4 = Neither Agree nor Disagree, 5 = Agree, 6 = Strongly Agree

however, that there were not many responses regarding the usefulness of these in-school visits due to the design of the survey instrument.

Communities of practice was also seen as a vital support mechanism for the program, yet its impact and influence was not as pervasive as anticipated. Although there were some mixed views regarding the effectiveness of the Facilitated Communities of Practice (FCOPs), some respondents praised their experience of their FCOP as being a valuable component of the program:

> Absolutely the best aspect of the program...was working with the people in my FCOP.

Finally, evaluation of workplace support was well received with a mean of 4.7 out of 5 (see Table 5.16). Ninety two percent of respondents reported they had received workplace support and encouragement to participate in the program. Most indicated this support and encouragement was strong, as reflected in the comments.

> My leadership strongly supported me and gave me time to complete tasks and to attend da... [Comment: This sentence appears to be missing the rest of the quote.]

DISCUSSION

The findings from this study overwhelming suggest that numeracy coaches perceive that the NCP impacted their knowledge, skills, and work in schools. The reported satisfaction indicates that numeracy coaches felt the NCP had helped them become better leaders in impacting, influencing, and challenging of existing school numeracy teaching and learning. This supports the research indicating that successful school leaders can both directly and indirectly affect student learning by influencing other people, the organization, and school processes (e.g., Darling-Hammond, La Pointe, Meyerson, Orr, & Cohen, 2007; Davis, Darling-Hammond, La Pointe, & Meyerson, 2005). Instructional numeracy coaches used their coaching and leadership approaches to build trust, support teachers, and build capacity (Erkins, 2008). They also were able to restructure approaches to curriculum and assessment and differentiation through their CliP projects in similar ways to what effective leaders do to create conditions for effective numeracy learning to occur (Leithwood et al., 2004).

Reflecting the power of using a blended learning approach (Oliver & Trigwell, 2005), the workshops, coaching sessions, and materials all received very high ratings. Slightly lower ratings were given to the poster sessions, the in-school project (the CLiP), and the school visits. Least successful was the WIKI, suggesting that future cohorts will need to experience this component as an essential part of the program, rather than as an add-on.

What Qualities and Roles Did Numeracy Coaches Develop Through the NCP?

Descriptive literature about teacher coaches (Killion & Harrison, 2006) indicates that instructional coaches are expected to fulfill many varied roles, some of which were developed in the NCP. First, they became relationship builders, who engaged teachers and built professional relationships with them (Killion & Harrison, 2006). Developing significant professional relationships as a numeracy coach were Bastow Tender priorities, focusing on mutual trust, respect, and teacher accountability. Clearly, for coaching to succeed, a strong professional relationship must develop between the partners, and within teams involved in the coaching relationship. Strong relationships emerge as partners begin to trust one another, share different perspectives, see problems as learning opportunities, provide emotional support, and strive to attain agreed-upon goals as part of a mutual accountability (Showers, 1985; Bloom, Castagna, & Warren, 2005).

Second, as data coaches, NCP participants were able to act as change agents and identify appropriate interventions for teacher learning (Killion & Harrison, 2006). For instance, they gathered small-scale formative assessment data in classrooms for math improvement and provided teachers with resources (Knight, 2006). In addition, paramount in the NCP design was the building of a community of practice for coaches to access a variety of data sources (individuals, COP regional groups, and peers within schools) to build their coaching tool kits. Geist and Hoy (2004) acknowledge that the topic of trust is somewhat elusive, but it must be earned in coaching environments through participating in a community of practice. The key was to have coaches become change agents and data coaches to identify appropriate interventions for teacher learning school relationships.

Third, effective instructional coaches model good teaching (Killion & Harrison, 2006). The elements of the Bastow Tender that were keys to this area focused on developing substantive conversations through modeling, promoting inquiry, developing of reflection, and using data and evidence for supporting informed decision-making. One of the most often-mentioned concepts associated with the numeracy coaching process was the importance that reflection has in stimulating individuals' thinking and actions, which proved vital to the success of the numeracy coaches (e.g., Brown et al., 2005; Conyers, 2004). As Barnett and O'Mahony (2007, 2008) note, the image of a successful coach is someone who encourages their coachees to become more reflective, inquiring professionals who undertake ongoing reflective inquiry and goal-setting, through ongoing learning conversations. Participants also used authentic case studies to explore coaching and leadership interventions through role playing of problem based learning (Bridges & Hallinger, 1995).

Numeracy Coaches as Instructional Teacher Leaders

Conceptually, the NCP was aimed at developing what Lieberman and Miller (1992) identify as three types of knowledge acquisition for improving practice. Regarding knowledge *for* practice, participants indicated the knowledge, content, design, delivery and of the program met their expectations and prepared them for their numeracy coaching roles. Although they were less positive about their ability to develop distributive leadership, their confidence and competence increased due to reading existing research, exploring best coaching practices, and being exposed to exemplary classrooms (Lieberman and Miller, 1992). The second area, knowledge *in* practice, emerged as coaches used the six capabilities to work with teachers. These skills were reinforced through modeling, sharing, guiding and collaborating about good practice (Gallucci et al., 2010; Lieberman & Miller, 1992). Finally, knowledge *of* practice was acknowledged by participants' use of the CLiP initiatives. As coaches engaged in and reflected on their own leadership, they recognized ways to improve their colleagues' numeracy teaching practices. The use of structures, such as communities of practice, online WIKIs, and workplace support, provided a network for coaches to access help and support in developing their knowledge of practice.

Future Research Agenda

To counteract the methodological and substantive omissions of this small-scale study, a variety of suggestions are offered to shape future research on teacher coaching. What types of research designs would be appropriate? As noted earlier, much of the research on teacher coaching leadership is piecemeal and based on perceptions of participants in individual coaching programs (Gallucia et al., 2010). Therefore, the advice of West and Milan (2001) is particularly relevant to expand the current research design. They recommend future studies should:

1. Increase the number of respondents sampled within and across programs by obtaining information from other stakeholders (e.g., principals, teachers, student) to reduce the subjectivity of only capturing,

coaches' impressions. An excellent illustration of this strategy was utilized by Leithwood, Jantzi, Coffin, and Wilson (1996), who examined teachers' perceptions of the leadership skills of teachers who attended specific leadership preparation programs.

2. Incorporate control groups of school coaches who have not been trained to be coaches. These types of quasi-experimental designs are rare; however, Strong, Barrett, and Bloom's (2003) study of coaching for first- and second-year leaders is a good example of how to incorporate control groups for comparative purposes.

3. Gather data on the effects coaches have on student learning. Studies such as the one conducted by Leithwood, Riedlinger, Bauer, and Jantzi (2003) show the potential for designing investigations that demonstrate how educators' involvement in professional development programs can impact student performance.

CONCLUSIONS

The NCP showed that for change to occur through school-based coaching, coaches need an organizational infrastructure in which to work and school policies that acknowledge the benefits of coaching. Fullan (2005) has argued for the recognition of the central importance of collaboration, collegiality, and cooperation among teacher leaders for the implementation of real change. The NCP showed that significant change depended on providing frequent opportunities to converse and interact about concrete observed practices, so that teacher leaders and coaches know what is expected in leading the change, why the change is important, and how to undertake it. The introduction of coaching and the development of a uniform school policy about the use of coaching are vital. As a way forward, contemporary theorists (e.g., Earl, Levin, Leithwood, Fullan, & Watson, 2001) argue that by building teacher capacity to implement leadership reforms, it is possible to improve mathematics instruction and to rebuild the school culture through enhanced collegiality and collaboration (DuFour, DuFour, & Eaker, 2008, 2009). The NCP revealed that coaches were able to access specific instruction to assist in their roles as relationship builders, change agents, data coaches, and instructional models.

The findings of this study suggest that coaches best develop with layers of learning coupled with a support network. Barnett and O'Mahony (2007) have argued that professional expertise develops through storytelling, modeling, feedback, reflection about experiences, and the guidance of mentors, coaches, and peers within a community of colleagues. These conditions need to permeate coaching programs if they are to thrive. The NCP demonstrated that there is no better substitute for the primacy of making time for coaching within the school timetable. In conclusion, the NCP's emphasis on helping teachers enact small-scale classroom changes in teaching and learning with the support of a peer coach was an effective strategy for impacting teacher growth that may indeed lead to improvements in student learning.

Thanks are expressed to the Bastow Institute of Educational Leadership permission to access and use Success Works and RMIT evaluation data gathered on the NCP.

APPENDIX

TABLE 5.1   Position

School—Accomplished Teacher	2	7.7%
School—Expert Teacher	2	7.7%
School—Leading Teacher	8	30.9%
School—Assistant Principal	3	11.5%
School—Teaching and Learning Coach	5	19.2%
School—Other Coach	2	7.7%
Network—Teaching and Learning Coach	3	11.5%
Other (please specify):	1	3.8%
Total	26	

TABLE 5.2   Time in Position

Less than 2 years	11	42.3%
Over 2 years and less than 5 years	11	42.3%
Over 5 years and less than 10 years	1	3.8%
Over 10 and less than 15 years	2	7.7%
Over 15 years	1	3.8%
Total	26	

TABLE 5.3   Age

<25 years	0	0.0%
25–29 years	2	7.7%
30–34 years	1	3.8%
35–39 years	5	19.2%
40–44 years	3	11.5%
45–49 years	5	19.2%
50–54 years	4	15.4%
55–59 years	6	23.2%
60–64 years	0	0.0%
65 years	0	0.0%
Total	26	

TABLE 5.4 Satisfaction with the Program (Means listed)

Content	4.1
Design	4.2
Delivery	4.2
Overall	4.3

TABLE 5.5 Satisfaction with the Program Content

I was satisfied with the content of the program

Strongly Disagree	0	0.0%
Disagree	2	7.7%
Neither Agree nor Disagree	2	7.7%
Agree	12	46.2%
Strongly Agree	10	38.4%
Total	26	
Mean	4.2	

TABLE 5.6 Satisfaction with the Program Design

I was satisfied with the design of the program

Strongly Disagree	0	0.0%
Disagree	3	11.5%
Neither Agree nor Disagree	1	3.8%
Agree	12	46.2%
Strongly Agree	10	38.5%
Total	26	
Mean	4.1	

TABLE 5.7 Satisfaction with the Program Delivery

I was satisfied with the delivery of the program

Strongly Disagree	0	0.0%
Disagree	2	7.7%
Neither Agree nor Disagree	1	3.8%
Agree	14	53.9%
Strongly Agree	9	34.6%
Total	26	
Mean	4.2	

TABLE 5.8 Satisfaction with the Program Overall

I was satisfied with the program overall

Strongly Disagree	0	0.0%
Disagree	1	3.8%
Neither Agree nor Disagree	1	3.8%
Agree	13	50.0%
Strongly Agree	11	42.4%
Total	26	
Mean	4.3	

TABLE 5.9 Achievement of Expectations

I achieved what I expected to achieve from the program

Strongly Disagree	0	0.0%
Disagree	1	3.8%
Neither Agree nor Disagree	3	11.5%
Agree	13	50.0%
Strongly Agree	9	34.7%
Total	26	
Mean	4.2	

TABLE 5.10

Data and Evidence	
Facilitating the collection of data	4.1
Identifying evidence	4.2
Supporting evidence-informed decision making	4.2
Substantive Conversations	
Eliciting teacher goals	4.3
Promoting enquiry	4.3
Using questioning and active listening techniques	4.6
Supporting the resolution of cognitive dissonance	4.3
Facilitating reflective practice	4.4
Purposeful Instruction	
Supporting improved instructional practice across all domains of e^5	3.6
Supporting effective planning for differentiation	4.0
Extending teacher content knowledge	4.4
School Improvement	
Advocating a school improvement agenda	4.3
Collaborating with leadership	4.2
Supporting professional learning teams	4.4
Self Development	
Reflecting on my own practice	4.4
Strengthening my own capacity	4.5

TABLE 5.11   Coaching Teachers in Effective Instruction

Capability	Upper	Lower	Mean
Self Development	4.8	4.1	4.5
Substantive Conversations	4.7	4.1	4.4
School Improvement	4.6	4.1	4.3
Professional Relationships	4.7	3.9	4.3
Data and Evidence	4.6	3.7	4.2
Purposeful Instruction	4.4	3.7	4.0

TABLE 5.12   Influence of Program Participation

How, if at all, has your participation in the program influenced your leadership aspirations?

I have actively sought promotion into a leadership role.	3	11.5%
I have been promoted into a leadership role since beginning the program.	8	30.8%
I have considered moving into a leadership role.	4	15.4%
I have decided NOT to seek a leadership role.	1	3.8%
The program has not influenced my leadership aspirations.	10	38.5%
Total	26	

TABLE 5.13   Impact of Workplace Project/Plan

My workplace project/plan achieved its aims and objectives.	4.1
My workplace project/plan has had a positive impact on my knowledge and skills.	4.5
My workplace project/plan has had a positive impact on my workplace.	4.1
I received adequate support from the program provider to achieve my project/plan's aims and objectives.	4.2

TABLE 5.14   Satisfaction with Allocation of Coach or Mentor

I was compatible with my coach/pair/mentor/shadow.	4.1
I was satisfied with the frequency of contact with my coach/mentor/pair/shadow.	4.1
My experience with my coach/mentor/pair/shadow has had a positive impact on my knowledge and skills.	4.1

TABLE 5.15 Usefulness of Online Component

I found the online component(s) useful in achieving the aims of the program.

Strongly Disagree	2	8.7%
Disagree	8	34.8%
Neither Agree nor Disagree	8	34.8%
Agree	5	21.7%
Strongly Agree	0	0.0%
Total	23	
Mean	2.7	

TABLE 5.16 Level of Workplace Support

My participation in the program received continued support and encouragement from my workplace.

Strongly Disagree	0	0.0%
Disagree	1	3.8%
Neither Agree nor Disagree	1	3.8%
Agree	3	11.5%
Strongly Agree	21	80.9%
Total	26	
Mean	4.7	

TABLE 5.17 Time Spent Coaching

Approximately how many hours have you spent coaching?

1–4 hours	1	4.3%
5–9 hours	1	4.3%
10–14 hours	1	4.3%
15–19 hours	0	0.0%
20–24 hours	2	8.7%
25–29 hours	3	13.0%
30 hours or more	15	65.2%
Total	23	

TABLE 5.18 Support for Coaching

Is your coaching timetabled or otherwise supported by the leadership team?

Yes	23	100.0%
No	0	0.0%

TABLE 5.19 Leadership Aspirations

Knowledge and skills to lead	4.1
Confidence to lead	4.2
Motivation to lead	4.2

REFERENCES

Barnett, B. G., & O'Mahony, G. R. (2006, October). *Peer coaching for experienced principals: Building their capacity as transformational leaders.* Paper presented at the annual convention of the University Council for Educational Administration, San Antonio, TX.

Barnett, B. G., & O'Mahony, G. R. (2007, April). *Developing productive relationships between coaches and principals: The Australian experience.* Paper presented at the annual meeting of the American Educational Research Association, Chicago, IL.

Barnett, B. G., & O'Mahony, G. R. (2008). Mentoring and coaching programs for the professional development of school leaders. In J. Lumby, G. Crow, & P. Pashiardis, P. (Eds.), *International handbook on the preparation and development of school leaders.* New York, NY: Routledge.

Barth, R. (1991). *Improving schools from within: Teachers, parents and principals make the difference.* San Francisco, CA: Jossey-Bass.

Becker, J. R. (2001). Classroom coaching: An emerging method of professional development. *Harvard Educational Review, 57,* 1–22.

Bloom, G., Castagna, C., & Warren, B. (2005). *Blended coaching: Skills and strategies to support principal development.* Thousand Oaks, CA: Corwin Press.

Booker, G., Bond, D., Briggs, J., & Davey, G. (1997). *Teaching primary mathematics.* Melbourne, Australia: Longman.

Bridges, E. M., & Hallinger, P. (1995). *Implementing problem based learning in leadership development.* Eugene, OR: University of Oregon, Educational Resources Information Center, Clearinghouse on Educational Management.

Brown, C. J., Stroh, H. R., Fouts. J. T., & Baker, D. B. (2005). *Learning to change: School coaching for systemic reform.* Seattle, WA: Fouts & Associates.

Bruner, J. (1960). *The process of education.* Cambridge, MA: Harvard University Press.

Caffarella, R. S., & Barnett, B. G. (1994). Characteristics of adult learners and foundations of experiential learning. *New Directions for Adult and Continuing Education, 62,* 29–42.

Coggins, C. T., Stoddard, P., & Cutler E. (2003, April). *Improving instructional capacity through school-based reform coaches.* Paper presented at the Annual Meeting of the American Educational Research Association, Chicago, IL.

Cohen, D. K., & Hill, H. C. (2000). Instructional policy and classroom performance: The mathematics reform in California. *Teachers College Record, 102,* 294–343.

Conyers, J. G. (2004). Thinking outside to support newcomers. *School Administrator, 61*(6), 18–21.

Darling-Hammond, L., La Pointe, M., Meyerson, D., Orr, M. T., & Cohen, C. (2007). *Preparing school leaders for a changing world: Lessons from exemplary leadership development programs.* Palo Alto, CA: Stanford University, Stanford Educational Leadership Institute.

Davis, S., Darling-Hammond, L., La Pointe, M., & Meyerson, D. (2005). *Review of research: School leadership study. Developing successful principals.* Palo Alto, CA: Stanford University, Stanford Educational Leadership Institute.

DuFour, R., DuFour, R., & Eaker, R. (2008) *Revisiting professional learning communities at work: New insights for improving schools.* Bloomington, IN: Solution Tree Press.

Earl, L., Levin, B., Leithwood, K., Fullan, M., & Watson, N. (2001). *Watching and learning 2: Second annual report of the British literacy and numeracy strategy.* Toronto: Ontario Education.

Erkins, C. (2008). Growing Teacher Leadership. In A. Buffum, C. Erkins, C. Hinman, S. Huff, L. Jessie, T. Martin et al. (Eds.), *The Collaborative Administrator: Working Together as a Professional learning Community* (pp. 39–54). Bloomington, IN: Solution Tree Press.

Fullan, M. (2005). The meaning of educational change: A quarter of a century of learning. In A. Lieberman (Ed.), *International handbook of educational change: The roots of educational change* (Vol. 1, pp. 202–216). Dordecht, The Netherlands: Springer.

Gallucci, C., & Swanson, J. (2008). *Aiming high: Leadership for district-wide instructional improvement: A partnership between the Center for Educational Leadership and Norwalk-La Mirada Unified School District, Interim research report and case summary.* Seattle, WA: Center for the Study of Teaching and Policy, University of Washington.

Gallucci, C., Van Lare, M., Yoon, I., & Boatright, B. (2010). Instructional coaching: Building theory about the role and organizational support for professional learning. *American Educational Research Journal 47,* 919–963.

Geist, J., & Hoy, W. K. (2004). Cultivating a culture of trust: Enabling school structure, teacher professionalism, and, academic pres. *Leading and Managing, 10,* 1–18.

Gibson, S. A. (2005). Developing knowledge of coaching. *Issues in Teacher Education, 14*(2), 63–74.

Glaser B. G. (1965). The constant comparative method of qualitative analysis, *Social Problems, 12,* 436–445.

Guskey, T. R. (2000). *Evaluating professional development.* Thousand Oaks, CA: Corwin Press.

Guskey, T. R. (2002). Professional development and teacher change: Teachers and teaching. *Theory into Practice, 8*(3/4), 381–399.

Guskey, T. R. (2003). What makes professional development effective? *Phi Delta Kappan, 84*(10), 748–750.

Guskey, T. R. (2005). Five key concepts that kicked off the process: Professional development provides the power to implement standards. *Journal of Staff Development, 26*(1), 36–40.

Hattie, J. (1992). Towards a model of schooling: a synthesis of meta-analyses. *Australian Journal of Education, 36,* 5–13.

Joyce, B., & Showers, B. (1982). The coaching of teaching. *Educational Leadership, 40*(1), 4–10.

Joyce, B., & Showers, B. (2002). *Student achievement through staff development.* Alexandria, VA: Association for Supervision and Curriculum Development.

Killion, J., & Harrison, C. (2006). *Taking the lead: New roles for teachers and school-based coaches.* Oxford, OH: National Staff Development Council.

Knight, J. (2006). Instructional coaching. *The School Administrator, 63*(4), 36–40.

Knowles, M. (1978). *Self-directed learning.* New York, NY: Association Press.

Lave, J. (1993). The practice of learning. In S. Chaiklin & J. Lave (Eds.), *Understanding practice* (pp. 3–32). New York, NY: Cambridge University Press.

Leithwood, K., Jantzi, D., Coffin, G., & Wilson, P. (1996). Preparing school leaders: What works. *Journal of School Leadership, 6,* 316–342.

Leithwood, K., Seashore-Louis, K., Anderson, S., & Walstrom, K. (2004). *How leadership influences student learning: A review of research for the Learning from Leadership Project.* New York, NY: Wallace Foundation.

Leithwood, K., Riedlinger, B., Bauer, S., & Jantzi, D. (2003). Leadership program effects on student learning: The case of the Greater New Orleans School Leadership Centre. *Journal of School Leadership, 13*(6), 707–738.

Lieberman, A., & Miller, L. (1992). Revisiting the social realities of teaching. In A. Lieberman & I. Miller (Eds.), *Staff Development: New demands, new realities, new perspectives* (pp. 92–109). New York, NY: Teachers College Press.

Lowenhaupt, R., & McKinney, S. (2007, April). *Coaching in context: The role of relationships in the work of three literacy coaches.* Paper presented at the Annual Meeting of the American Educational Research.

Mangin, M. M. (2005, April). *Designing instructional teacher leadership positions: Lessons learned from five school districts.* Paper presented at the annual meeting of the American Educational Research Association, Montreal, Canada.

Mangin, M. M., & Stoelinga, S. R. (2008). Teacher leadership: What it is and why it matters. In M. M. Mangin & S. R. Stoelinga (Eds.), *Effective teacher leadership: Using research to inform and reform* (pp. 10–35). New York, NY: Teachers College Press.

Marsh, J. A., McCombs, J. S., Lockwood, J. R., Martorell, F., Gerwhwin, D., Naftel, S. et al. (2008). *Supporting literacy across the sunshine state: A study of Florida middle school reading coaches.* Santa Monica, CA: Rand.

Martin, M. O., Mullis, I. V. S., & Chrostowski, S. J. (Eds.). (2003). *TIMSS 2003 Technical report: Findings from EA's trends in international mathematics and science study at the fourth and eighth grades.*

McGatha, M. (2008). Levels of engagement in establishing coaching relationships. *Teacher Development, 12*(2), 139–150.

Merriam, S. B., & Caffarella, R .S. (1999). *Learning in adulthood: A comprehensive guide* (2nd ed.). San Francisco, CA: Jossey Bass.

Neufeld, B., & Roper, D. (2002). *Off to a good start: Year I of collaborative coaching and learning in the effective practice schools.* Boston, MA: Education Matters, Inc.

Neufeld, B., & Roper, D. (2003). *Coaching: A strategy for developing instructional capacity: Promises & practicalities.* Boston, MA: Education Matters, Inc.

Newman, F. M., King, M. B., & Youngs, P. (2000). Professional development that addresses school capacity: Lessons from urban elementary schools. *American Journal of Education, 108*(4), 259–299.

O'Mahony, G. R., Matthews, R. J., & Barnett, B. G. (2009). *The power of coaching for school improvement: Nurturing talent and building capacity.* Cheltenham, Victoria: Hawker Brownlow Education.

O'Mahony, G., & Barnett, B. (2008). Coaching relationships that influence how experienced principals think and act. *Leading & Managing, 14*(1), 16–37.

Oliver, M., & Trigwell, K. (2005). Can 'blended learning' be redeemed? *E-Learning, 2*(1), 17–26.

Organisation for Economic Co-operation and Development. (1999). *Measuring student progressive achievement tests in mathematics: First results form PISA 2000 (Education and Skills).* London: ACER Press

PISA. (2006). *PISA 2006 national report.* London: ACER Press.

Poglinco, S. M., Bach, A. J., Hovde, K., Rosenblum, S., Saunders, M., & Supovitz, J. A. (2003). *The heart of the matter: The coaching model in America's Choice schools.* Philadelphia: Consortium for Policy Research in Education, University of Pennsylvania.

Schwab, J. (1978). *Science, curriculum and liberal education: Selected essays Joseph J. Schwab.* In I. Westbury & N. Wilkof (Eds.), Chicago, Il: University of Chicago Press.

Showers, B. (1985). Teachers coaching teachers. *Educational Leadership, 42*, 43–48.

Shulman, L. S. (1986). Those who understand: Knowledge growth in teaching. *Educational Researcher, 15*(2), 4–14.

Siemon, D. (2000, October). *Researching numeracy in the middle years—The experience of the Middle Years Numeracy Research Project.* Paper presented to ACER Research Conference. Brisbane, Australia.

Siemon, D., Virgona, J., & Corneille, K. (2001, May). *The middle years numeracy research project: 5–9, final report.* A project commissioned by the Department of Education, Employment and Training, Victoria, Catholic Education Commission of Victoria and Association of Independent Schools of Victoria. RMIT University. Retrieved December 19, 2003, from http://www.sofweb.vic.edu.au/mys/research/MYNRP/index.htm

Siemon, D. E., & Virgona, J. (2001). *Roadmaps to numeracy: Reflections on the Middle Years Numeracy Research Project.* Paper presented to Australian Association for Research in Education Conference Fremantle, Perth.

Siemon, D. E. (2005). *Developing the "big ideas" in mathematics.* Paper prepared for Victorian Schools, Victoria, Australia.

Siemon, D. E. (2009). Developing mathematical knowledge keepers: Issues at the intersection of communities of practice. *Eurasia Journal of Mathematics, Science & Technology, 5*(3), 221–234.

Smith, A. T. (March, 2009). Considering literacy coaching responsibilities in terms of teacher change. *Literacy Coaching Clearinghouse.* Retrieved August 1, 2009, from http://www.literacycoachingonline.org/briefs/coaching_trajectory_a_smith.pdf

Strong, M., Barrett, A., & Bloom, G. (2003, April). *Supporting the new principal: Managerial and instructional leadership in a principal induction program.* Paper presented at the annual meeting of the American Educational Research Association, Chicago, IL.

Success Works-Post-Program Draft Report. (2010, December). *Numeracy coaching program. Annual report for Bastow Institute of Educational Leadership.* Melbourne, Victoria, Australia.

Tung, R., Ouimette, M., & Feldman, J. (2004). *The challenge of coaching: Providing cohesion among multiple reform agendas.* Boston: Center for Collaborative Education, University of Chicago Press. (Original work published 1961)

Vincent, J., & Stacey, K. (2008). Do mathematics textbooks cultivate shallow teaching? Applying the TIMSS Video Study criteria to Australian eighth-grade mathematics textbooks. *Mathematics Education Research Journal, 20*(1), 81–106.

Waters, J. T., Marzano, R. J., & McNulty, B. A. (2003). *Balanced leadership: What 30 years of research tells us about the effect of leadership on student achievement.* Aurora, CO: Mid-continent Research for Education and Learning.

West, L., & Milan, M. (2001). *The reflecting glass: Professional coaching for leadership development.* Basingstoke, England: Palgrave.

CHAPTER 6

RESPONDING TO A CHANGING WORLD

Challenges and Early Findings in Orchestrating a Principal Professional Development Program in Indonesian Schools

Khairan Indriani, Luana Zellner, and Steven Rose

This chapter will provide the reader with a detailed description of the developmental journey that is taking place in Indonesia's efforts to build an effective school leadership preparation program. Focus is placed on the results of implementing the initial stages of a new program for the recruitment and preparation of transformational instructional principals based on Indonesian Ministerial Education Regulation No. 28/2010: The Institution of Development and Empowerment of (school) Principal of Indonesia (LPPKS) (See Appendix A-1) and principal professional development. Indonesian education reform strategies were prompted by the need for a highly trained population ready to address rapid global changes in technology, communication and social networking, and the international/na-

The Changing Nature of Instructional Leadership in the 21st Century, pages 125–162

tional economies. The initial stages of the new ministerial regulation had two components: the Principal Professional Program (PPP) for the identification and training of candidates, and the Continuing Professional Development (CPD) for practicing principals. The intent was to pilot these components in a select setting and evaluate the outcome. The program design was evaluated with respect to viability across the many socially and economically diverse administrative districts in Indonesia. Once this task is completed, the findings will be applied to implementation throughout Indonesia with respect to its diverse culture, language, and geography. Collected data on trainer and participant perceptions of the program and their training experiences were used to assess the effectiveness of the piloted procedures and the relevance of the training. In the first pilot 186 aspiring principals (teachers) were recruited from five Indonesian administrative districts and participated in the training phase of the initial PPP. In a second pilot, 420 principals-in-practice from six districts participated in a training trial of the CPD. Initial findings indicated that the first training trial of the PPP program helped participants gain confidence and needed skills in preparing for school leadership roles. Similar results were found for the principals-in-practice who participated in the CPD training trial. Since the new ministerial program model is employing an iterative cycle of development and evaluation, a more definitive measure of its success will be available after participants have practiced their newly acquired knowledge in their workplace.

HISTORICAL FRAMEWORK OF INDONESIAN EDUCATION SYSTEM AND PRINCIPAL PREPARATION

In 2006 the Australia Indonesia Basic Education Program (AIBEP) was initiated. The AIBEP program supports the Government of Indonesia's (GoI) efforts to increase access for all Indonesians to a basic education as well as the GoI's efforts to develop and implement a model that will provide continuity and quality education in all Indonesian territories. One of the products of the program initiative is the development of standardized education regulations for principals (See Appendix A-2). Three regulations (laws) primarily dictate the required principal and superintendent competencies, qualifications for licensure, roles, responsibilities, and professional development expected by the Indonesian Ministry of Education (See Appendix A-3). In 2010, limited trials were conducted in five Indonesian education districts where professional development existed for both school principals and district supervisors. The study described in this chapter covers the preliminary findings from the initial trials focused on a select group of Continuing Professional Development (CPD) components associated with the

AIBEP program as well as the recruitment process and preparation training covered in the Principal Preparation Program (PPP) component. To understand the significance of the transformation that is taking place in Indonesia's education system, it is important to take a look at the challenges the country has faced since 1945.

In most countries there is increasing governmental awareness of the rapid changes taking place around the world. With rapid change comes challenge in how to prepare citizens for functioning in a global society. Indonesia is addressing the challenge of producing a more educated citizenry by reviewing and reforming its education policies. A major challenge for Indonesia is its geography. Indonesia is a vast island nation in South East Asia with widespread territorial and cultural differences. The country shares borders with Papua New Guinea, East Timor, Malaysia, Singapore, Philippines, Australia, the Indian territory of the Andaman and Nicobar Islands. It consists of 17,508 islands that are scattered over both sides of the equator. There are around 300 distinct native ethnicities in Indonesia, and 742 different languages and dialects, each with cultural identities developed over centuries, various religions, and influence by Indian, Arabic, Chinese, and European sources (Indonesia, 2011). Thus, education reform is a tremendous undertaking on the part of the Indonesian government.

The country has made significant strides since its independence in 1945 through several reforms, with each reform responding to a different need of the country. At the beginning of Indonesian independence, the country's focus was on creating a mechanism for serving a nationalistic purpose by integrating societal differences of race, ethnicity, and class (Christano & Cummings, 2007). In the late 1970s until the 1990s, the government primarily focused on providing increased access to schools, particularly primary schools. In 1994, through a presidential mandate, access to schools extended to the secondary level. At this time, students are provided nine years of compulsory education (See Appendix A-4).

Over the last decade, the Indonesian government has gradually moved its focus to not only improve access to basic education, but to increase the quality of the education it offers its citizens. The government of Indonesia put in place a particular law that provides legal regulations that support a new direction for the Indonesian National Education System (See Appendix A-5). In the Ministry of Education document, the government states:

> National education should ensure equal opportunity of education, improve its quality, relevancy, and efficiency of education management to respond to the challenges and change at the local level, national, and global level. Thus, an education reform is needed with continuous systematic planning, direction, and it is sustainable.

Upon the urging by internal political reforms in 1998, the decentralized system was legalized by 1999. At this point in time, Indonesia set a platform of education reform focused on redeveloping its curriculum to reflect local cultural values, educational differences, and diverse needs of its student population. The platform also set national education facility standards and teaching/learning process standards. Implementation of the standards was designed to be monitored for quality assurance by a designated government approved institution. The platform included setting professional qualification standards for education personnel, school based management, and an open and multi entry education system. Besides, the national government regulation mandates, districts were required to allocate at minimum 20% funding for education (Government of Indonesia Law, 2003).

Currently, the National Education System of Indonesia has five missions focused on improving the quality of education for its citizenry (See Appendix A-6). To achieve the missions, the national system suggested 13 strategies for national education development. Increasing the professionalism of its education personnel was one of the 13 strategies.

With focus on improving educational outcomes for all Indonesian children, the GoI is moving toward embracing a model of education quality assurance and improvement (See Appendix A-5). Among the mandated regulations are:

1. Laws that cover roles and responsibilities of teachers and instructional practices within the national education system,
2. Laws that cover the National Standard of Education,
3. Laws that focus on the Educational Quality Assurance System, and
4. Laws that explain the Minimum Service Standard of Education.

Within these efforts, the Government of Indonesia has created a set of new mandated National Education System regulations to increase professional development of its teachers, principals, and school supervisors (See Appendix A-7). These particular regulations define the required qualifications, competencies, roles, and responsibilities personnel in the field of education will need. Additional standards apply to principals in both public and religious community based schools (See Appendix A-8). Indonesia has two types of public schools—general public schools that are run by the Ministry of National Education (MoNE) and religious community based public schools or madrasahs directed by the Ministry of Religious Affairs (MoRA) (See Appendix A-9). Eventually both education systems will assign competency-trained teachers to principalship positions. During the first six months of 2011 the Continuing Professional Development (CPD) program was used to further develop principal and supervisor instructional leadership skills. The CPD Level One was the first of three CPD training phases to be developed and went through a number of trials in selected Indonesian administrative districts.

Even with the new GoI education system framework and policies, the MoNE has yet to produce a well developed system and process that translates the new education policies to operational levels throughout the country. With the government expecting full program implementation in over 530 administrative districts by 2013, the pressure is on to quickly establish a quality recruitment and professional development program model for both aspiring and practicing principals (See Appendix A-10). This need leads us to the purpose and importance of the study covered in this chapter.

PURPOSE OF THE STUDY

The purpose of the study was to examine initial implementation trials of two components in the Indonesian Ministerial Regulation of National Education No. 28/2010, the Principal Preparation Program (PPP) and the Continuing Professional Development (CPD) program, to evaluate the effectiveness of the various procedures, training techniques, and training materials. These initial trials focused on the recruitment, selection, and training processes covered in the PPP component as well as testing a select group of training modules in the CPD component as a means of providing insight into the challenges and opportunities the two components will provide the Indonesian Ministry of National Education. The overall iterative design of the programs will benefit from this initial evaluation of the materials and the implementation procedures to insure success in the next steps in extending the CPD and PPP programs throughout the breadth of the Indonesian education system.

In addition, professionals in principal training programs in locations other than Indonesia may benefit by learning how the Indonesian program model addressed the challenges of assessing, orchestrating, and implementing training in differing social contexts and settings. Implementing a set of government mandates in multiple contexts is an issue that many western developed countries currently face. For example, the 2003 No Child Left Behind (NCLB) program in the United States and the Australian Institute for Teaching and School Leadership (AITSL) initiative are both instances where government mandated education programs require implementation at the local (district) level. Since the CPD Level One program model is based on the iterative design components of the AITSL program, the initial findings may help refine the implementation processes to insure success in the subsequent implementation steps for the PPP and CPD programs and may offer insights for similar implementations in other settings.

LITERATURE REVIEW

Within educational leadership research, instructional leadership and trans-formational leadership are often presented separately, though recent re-search indicates they are tightly connected. The conceptual attributes and linkages of both leadership strategies are a major part of the newly devel-oped Indonesian principal CPD.

Goddard, Neumersky, Goddard, Salloum, and Berebitsky (2010) clearly summarized the attributes of instructional and transformational leadership as well as their linkage to instructional leadership in their work, which links instructional leadership to the management and improvement of teaching and learning as well as the work principals engage in to support improve-ment. Similarly, Marks and Printy (2003) also found that the combination of the two approaches can be very effective. Transformational leadership is primarily related to the work leaders do to deepen motivation, commit-ment, and dedication of group members when striving to reach organiza-tional goals (Bass & Avolio, 1994). This form of leadership is achieved by empowering the members of a group (Knight & Erlandson, 2003).

A variety of definitions have been associated with instructional and trans-formational leadership practices over the last 30 years. During the 1970s early work with the *Effective Schools Project* linked effective schools to instruc-tional leadership practices by school administrators (Brookover & Lezotte, 1979; Edmonds & Frederiksen, 1978; Lezzote, 2001) (See Appendix A-11). A more explicit definition of instructional leadership was given by Hallinger (2005) in his conceptualized model. This particular model includes three dimensions: a) defining the school's mission, b) managing the instructional program, and c) promoting a positive learning climate. Several researchers in the area of instructional leadership agree that principals should coordi-nate instruction and curriculum, include supervision as well as monitoring teaching and learning activities, and have expertise in teaching in order to do so. Principals should also promote a positive learning climate to support instructional improvement, develop and maintain high expectations and standards, and provide incentives for learning (Darling-Hammond, 1997; Donaldson, 2008; Glickman, 2002; Hord, 2004; Knight & Erlandson, 2003; Lambert, 2005; Zellner & Erlandson, 2002).

Transformational leadership, originally introduced by Burns (1978), im-plies that this particular leadership strategy is the ability to foster capacity and personnel commitment, transform the follower by increasing motiva-tion, increasing their performance, and supporting one another to achieve the goals of their organization. Hallinger (2003) describes a transforma-tional leader as one who is a "leader of leaders, who emphasizes collabora-tive problem solving and capacity building of all staff" (p. 330). Transfor-mational leaders are said to be more influential when inspiring followers to achieve organizational goals (Marks & Printy, 2003). Further, the work of Bass and Avolio (1994) and Leithwood (1994) supports these same attributes in developing a strong school leader. Bass and Avolio (1994) proposed the four I's of transformational leadership: 1) idealized influence, in which leaders build trust to make organizational change and become a role model of their followers (Avolio, 1994; Bass, Avolio, Jung, & Berson, 2003; Bass & Riggio, 2006); 2) inspirational motivation, in which transformational leaders develop an attainable vision, motivate, and inspire their followers to increase their capacity (Avolio et al., 1999; Hoy & Miskel, 2005); 3) intellectual stimulation, in which transformational leaders use innovation and creativity to encourage followers to question traditions and try new approaches to their work without criticism (Bass & Avolio, 1994); and 4) consideration of the individual, where transformational leaders act as coaches or mentors, establishing learning opportunities, active listening, and encouragement to take responsibility for their own development (Antonakis, Avolio, & Sivasubramaniam, 2003; Bass & Riggio, 2006; Marks & Printy, 2003). Additionally, Leithwood and Jantzi's (2005) work provides a philosophical conceptualization of transformational leadership by formulating six components of transformational leadership: 1) holding high performance expectations, 2) building school vision, 3) providing intellectual stimulation, 4) offering individualized support, 5) symbolizing professional practices and values, and 6) developing structures to foster participation in school decisions.

In recent leadership studies covered by Goddard et al. (2010) and supported by Marks and Printy (2003), transformational leadership should not be viewed in isolation, but rather as being mutually supportive when integrated. Their views call for a shared instructional leadership perspective between leaders and followers. In their view (Marks & Printy, 2003) and in the view of others (Donaldson, 2006; Knight & Erlandson, 2003), transformational and instructional leadership are interdependent and insufficient on their own. The core view is that transformational leaders focus on building a common vision and promote collaborative member involvement; however, they lack attention to teaching and learning in their definition. In contrast, instructional leaders primarily focus on instruction, curriculum, and assessment, without emphasizing how to motivate teachers and staff. In the work of Goddard et. al. (2010) and Marks, Zaccaro, and Mathieu, (2000), transformational leadership is said to be a necessity in leading schools through reform, but an insufficient approach with the absence of instructional leadership as its partner. When these two types of leaderships coexist, teachers become participants sharing in leadership functions. "Principals are observed leading teachers toward engagement in commitment, professional involvement, and wiliness to innovate" (Goddard et. al., 2010 p. 338). Marks et al. (2000) theorized that efficacious principals are skilled at both types of leadership. Erlandson, (1997) and Knight and Erlandson (2003) further support this view with their research on the strengths of participatory leadership where both teachers and principal collaboratively work together in addressing the needs of the learning community (students, teachers, and parents). Moreover, Bill Mulford (2003) found the combination of instructional and transformational leadership to be more beneficial in a decentralization system, such as the one existing in Indonesia. Overall, the literature supports an integrated approach that includes both instructional and transformational leadership practices and suggests that this integrated approach is more effective in producing positive student outcomes and enabling school improvement.

The two leadership practices covered in this review of literature are ones that can be applied within any cultural context. However, selecting principal candidates who exemplify these practices becomes another issue. In the work of Tooms, Lugg, and Botch (2010), the authors advise leadership preparation programs to "create spaces for new understanding as to what leadership is based on, the recognition of embedded elements in our society that drive how we frame who is and is not leadership material" (p. 122). They further suggest that leadership preparation programs include within the curriculum, activities that "help aspiring administrators understand the connections between school leadership as discussed in academe and school leadership as it is practiced in their place of employment" (Tooms et al., 2010, p. 122). The Indonesian principal preparation program isn't alone in the challenges it faces regarding linking its training to the field. Besides challenges in recruitment and preparation of candidates, finding the best *fit* for the job can be challenging. Employing competent qualified candidates fit for school leadership is a universal issue shared by many cultures and countries around the world (Tooms et al., 2010). To understand the design and evaluation issues the GoI faced within this study, a more detailed description of the Indonesian principal CPD follows.

THE INDONESIAN PRINCIPAL PROFESSIONAL DEVELOPMENT PROGRAMS: INTEGRATING A LEADERSHIP PHILOSOPHY TO PRINCIPAL STANDARDS AND PRACTICES IN INDONESIA

In Indonesia, the Ministerial Regulation of Education defines what the qualifications and competencies of Indonesian principals should be (See Appendix A-12). In the regulation (law), there are five major dimensions comprising 33 items of required principal competencies that combine qualities of both transformational and instructional leadership constructs. The five dimensions are personality, managerial, entrepreneurship, supervision, and social competency. The dimensions of personality, entrepreneurship and social competencies comprise the transformational leadership qualities, whereas the managerial and supervision dimensions comprise qualities associated with instructional leadership. The integrated approach reflects the values of Indonesia's national education system that was designed to encourage a sharing of responsibilities by the school's stakeholders. The approach also includes legalizing and promoting community participation for the purpose of achieving an educated Indonesian society. This approach has standards and practices similar to those that most U.S. school leadership training programs reference in their National Policy Board for Educational Administration (NPBEA) Interstate School Leaders Licensure Consortium (ISLLC) standards of practice (Council of Chief State School Officers, 2008).

Indonesian principals are expected to raise student outcomes by working collaboratively with different stakeholders, such as teachers, parents, and community. However, communities in Indonesia are unique and diverse in their ethnicity, culture, religion, and economics. Their diversities present several obstacles and challenges to professional training in leadership. One obstacle is the extreme variability in access and delivery of training that results from Indonesia's widespread geography and government decentralization policy. Geography and government decentralization have negatively affected the ability to provide adequately trained staff as well as continuity among those who govern Indonesian schools. In such a diverse country, instructional leadership alone would be inadequate. Besides being instructional leaders, principals need skills in communication and social networking to maintain good relationships with diverse communities and cultures (Rose & Indriani, 2011b). They need training in how to build commitment, motivate teachers, and nurture an open, supportive school environment. They need to be able to infuse an entrepreneurial spirit focused on addressing challenges that hinder the effectiveness of their staff and the education of their students (Rose & Indriani, 2011b). The Indonesian principal needs all the above-mentioned skills and traits to become a trusted professional for teachers and community to follow. The principal traits and skills described are adapted from the Australian ITSL professional development framework (Timperley, 2011) and are the basis for the entire Indonesian principal preparation program model.

Unfortunately, at this time, Indonesia does not have a completely operationalized professional development program for preparing principals in the competencies described. In recent years the decentralization of government services shifted responsibility for providing education services from the national level to the district administrative level. Currently, districts have different mechanisms for selecting, training, and appointing principals. Historically, the common practice has been one where the district supervisor/program coordinator proposes a list of candidates to the district head of the education office (See Appendix A-1). Once the list of applicants was approved, the candidates participated in a selection process. Compared to candidate selection processes in the U.S. and other western countries, selected candidates were provided with minimal training. Once candidates completed their training, the district Mayor assigned their principal appointment. Seniority was an important consideration during the selection process, and politics historically influenced the process. Training, if provided at all, was generally ad hoc and primarily based on content mastery rather than the leadership skills needed for the job. Appointed principals received little or no additional professional development after their assignment. This practice resulted in high disparity in the number of qualified leaders among Indonesian principals (Ministry of National Education Indonesia, 2010).

Thus, the newly developed mandated principal preparation program is intended to standardize a principal professional development mechanism that will assure that future Indonesian principals in all districts have met the required competencies before certification and placement in schools (See Appendix A-2).

PREPARATION AND PROFESSIONAL DEVELOPMENT PROGRAMS (MINISTERIAL REGULATION OF NATIONAL EDUCATION/MRONE NO. 28/2010)

There are four general concerns for adequate professional development: recruitment of potential principals, initial training or preparation acceptability, continuing development of practicing principals, and principal performance appraisal. Presently, developing and providing training materials that cover all 33 principal competencies prescribed in the new Ministry of Education mandate is a daunting task in terms of labor and time (See Appendix A-2). For this reason priority was given to the more crucial management competencies of leadership. Basic leadership skills were embedded in all training activities. Skills included management of school planning, facilities, curriculum, student, teacher, and supervision. Learning materials covered core leadership competencies needed by all program participants whether they were aspiring or practicing principals.

PRINCIPAL PREPARATION PROGRAM

The Principal Preparation Program (PPP) was designed for the identification, recruitment, and initial training of potential principals. The Government of Indonesia's education mandate required that the PPP component of the leadership program was to adopt a new instructional model called *in-on-in*. The aim of the training model was to provide both a theoretical foundation, and, most importantly, the opportunity for candidates to "practice" their learning in selected areas (school settings) during their principal internship. The requirement was designed to insure that candidates develop the needed competencies to do the job. A minimum of 100 hours of face-to-face in-service training as well as a minimum of three months of on-the-job training (OJT) in a school setting is a major requirement of the in-on-in model. The in-service training included two training sessions: Inservice One, and Inservice Two. Inservice One training provided candidates with an overview of the program and materials to be learned. Candidates were then required to demonstrate their knowledge and leadership qualities during their three month OJT period in an applied school setting. Upon completion of this phase, candidates participated in their second in-service training, Inservice Two. During this phase of their training, participants were required to reflect on their learning and achievement. When compared to the principal preparation and professional development programs in countries such as the United States, United Kingdom, and Australia, the in-on-in training model is utilized due to the fact that Indonesia is currently economically unable to offer a set of cost effective university courses to prospective school principals. For this reason, the initial training was limited to these two intensive in-services and the OJT period. Once completing the new preparation program, candidates will go through a placement process where a joint team of certified principals, officials from a district office, and school committee members conduct the selection and placement of candidates in schools (See Appendix A-13).

CONTINUING PROFESSIONAL DEVELOPMENT (CPD) PROGRAM

The Principal Continuing Professional Development (CPD) program is based on Ministerial Regulation of Education No. 28/2010 (President of Indonesia Instruction, 2010). The CPD is one part of the overarching School/ Madrasah Principal Quality Assurance System, and its components are outlined in relation to the PPP program in Figure 6.1.

The PPP was designed for recruitment and initial training of principals, and the CPD was designed for long-range, continuing training for current principals as well as those advancing from the PPP. The major difference between training introduced in the PPP component and the CPD component is that training in the CPD includes additional contextually designed activities that are appropriate to newly hired and experienced principals. The CPD component of the MRoNE No. 28/2010 program offers a per-

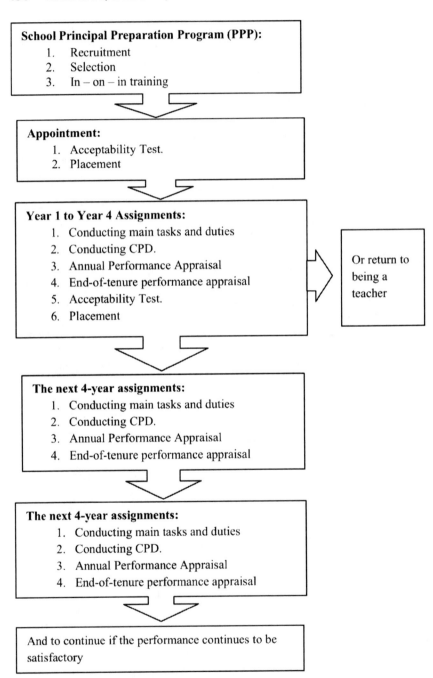

Figure 6.1 School/Madrasah principal quality assurance system: The sequence of steps in the principal recruitment and certification program.

spective that differs from past Indonesian practices. Historically, the view was that every candidate for principalship learned at the same pace and needed the same training and knowledge. Emphasis was on content knowledge, and training resembled teacher preparation, rather than leadership preparation strategies. The CPD program will provide a different training paradigm based on individual professional development needs, level of expertise, ownership of one's self-improvement, and focus on demonstrated performance (improved leadership), not just knowledge about leadership.

The following principles will be utilized through the development and final design of the CPD: 1) The new component of the ministerial regulation program will be integrated within the current existing system; 2) an active learning approach will be utilized; 3) performance will focus on continuous improvement; 4) principal training and support will be accessible; and 5) the program will be sustainable and the cost affordable by the Indonesian government (Casteel & Rose, 2011). In the meantime, the CPD program will work on fine-tuning the process before complete deployment throughout the country (See Appendix A-10). Figure 6.2 illustrates the components of the CPD process.

The CPD focuses on three levels of training: level one for beginner, level two for intermediate learning, and level three for the highly competent

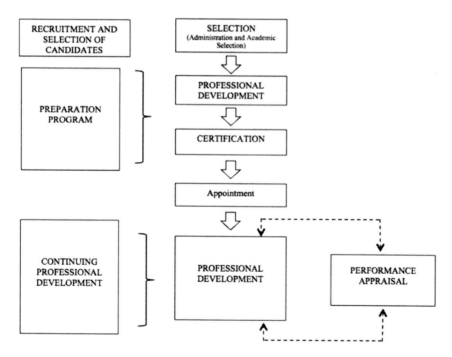

Figure 6.2   Principal continuing professional development (CPD) Indonesia ministerial regulation of education no. 28/2010 (Casteel & Rose, 2011).

Figure 6.3 The CPD implementation process, an iterative cycle for continuous program ministerial development and improvement.

principal. Currently only one of three training levels is operational. In this particular training design, it is assumed that a principal is likely to qualify for more than one level of training expertise at the same time. Learning progress is based on demonstrated improved competence rather than attending and/or completing one level of professional development before stepping on to the next level (Rose, 2010). Figure 6.3 illustrates the CPD Iterative Implementation Process for Principal Preparation by the Ministry of National Education Indonesia (2010).

ONGOING PRINCIPAL PERFORMANCE ASSESSMENT

Practicing principals admitted to the CPD component and those who complete the PPP component are subject to a series of appraisals. The first appraisal of the principal's performance is completed within a period of one year (annual appraisal) and again after four years (fourth-year appraisal). The sequence of four-year cycles is illustrated in Figure 6.1 above. There are three leadership standards assessed, with each practice representing the following key features: a) leadership in the framework of school/madrasah development; b) progress made on Continuous Professional Development: CPD Planning, CPD Practice, CPD Implementation; and c) principal/

madrasah's leadership in orchestrating school improvement and student achievement. Leadership quality is based on eight national education standards grouped under learning quality or management and resource quality (See Appendix A-14). Presently, only the PPP component of the MRoNE 28/2010 has been assessed. The program components of acceptability, professional development, and performance appraisal are not fully designed and ready for implementation at this point in time. However, a limited trial was recently conducted to assess the use of learning materials at the first level of training exercises in CPD level 1. The materials were designed to include activities that were relevant, accessible, and primarily based on collaborative learning activities. Having accessibility to high quality learning materials (Unit of Learning) is one of the important elements in this model. Accessibility will allow participants to interact, learn, and build their competencies (Tooms, Lugg, & Bogotch, 2010). The major element of accessibility will determine the system's success in its ability to incorporate the proposed CPD training format. This leads us to the question the study addressed: In consideration of the differences in Indonesian culture, language and geography, what are the perceived challenges to the replication of the PPP and CPD Level One components in the Ministerial Regulation of National Education No. 28/2010 training program?

METHODOLOGY

An iterative cycle of assessment, development, and redesign is currently used for examining Indonesia's progress in implementing two component programs in the principal preparation program. Collected data on trainer and participant perceptions of the program and their training experiences were used to assess the effectiveness of the piloted procedures and the relevance of the training in which participants were engaged. The first component, the PPP, only covers the recruitment process and preparation training for in-on-in. The second component, the CPD, covers professional development and assessment of the principals after they are placed in a principalship position. The CPD is the one component of the MRoNE 28/2010 program that has been piloted using the iterative process. The plan of the CPD is to cover principal certification/licensure, placement, professional development, and appraisal of on-the-job performance. The study specifically covers the early administration process in the recruitment of candidates for the PPP, preparation for the training, and the seven introductory training modules. During the principal's first year on the job, the first CPD in-services occur in CPD Level One.

This phenomenological study employed qualitative research methods as described in work by Creswell (2007); Erlandson, Harris, Skipper and Allen,

(1993); and Leech and Onwuegbuzie, (2007). The study considered the experiences of the participants about a phenomenon, in this case, the pilot principal CPD program. Social science and psychology have used the phenomenological approach and the social constructivist paradigm repeatedly over time, making these approaches a good match to research in education in general, and training in particular. In the case of this study, a social constructivist paradigm refers to how acquisition of knowledge by participants was influenced by their individual social and cultural constructs (Blanck, 1992). The objective was to uncover participants' perceptions of their learning as well as their application of new knowledge within their social context.

In analyzing the data, qualitative analysis procedures were utilized in using collated data from a range of locations and a number of respondents. Themes were discerned from the experiences revealed in the data collection. In checking accuracy, validity, and trustworthiness of the data, member checking was utilized where all participants (candidates, trainers, and administrators) were given opportunity to read and review their statements, themes of discussion, researcher interpretations, assertions and findings (Creswell, 2007; Leech & Onwuegbuzie, 2007). The goal was to obtain a rich and detailed view of participants' understanding of the program's benefits and knowledge base. The research activities focused on data collected through semi-structured and structured focus group interviews (See Appendix B), trainer observations, written reviews completed by participants, as well as results of a questionnaire completed by program participants at the end of their on the job training (OJT) experience (See Appendix C). Themes emerged through constant comparison of the data and packaging of shared experiences and views. These themes were based on key areas of inquiry, program organization, program implementation, learning by participants, and the assessment process of the CPD Level One training. Additionally, reported pass/fail rates of participants in the pilot PPP program were included in the study.

During this stage of the program, not all components of the Indonesian principal preparation program were ready for review. The study in this chapter looked at two program components that are being piloted. They include the PPP component focused on the recruitment process, candidate selection, and program pedagogy and the CPD Level One program component focused on continuous professional development of the first year principal candidate. Other elements such as acceptability, certification, and assessment will be trialed (assessed) at a later date. Of special interest is learning how the PPP program is impacting recruitment, candidate selection, and in-on-in training.

After successfully completing the preliminary administration selection process, 186 teachers from five self-selected districts participated as candidates in the assessments (trials). Twenty-eight percent of the participants were elementary school teachers, 29% were junior high school teachers, 22% were senior high teachers, and 7% taught in a vocational school. The five self-selected districts participated in the pilot program assessments from January through May of 2011 (See Appendix A-15). A concurrent assessment was conducted with seven core-learning materials at the CPD Level One. The learning materials primarily cover instructional materials focused on managing school scheduling, curriculum, students, teachers, school facilities, finance, and supervision of staff. The research was designed to gain feedback on the use of learning materials by recently appointed principals. The materials, designed around the in-on-in model, link course work to practice in the field.

Six school districts from three provinces selected by Pusbang Tendik (The Development Center of Education Personnel) participated in the pilot covered in this portion of the study (See Appendix A-15). Participants had to meet the following criteria set by the government: a) predominantly elementary principals, b) new school principals with less than three years of experience who have had minimal or no prior professional development, c) willing to work on one leadership topic that they haven't mastered, and d) must live within two hours distance from the site of the pilot program. Selection criteria for local facilitators was based upon their credentials (certification as a school principal or supervisor), their competency/mastery of the content in each unit of learning, their experience as a facilitator, and their enthusiasm for participation in the pilot program.

Participant's use of, and comfort with, the learning materials were assessed (trialed) during implementation of the in-on-in model. The in-on-in activities included three days for in-service one (April 24–30, 2011), one month of on the job training (end of April through May, 2011), and two days of in service (early to mid June, 2011). Seventy principals from each of six participating administrative districts participated, making a total number of 420 participating principals. The 70 principals in each participating district were then divided into seven learning groups, with each group covering one specific unit of learning. Seven local facilitators lead each group, with a total of 42 facilitators leading the training sessions.

During focus group interviews held in 11 administrative districts, 186 participating principal candidates and 420 principals shared their views about the program with 60 designated program facilitators/assessors and 16 district officers. Besides interviews, program facilitators and district administrators conducted structured observations during training sessions. Their collective response was that the program provided new strategies, skills, and content knowledge that clearly related to the tasks principals will encounter.

RESULTS

The aim of the trials for both the PPP and CPD programs, as modeled in MRoNE 28/2010, was to identity processes, materials, or activities that should be replicated. We wanted first to observe PPP events in action to gain a better understanding of how the program can be implemented in an effective manner, and second, to gain input regarding the quality and relevance of the materials (units of learning). The PPP and CPD Level One training programs received positive responses from participating districts and individual participants (candidates and practicing principals). Reflections and recommendations were gleaned from data collected during district observations, focus group interviews, and a CPD Level One survey administered at the end of the participants' on the job training experience (See Appendix B for CPD-1 Survey). Participants included principal candidates, practicing principals, district level administrators (officers), as well as program facilitators/assessors. Important themes emerged in the assessment of five program topics under review in both PPP and CPC Level One pilot programs. The five topics included: a) program organization and implementation, b) recruitment and selection, c) units of learning (UoL) in the CPD Level One program, d) assessment, and e) organization and implementation challenges. Summaries of the salient themes as well as examples of comments made by program participants follow under each topic. (Because of language interpretation differences, presentation of comments in western style English in the examples that follow cover the points made, not the necessarily exact translations.)

Program Organization and Implementation

Time, access to materials, and clarity on the role of bureaucracy in administration of both the PPP and CPD Level One components of MRoNE 28/2010 were the themes derived from the data. During focus group discussions between participants and program facilitators it was agreed that if both PPP and CPD Level One programs were to be successful, primary consideration should be given to the academic calendar and times available for program implementation. Regarding access to materials, program facilitators agreed that time should be allowed for all materials to be printed and distributed to participants prior to training sessions. Several program facilitators and district administrators stated that due to limited access to training materials, availability of hard copies is more convenient when materials are needed among principals and administrative districts. Regarding clarity on the role of bureaucracy in administration of both the PPP and CPD components of MRoNE No. 28/2010, the following comments were made:

"Effective coordination and consistency in communication is important for successful program implementation." "There is a need to have roles and responsibilities clearly defined at all administrative levels." "The Government of Indonesia is now taking the lead, but it is not sustainable in the long-term." and "District administrators require training to improve their ability to plan, coordinate and implement the PPP and CPD programs." Program facilitators agreed that there needs to be less bureaucracy for the CPD to be effective. One facilitator said, "Less bureaucracy was the main reason why participants (practicing principals) chose to participate in the CPD Level One program."

A majority of participants, especially district administrators, said they preferred the system of direct funding from the government to implement the program components (PPP and CPD). This concern is similar to what state education agencies and organizations within the United States are concerned with in the mandated funding of NCLB (U.S. Department of Education NCLB Funding Report, 2010). Other comments included, "It is important that all district stakeholders are informed and comfortable with Regulation 28/2010, including the PPP process and the CPD Level One later on" (See Appendix A-16). It was suggested that the administrative district and/or a principal cluster forum might provide this opportunity.

One participant from the training said, "I was more aware of the responsibilities to be a principal and I felt more prepared both in knowledge and confidence to be one." Another participant comment made during OJT was, "... too early to accurately assess, but we feel confident that the PPP and OJT will prepare us well and give us the confidence and foundation to be good starting principals." Principals interviewed expressed satisfaction with PPP and saw the benefits to the individual, the school and the children. "Before there was no guide on how to undertake the role and responsibilities of a principal—you just learned on the job. Now [prospective] principals are selected on merit and provided with some training and support to get started. By following the program they are well prepared."

Recruitment and Selection

The main theme centered on the need for national alignment of rules regarding recruitment and selection of candidates for the new ministerial program. Interviews with district officers from each of the 11 administrative districts were the main source of information for the following suggestion: "For PPP to be successfully implemented, there needs to be an alignment between the local governing regulations for principals and the PPP and CPD Regulation 28/2010." In this case, reference was made to all three levels of the CPD program (See Appendix A-17). Another suggestion was,

"Particular priority should be given to schools in remote areas to ensure equal opportunity." Because of the challenges distance can create, teachers in remote area schools don't always have access to information about the CPD program. Lack of access will potentially hinder the ability of aspiring principals to complete requirements for participation in the candidate selection process.

The Professional Development Program: Units of Learning (UoL)

The themes in this topic were a) candidates' ability to do academic work, b) the need for revising the units of learning (UoL), and c) a need for trained program facilitators. The following are comments were made by program facilitators: "Principal candidates had difficulty understanding instructions for writing an academic paper as well as the tasks presented in the Leadership Potential Assessment instruments." Facilitators agreed that feedback from principal candidates, trainers, and program assessors would assist in improving the instructions in the future. Comments referring to the UoL were: "Planning, writing and producing learning materials are difficult and complex tasks that require a significant amount of time to complete. Further review and revision of the materials based on feedback from candidates, facilitators and assessors will assist this process." "The amount of time allocated to each learning module is generally insufficient for participants to adequately complete all tasks. Review and revision of the modules as well as adjustment to the time allotted for activities and tasks should improve the delivery and learning process." "There needs to be a review and refinement of the materials so there is consistency across PPP, CPD Level One, CPD Level Two and eventually CPD Level Three. Responsibilities for development should be clearly orchestrated."

Regarding the third theme in this topic, the need for facilitator training, the following comments represent the views of participants, both facilitators and principal candidates: "Facilitators need ongoing professional development to help them identify 'best practices' in facilitating the training process during PPP and CPD learning sessions." "Participants need mentoring by qualified people with a good understanding of topics covered in the PPP learning units and CPD during On Job Learning and Training (OJL/T). Supervisors are well positioned to provide this support, but are not yet informed or trained in the PPP/CPD process and units of learning." "More time should be allocated to on-the-job learning activities. This would allow participants a period of time to put into practice what they learned in their training rather than devoting most of the time to planning and preparing reports." "Candidate placement in their current school for OJL/T is a more efficient and effective approach to training than being located in a second school."

Assessment

In reviewing the themes that emerged regarding assessment, the following comments are examples of views expressed by participants and facilitators: "The focus of the second PPP in-service was almost entirely on assessment of the candidate rather than the candidate's competence." "The processes did not encourage candidates to participate in active learning. The final in-service is an opportune time to engage in active learning by reinforcing and summarizing what was covered in the modules." Examples of comments made during the final in-service in the CPD Level One program were: "We should be listening to each other and discussing issues about learning." "Review assessment tools in PPP were focused on assessment of data collection and content recall rather than assessing if we [participants] put our knowledge into practice."

During the final in-service training, participants apparently did not fully agree with the assessment process. The following comment from a participant is insightful in the fact that it represents some of the comments made during focus group interviews with participating candidates: "There is far too much assessment collected. This limits actual learning—all that candidates do is have tests on their knowledge in order to pass." Comments such as this provided the research team with valuable information to be used in further program development. The following facilitator comment provides additional support for this conclusion: "Consideration should be given to focusing on assessment that builds skills and higher-level thinking rather than only knowledge and content (Example: Application of Bloom's Taxonomy, 1956)."

The following comment represents views expressed by both candidates and program facilitators: "There is a considerable amount of time devoted to the completion of assignments. Consideration could be given to direct the candidate to focus on one topic rather than all eight core modules." The facilitators also agreed that there is a need to create an assessment process that can be used by both facilitators and learners while measuring principal competencies. Assessments should be conducted upon the completion of each module.

Overall, the initial pilot programs (PPP and CPD Level One) received positive feedback in regards to meeting the professional development needs of both program candidates and practicing principals. Participants in both training programs (PPP and CPD) conveyed confidence in their ability to carry out leadership responsibilities of the principalship in the future.

However, several important challenges were identified during trials of the pilots for beginning principals. A description of these challenges follows.

Organization and Implementation Challenges

The predominant theme focused on issues that need resolution before implementation and replication of the PPP and CPD Level One program components. The following is a summary of the comments shared during focus group interviews with facilitators and district administrators.

Districts have different capabilities and resources, especially in the areas of human resource planning, securing financial resources, and overall management and coordination of services. These differences also include managing facilities and access to information about the instructional and managerial leadership competencies of practicing principals. This situation will create a significant challenge to the full implementation and sustainability of the CPD preparation program in future years if support is not provided to districts experiencing specific deficits. One issue is the widespread lack of understanding of the Ministerial Regulation No. 28/2010 components. Another issue is development of a quality standardized national principal preparation program that achieves a balance between the national standard and the need for district autonomy. The challenges associated with geography, equity and access to resources, materials, and effective local organizations on a national scale will be daunting. Clear roles and responsibilities will be needed to guarantee schools in remote areas will have the opportunity to participate in the new ministerial program.

Some risks and challenges ahead for program development are: a) the scope and scale of program development across Indonesia, b) program sustainability might be hindered by regional and/or district politics, c) the limited capacity of government to ensure program alignment over all of Indonesia, d) an up to date communication infrastructure for program coordination, and e) potential delays in issuing supervisor regulations and principal certification may hinder progress and alignment of program components.

There were many limitations in this study that were quickly noted and will be addressed in the next round of pilots and assessments. For example, the pilot programs did not have all the recommended training components and lacked the needed number of enough well-trained program facilitators. The deliberate artificiality of the settings within hotels instead of schools as well as the short time between trainings affected the principal certification process. The hurried approach more than likely will impact the readiness of participants for leadership roles in the districts they will serve. Therefore, the process needed for establishing internal validity of the pilot assessments was low. Only 50% of the 186 participant candidates passed their exams and were certified as principals. This is a major issue facing administrative districts that desperately need more qualified school leadership. A deeper understanding of the reasons for the discrepancy and the development of practical and sustainable strategies will be important if the issue is to be resolved.

Though the study had many limitations, piloting and assessing the initial PPP and CPD Level One programs has helped the Indonesian Government advance in its efforts to establish effective preparation for school leadership. The pilot programs speeded up creation of professional development materials and activities for prospective principals. Presently, Indonesia is continuing its engagement in piloting the training described in this chapter while developing other components of the entire Indonesian Principal Professional Development program of MRoNE No. 28/2010.

DISCUSSION

Regarding the nature of principal preparation and field experiences, the work of Zhixin Su, David Gamage, and Elliot Mininberg (2003) indicated that both American and Australian school principals placed less importance on formal training programs because most have learned to become principals in an apprenticeship model that required them to immerse in everyday, real school field experiences. Within the study, Australian and American principals agreed that training programs should emphasize a closer connection between theory with practice. Interestingly, Australian principals have little or no pre-service training before they take school leadership positions, whereas American principals must have completed formal credential training on a university campus or state approved program prior to applying for leadership positions in schools (Su et al., 2003). Findings from this particular study (Su et al., 2003) as well as other comparative studies (Daresh & Male, 2000; Sharpe, 1991; and Su, Adams, & Mininberg, 2000) demonstrate that nations may differ in the theories and practices they use, but *all* recognize school leaders (headmaster, lead teachers, principals) to be the center of school improvement efforts (Su et al., 2003). Consequently, the successful implementation of effective principal training programs is essential to successful educational reform in Indonesia.

Speaking from a global perspective, many of the planning, recruitment, and training issues covered in the study are not unique to Indonesia. In general, principal preparation programs in developed and developing nations face similar challenges in administering education reform. The pace at which Indonesian education reform is intended to take place over the next four years is daunting; however, through the development of a comprehensive iterative assessment model, Indonesia is well on its way to achieving its goal of education reform. The strength of this program is its emphasis on principal candidates applying what they learn in training during field experiences while under the watchful support of a local administrator. This model resembles other principal and headmaster preparation programs and combines national standards with local control and facilitation.

The dynamics of the paradigm shift from the traditional way principals were prepared for school leadership in Indonesia are unique due to the fact that administration of their reform efforts must occur by 2013 in approximately 530 administrative districts in 33 provinces (similar to states). The need to adapt program resources to serve 300 distinct native ethnicities as well as 742 different languages presents additional challenges to program implementation. With the goal of creating a larger educated citizenry, the shift in responsibility for implementing leadership-training programs from central government control to local district control makes sense in terms of cost and management. The initial program pilots and implementation of selected program components in the Indonesian Principal Professional Development Program, mainly the PPP component and its limited use of learning materials for CPD Level One, were successfully completed during the first six months of 2011. The analyses of participant progress and perceptions in the pilot training and skill assessment program provided invaluable insight into the workability of the initial program modules and training. Participating candidates and practicing novice principals said they felt more confident and better prepared for the leadership role they would play as principal. However, as in most principal training programs, the true test of preparedness can only be measured when the candidates are appointed as principals and their students have successfully demonstrated academic achievement (Rose & Indriani, 2011a, 2011b). Based on these findings the developers can continue implementation of the basic program model emphasizing resource refinement and improved facilitator training.

APPENDIX A:
DEFINITIONS AND ELABORATIONS OF PROGRAM
COMPONENTS

1. The Institution of Development and Empowerment of the (school) Principal of Indonesia (LPPKS). The Institution of Development and Empowerment of (school) Principals of Indonesia (IODEPI) is the English translation of the Indonesian principal preparation Program. Lembaga Pengembangan dan Pemberdayaan Kepala Sekolah (LPPKS). For continuity purposes among chapter documents, the Indonesian abbreviation (LPPKS) will be used instead of the English abbreviation IODEPI.

2. Principal preparation is based on the standardized education regulations included in the Ministerial Regulation of National Education No. 28/2010 as the continuation of policy framework mandated by Indonesian National Education System Law No. 20/2003.

3. Three regulations (laws) primarily dictate the required principal and superintendent competencies, qualifications for licensure, roles, responsibilities, and professional development expected by the Indonesian Ministry of Education. They are: Ministerial Regulation of Education No. 28/2010, GoI Law/UU No. 14/2005 that covers roles and responsibilities of teachers and instructional practices within the national education system, GoI Regulation/PP No. 19/2005 that covers the National Standard of Education, Ministerial Regulation of Education No. 63/2010 that focuses on the Educational Quality Assurance System, and Ministerial Regulation of Education No. 15/2010 that explains the Minimum Service Standard of Education.

4. Presidential Instruction No. 1 1994 extended access to schools to the secondary level.

5. To achieve the mandated goal of Government of Indonesia (GoI) Law No. 20/2003, the GoI produced new regulations that will improve the education system.

6. The national education system missions include: a) extend and increase access to quality education for all of Indonesian citizens; b) support and facilitate full development of children from early childhood on to create a life long learning community; c) increase an education process that will optimize morale ethical character development; d) improve professionalism and accountability of Indonesian institutions of education by creating organizations that develop knowledge, skills, experiences, positive attitudes toward learning, and values based on national and global expectations; and e) Empower community participation in implementing education

based on principles of autonomy within contexts of the Indonesian Republic.

7. This is one of many mandated strategies covered in GoI Law No. 20/2003 of the National Education System. The professional development strategies covered in this law are primarily designed for teachers, principals, and school supervisors.

8. Regarding standards for school principals, Ministerial Regulation of Education (MRoE) No. 13/2007 defines the needed qualifications and competencies principals will need to perform their position as a school leader.

9. In Indonesia, Madrashas are Islamic religious schools. In its common literal usage, madrasha or madrasa simply means "school". In its secondary meaning, a madrasha is an educational institution offering instruction in Islamic subjects including, but not limited to, the Quran and the Prophet Muhammad. In this paper, the term madrasha refers to Islamic religious schools at the primary and secondary levels. Historically, madrashas were distinguished institutions of higher learning and exited in contrast to more rudimentary schools that taught only the Quran. Indonesia is home to the largest number of Muslims in the world with almost 20%–25% of its children attending Islamic religious schools (*pesantrens*). Indonesian pesantrens have been noted for teaching a moderate form of Islam, one that encompasses Islamic mysticism or Sufism (Luckens-Bull, 2001). See "Madrasa" in the *Encyclopedia of Islam,* new ed (Leiden: E.J.Brill, 1965–); "Madrashah," in the *Oxford Encyclopedia of the Modern Islamic World* (New York: Oxford Univ. Press, 1995).

10. Ministerial Regulation of Education No. 28/2010 requires full implementation of the Principal Preparation Program and Principal Continuous Professional Development (CPD) Program. The program is part of the overarching Institution of Development and Empowerment of Indonesian School Principals (LPPKS) program.

11. Effective Schools research emerged in response to the 1966 Coleman report, the *Equity of Educational Opportunity* study led by James S. Coleman (Coleman, Campbell, Hobson, McPartland, Mood, Weinfeld et al., 1966). When researchers compared high-performing schools to low-performing schools serving the poor, it was found that "Effective Schools" could be distinguished by a common set of characteristics. Effective Schools research to improve schools eventually evolved into the *More Effective Schools* (MES) model. In 1989 Ben Birdsell founded the non-profit Association for Effective Schools (AES), Inc. Since its founding, more than 405 schools in the United States have implemented the model with similar success.

12. Permendiknas (law) No. 13/2007 of the Indonesian Principal Standards defines what the qualifications and competencies of Indonesian principals should be.

13. A major component of the Principal CPD program can be found in regulation No. 28/2010. This particular regulation covers candidate acceptance into the CPD program.

14. Quality is based on eight national education standards that are grouped as follows: a. Quality of learning, which includes: content standards, process standards, graduates' competency standards, and assessment standards, b. Quality management and resources, which include: management standards, teachers and educational personnel standards, equipment and facility standards, and financing standards.

15. The self-selected school districts included Banjarmasin and Kotabaru (South Kalimantan Province), Kota Waringin Barat (Central Kalimantan), Singkawang (West Kalimantan), and Kutai Kertanegara (East Kalimantan). The assessments (trials) of the pilot were coordinated by the newly created institution of Development and Empowerment Principal of Indonesia (LPPKS).

16. The PPP in Regulation 28/2010 includes recruitment, admission, training, placement, assessment, and certification of principals. Similar training is covered in the CPD Level 1, but designed for re-certification of practicing principals.

17. The Ministry of Education wants *all* school leaders to eventually master all 3 levels of the CPD component in the LPPKS program whether they are candidates for leadership positions or experienced practicing principals. CPD Level 1 covers the fundamentals of school leadership; CPD Level 2 will cover additional duties and responsibilities in leadership; and CPD Level 3 will cover more advanced leadership strategies and activities. Each level of the CPD program will build on the knowledge and skills of the participant

APPENDIX B:
PILOT PREPARATION PROGRAM—FOCUS GROUP
DISCUSSION—2ND "IN-SERVICE"

District _____ Date _____

Key Questions to Lead Discussion

Calon Participants

1. Second In Service
   Learning materials—portfolio
   Learning process—facilitation, interaction, learning activities, reflection
   Calon assessment process
   Challenges
   Benefits
   Improvements
2. Overall PPP

   What are your general impressions of the principal preparation program now that you have completed the training?

   What do you think were some of the highlights of PPP?

   What do you think was the most important/useful knowledge you have gained during the PPP pilot? Why?

   What do you think has been the least useful part of the pilot? Why?

   What issues/ processes concerned do you have of the PPP? How can these be addressed?

   Do you have any suggestions on how the PPP can be improved?
   – Admin selection
   – Academic selection
   – In service 1
   – OJL (On the Job Learning)
   – In service 2
   – Organization
   – Assessment
   – Is there a general consensus regarding the suggestions/ recommendations made?

   How well do you think you are now 'prepared' to be a principal?

   Provide suggestions for how your preparation could be improved.

   As a result of the PPP training, what are your future goals?

   What are the implications for you in your workplace? What do you intend to do?

What (if any) changes have you facilitated in your school as a consequence of the PPP training?

Are there any other comments that you would like to make that might help with further planning of the PPP program?

District Facilitators/Trainers

How did you plan the 2nd in-service?

How have you coordinated program activities during the 2nd in-service?

What plans do you have for continuing PPP after the pilot?

What benefits do you believe can be gained by the Calon/school/district?

What are the key challenges you have experienced so far?

What challenges do you think you will have for implementing and sustaining the PPP?

What training do you think your district might need to support implementation in the future?

What are the plans for permanently implementing the PPP?

What are the funding implications for the implementation of PPP in your district?

What do you see as the most useful material for Calon?

What delivery model will best suit your District? How do you think this could be implemented?

What is your understanding of Regulation 28 2010 now? How has it changed since the beginning of the pilot program?

What are the implications for implementation of Regulation 28 in your District?

What approach will your District undertake for implementation of PPP next year and beyond?

APPENDIX C

CPD Level 1 OJL (On the Job Learning) Questions: Participants

Is the OJL approach providing the best way of learning, practicing and enhancing the new knowledge learned during the in training?

What problems have been experienced during the process?

What successes have been achieved so far?

What support has been provided to you?

What further support do you think is needed?

Was the 'in' training material appropriate and useful for you during the OJL?

What other materials do you think would have been useful?

What has stopped you from implementing your action plan?

How could the OJL be improved in the future?

What do you see as the benefits to you and to your school through OJL process?

CPD Overall Questions: Participants

What are your general impressions of the CPD at this stage of the trial?

What do you think were some of the highlights of CDP?

What do you think are the most important/useful knowledge you have gained during the CDP trial? Why?

What do you think has been the least useful part of the trial? Why?

What issues/ processes concerned you most about the CDP? How can these be addressed?

Do you have any suggestions on how the CDP can be improved?
- Materials
- Workshop program
- Workshop processes and facilitation
- OJL
- Organization
- Assessment

How well do you think you think the CPD training has improved your capacity as a principal? What ways (if any) have you improved because of the CPD?

What are your expectations for you in the future as a consequence of the CPD training?

What are the implications for you in your workplace? What do you intend to do?

What (if any) changes have you facilitated in your school as a consequence of the CPD training?

Are there any other comments that you would like to make that might help with further planning of the CPD program?

CPD Overall Questions: Participants: Districts

How have you planned and coordinated OJL?

What plans do you have for continuing CPD after the pilot?

What benefits does this program provide your principal/school/district?

What challenges have you experienced so far?

What challenges do you think you will experience when permanently implementing CPD?

What training do you think your district might need to support implementation?

What are the funding implications for implementation of CPD in your district?

What do you see as the most useful material for principals so far?

What delivery model will best suit your District?

APPENDIX D:
MONITORING OF PPP TRIAL (PILOT) PROGRAM—
1ST 'IN' (IN-SERVICE) TRAINING PROGRAM

Kalimantan Districts

1. Intent of Monitoring Activities

   |To monitor, observe and gain constructive feedback on PPP trial (pilot) processes during the training phase.

2. Proposed Outputs

   Activity monitoring report including key findings and lessons learned on all key areas of enquiry.

3. Approach

   The LPPKS *(Lembaga Pengembangan dan Pemberdayaan Kepala Sekolah) monitoring team developed a number of monitoring and evaluation instruments to use during the training phase of the PPP trial (pilot). Our approach is to support the monitoring team (in 2 locations) in administering the instruments, gain qualitative data on the PPP pilot, and review the efficacy of the LPPKS instruments. It is intended to provide ongoing support and advice to the LPPKS monitoring team throughout the next phases of the trial (pilot).

4. Stakeholders
   – Candidates
   – LPPKS monitoring
   – District staff
   – MT/Assessors

5. Key Areas of Enquiry
   5.1 District implementation of training program
   5.2 Units of learning materials
   5.3 Units of learning delivery

6. Monitoring Activities

   It is expected that the monitoring team members will undertake focus meetings and semi-structured interviews during and at the conclusion of the 'in' training. MCPM role is to support and demonstrate how these approaches can be undertaken and how to record data. During the training program our role will be observation—taking note of how the activities are undertaken- noting anything that may help us understand how the process is actually being undertaken. Towards the end of the training program there will be an opportunity for a feedback and reflection activity. We can undertake this in partnership with the LPPKS counterpart. Facilitated debriefing sessions can be conducted (informally) with trainers and the LPPKS monitoring staff at the end of the day. This is an effective way to discover highlights, challenges and lessons learned. It is also important to capture any feedback regarding the usefulness of the monitoring instruments. This can be achieved through administering them ourselves and reviewing feedback from monitoring by team members.

7. Possible Questions to be asked during interviews and focus/feedback sessions

These are questions to assist in discussion and clarification. It is not intended that all questions will be asked or that there is any order to the questions i.e., the questions are prompts to help the process.

7.1 District Implementation of training program

What do you see as being the role of the District with regard to the PPP training program?

How has the district planned, prepared and coordinated the 1st 'IN' training program?

What have been the challenges and highlights?

What improvements could you make in the future?

What support do you think you need to improve the IN' training in the future?

What is your impression of the UoL (Unit of Learning) so far?

Are there ways that you think the UoL could be improved?

Are there other UoL that you think would be useful for calon to undertake?

What plans do you have in place for the 'OJL' phase of the training?

What challenges/problems have you experienced in planning and coordinating the 'OJL'

What support processes have you put in place to assist **calon during the OJL?

Do you have a mentoring system in place to support calon? How will this work?

Can you think of some benefits that you can see for the District in implementing the PPP selection process?

* LPPKS: Lembaga Pengembangan dan Pemberdayaan Kepala Sekolah, is an Indonesian phrase meaning Institution of Development and empowerment of Indonesian School Principals.

** The word *calon* is an Indonesian term for "candidates for principalship"

7.2 Units of learning—Materials

Are the materials written to the appropriate level for the calon? If not, how should they be modified?

Is the use of language in the units of learning appropriate? How could language be improved?

Which parts of the activities are best received/appreciated and appear most effective with the calon?

What does the calon perceive as being most useful to them and why?

How could the training material be improved?

Does the material adequately prepare candidates for the OJL?

What evidence of learning can you see? Evidence?

7.3 Units of learning—Delivery

Was the time allocation for the UoL appropriate—how could it be improved?

Is there evidence of active learning and/listening—how is this happening?

Has the facilitation/training activities adequately prepared the calon for OJL?

Is there evidence of learning happening? Evidence?

REFERENCES

Antonakis, J., Ciancolo, A. T., & Sernberg, R. J. (2004). *The nature of leadership.* Thousand Oaks, CA.: Sage

Avolio, B. J. (1994). The "natural": Some antecedents of transformational leadership. *International Journal of Public Administration, 17,* 1559–1581.

Avolio, B. J., Bass, B. M., & Jung, D. I. (1999). Reexamining the components of transformational and transactional leadership using the multifactor leadership questionnaire. *Journal of Occupational and Organizational Psychology, 72,* 441–462.

Bass, B. M. & Avolio, B. J. (Eds.). (1994). *Improving organizational effectiveness through transformational leadership.* Thousand Oaks, CA: Sage Publications.

Bass, B. M., Avolio, B. J., Jung, D. I., & Berson, Y. (2003). Predicting unit performance by assessing transformational and transactional leadership. *Journal of Applied Psychology, 88*(2), 207–218.

Bass, B. M. & Riggio, R. E. (2006). *Transformational leadership* (2nd ed.) Mahwah. NJ: Lawrence Erlbaum Associates.

Birdsell, B. (2004). More effective schools: Kentucky cohort implementation 1990–1994. Albany, NY: Association for Effective Schools, Inc.

Blanck, G. (1992). Vygotsky: The man and his cause. In L. C. Moll, *Vygotsky and education: Instructional implications and applications of socio-historical psychology* (pp. 31–58). Cambridge, UK: Cambridge University Press.

Bloom, B. S. (1956). Taxonomy of educational objectives. Boston, MA: Allyn and Bacon.

Brookover, W. B. & Lezotte, L. W. (1979). Changes in school characteristics coincident with changes in student achievement. East Lansing Institute for Research on Teaching, Michigan State University. (ERIC Document Reproduction Service No. ED 181005)

Burns, J. M. (1978). *Leadership.* New York, NY: Harper & Row Publications.

Casteel, V. & Rose, H. (2010). *A strategy for quality improvement of school principals: Building a system for continuing professional development.* Program design paper and presentation of CPD in Indonesia. Jakarta, Australia Indonesia Basic Education Program.

Casteel, V. & Rose, H. (2011). *CPD, preparation and link to CPD, a new approach.* Program Design Paper and Presentation of CPD in Indonesia. Jakarta, Australia Indonesia Basic Education Program.

Christano, R. O. & Cummings, W. K. (2007). Schooling in Indonesia, In G. A. Postiglione & J. Tan (Eds.). *Going to school in East Asia* (pp. 122–141). Westport, CT: Greenwood Press.

Coleman, J. S., Campbell, E. Q., Hobson, C. J., McPartland, F., Mood, A. M., Weinfeld, F. D., et al. (1966). *Equality of educational opportunity.* Washington, DC: U.S. Government Printing Office.

Council of Chief State School Officers. (2008). Educational Leadership Policy Standards: ISLLC 2008 as Adopted by the National Policy Board for Educational Administration. Washington, DC: Author.

Creswell, J. W. (2007). *Qualitative inquiry & research design: Choosing among five approaches* (2nd ed.). Thousand Oaks, CA.: Sage Publications.

Daresh, J. & Male, T. (2000) Crossing the border into leadership: Experiences of newly appointed British headteachers and American principals. *Educational Management and Administration, 28*(1),89–101.

Darling-Hammond, L. (1997). *The right to learn: A Blueprint for creating schools that work.* San Francisco, CA: Jossey-Bass.

Donaldson, G. (2006). *Cultivation leadership in schools: Connecting people, purpose, and practice.* New York, NY: Teachers College Press.

Donaldson, G. (2008). *How leaders learn: Cultivating capacities for school improvement.* New York, NY: Teachers College Press.

Edmonds, R. R. & Frederiksen, J. R. (1978). *Search for effective schools: The identification and analysis of city schools that are instructionally effective for poor children.* Cambridge, MA: Center for Urban Studies.

Erlandson, D. (1997). Principals for the schools of Texas: A seamless web of professional development. A report sponsored by the Sid W. Richardson Foundation Forum. Ft. Worth, TX.: Sid W. Richardson Foundation.

Erlandson, D., Harris, E. L, Skipper, B. L., & Allen, S. D. (1993). *Doing naturalistic inquiry: A guide to methods.* Thousand Oaks, CA.: Sage Publications.

Glickman, C. (2002). *Leadership for learning: How to help teachers succeed.* Alexandria, VA: Association for Supervision & Curriculum Development.

Goddard, R. Neumersky, M. C., Goddard, D. R., Salloum, J. S., & Berebitsky, D. (2010). A multilevel exploratory study of relationships between teacher's perceptions of principals' instructional support and group norms for instructional elementary school. *The Elementary Journal, 111*(2), 337–357.

Government of Indonesia Law. (2003). Government of Indonesia Law No. 20/2003 of the National Education System. Jakarta: Government Indonesia.

Hallinger, P. (2003). Leading educational change: Reflections on the practice of instructional and transformational leadership. *Cambridge Journal of Education, 33*(3), 329–351.

Hallinger, P. (2005). Instructional leadership and the school principal: A passing fancy that refuses to fade away. *Leadership and Policy in Schools, 4*, 221–239.

Hord, S. M. (2004). *Learning together, leading together: changing schools through professional learning communities.* New York and Oxford: Teachers College Press.

Hoy, W. K. & Miskel, C. G. (2005). *Educational administration: Theory, research, and practice* (7th ed.). Boston: McGraw Hill.

Indonesia. (2012). In *Wikipedia, The Free Encyclopedia.* Retrieved from http://en.wikipedia.org/w/index.php?title=Indonesia&oldid=486060751

Knight, S. L. & Erlandson, D. A. (2003). Harnessing complexity: A framework for analyzing school reform. *Planning and Changing, 34*(3/4), 178–196.

Lambert, L. (2005). Leadership for lasting success. *Educational Leadership, 62*(5), 62–65.

Leech, N. L. & Onwuegbuzie, A. J. (2007). An array of qualitative data analysis tools: A call for data analysis triangulation. *School Psychology Quarterly, 22*(4), 557–584.

Leithwood, K. (1994). Leadership for school restructuring. *Educational Administration Quarterly, 30*(4), 498–518.

Leithwood, K. & Jantzi, D. (2005). A review of transformational leadership research 1996–2005. *Leadership and Policy in Schools, 4*(3), 177–200.

Lezotte, L. W. (2001). *Revolutionary and evolutionary: The effective schools movement.* Okemos, MI: Effective Schools Products.

Luckens-Bull, R. A. (2001), Two sides of the same coin: Modernity and tradition in Islamic education in Indonesia. *Anthropology and Education Quarterly, 32*(3), 353.

Marks, H. M. & Printy, S. M. (2003). Principal leadership and school performance: An integration of transformational and instructional leadership. *Educational Administration Quarterly, 39*(3), 370–397.

Marks, M. A., Zaccaro, S. J., & Mathieu, J. E. (2000). Performance implications of leader briefings and team-interaction training for team adaptation to novel environments. *Journal of Applied Psychology, 85,* 971–986.

Ministry of National Education Indonesia. (2010). National Strategic Plan of Education Indonesia 2010–2014. Jakarta: Ministry of National Education, Indonesia.

Ministerial Regulation of Education Indonesia. (2007). Ministerial Regulation of Education No. 13/2007 of Principal Standard. Jakarta: Ministry of National Education Indonesia.

Ministerial Regulation of Education Indonesia. (2010). Ministerial Regulation of Education No. 28/2010 about Teacher as Principal. Jakarta: Ministry of National Education Indonesia.

Mulford, B. (2003). School leaders: Changing roles and impact on teacher and school effectiveness. A paper commissioned by the Education and Training Policy Division, OECD, for the Activity Attracting, Developing and Retaining Effective Teachers.

President Indonesia Instruction. (February, 2010). Instruction of President Indonesia No. 1 About Capacity Enforcement of Principals and Supervisors. Jakarta: Government of Indonesia.

Rose, S. & Indriani, K. (2011a). Final monitoring report of CPD level 1. Program Report of CPD in Indonesia. Jakarta: Australia Indonesia Basic Education Program.

Rose, S. & Indriani, K. (2011b). Final monitoring report of principal preparation program. Program Report of CPD in Indonesia. Jakarta: Australia Indonesia Basic Education Program.

Sharpe, P. (1991). Selecting a high school principal in the US and Australia: A comparative study. *OSSC Bulletin, 19*(9). ED123739. Retrieved from http://www. eric.ed.gov/PDFS/ED123739.pdf

Su, Z., Adams, J., & Mininberg, E. (2000). Profiles and preparation of urban school principals: A comparative study in the U.S. and China. *Education and Urban Society, 32*(4), 455–480.

Su, Z., Gamage, D., & Mininberg, E. (2003). Professional preparation and development of school leaders in Australia and the USA. *International Education Journal, 4*(1), 42–59.

Timperley, H., (October, 2011) A background paper to inform the development of a national professional development framework for teachers and school leaders. A report commissioned by The Australian Institute for Teaching and School Leadership (AITSL). Melbourne, Australia. Retrieved from http:// www.aitsl.edu.au/verve/_resources/Background_paper_inform_the_development_of_national_professional_development_framework_for_teachers_and_school_leaders.pdf

Tooms, A. K., Lugg, C. A., & Bogotch, I. (2010, February). Rethinking the politics of fit and educational leadership. *Educational Administration Quarterly, 46*(1) 96–131.

U.S. Department of Education (2010) U.S. Department of Education NCLB Funding Report, National Education Association (NEA). Retrieved from www.nea.org/assets/docs/HE/NCLBFunding.pdf

Zellner, L. & Erlandson, D. (2002). Leaders for Our Schools: Reshaping School Leadership Preparation for the Recruitment of Principals, In F. Kochan (Ed.), *The organizational and human dimensions of successful mentoring: Programs and relationships* (pp. 153–167). Greenwich, CT: Information Age.

SECTION III

OBSTACLES AND CONSTRAINTS CONFRONTING
INSTRUCTIONAL LEADERS

CHAPTER 7

LEADING WITH LESS

Principal Leadership in Austere Times

Chad R. Lochmiller

Resource allocation decisions are an important aspect of principal leadership. School principals make critical decisions about the configuration of staff and the use of resources in their schools. These decisions ultimately shape the conditions for teaching and learning in the school (Darling-Hammond & Snyder, 2003; Grissom & Loeb, 2011). Surprisingly, education researchers have not thoroughly examined principal leadership in relation to school resources; instead, they have focused on state and district-level resource allocation strategies (Fuller, Loeb, Arshan, Chen, & Yi, 2007; Plecki et al., 2009; Rubenstein, 1998). The research is especially sparse with respect to the actions that school principals take when their schools are faced with budget reductions. The absence of research in this area is somewhat disconcerting given the unprecedented financial challenges that school districts throughout the United States are currently facing.[1] The current fiscal context surrounding schools elevates the importance of understanding how principals manage school resources and to what extent, if at all, principals use their leadership to prepare their schools for budget reductions.

The Changing Nature of Instructional Leadership in the 21st Century, pages 165–186
Copyright © 2012 by Information Age Publishing

165

In this chapter, I present a case study of an urban school principal in the United States whose school is facing district-imposed budget reductions caused by reduced state education funding, as well as declining student enrollment. Working from a U.S. education context, the chapter explores what the principal did to prepare her staff and school for the district-imposed budget reductions. The research presented in this chapter addresses three questions. First, what does the principal do to prepare her school for the budget reductions? Second, how does the principal engage the staff in making decisions about the school's resources? Finally, how do the principal's actions challenge existing conceptions of principal leadership as it relates to resource allocation? I begin the chapter with a brief review of the relevant literature. Next, I describe the qualitative research methods that I used to complete this analysis. Finally, I present the findings from my research and conclude by discussing these findings and their implications for the field of educational leadership with respect to practice, preparation, and policy.

RELEVANT LITERATURE

School districts throughout the United States currently face unprecedented fiscal challenges caused by the worst national recession since the Great Depression. The federal government has provided roughly $100 billion to help school districts close budget gaps, retain classroom teachers, and preserve education programs (Ellerson, 2009; Mead, Vaishnav, Porter, & Rotherham, 2010).[2] Despite this federal assistance, school districts continue to face significant budget challenges. Several organizations have taken an interest in the fiscal challenges facing school districts in the United States. The American Association for School Administrators (AASA), for example, has surveyed district administrators throughout the recession to document the effects that the recession is having on school districts and individual schools. Their survey research revealed that the current crisis has had an unprecedented impact on schools and school districts. Two-thirds (66%) of the respondents to a December, 2010 survey indicated that their school district was preparing to lay off additional employees to compensate for declining state resources (Ellerson, 2010a). At one point, the AASA projected that as many as 275,000 classroom teachers could be laid off (Ellerson, 2010b). The situation facing school districts is nothing short of a "fiscal tsunami" that threatens to upend decades of stable education funding (Guthrie & Peng, 2011, p. 19).

Unlike many other countries, the United States Constitution explicitly limits the federal government's role in public education (Wong, 1999). This constitutional framework means that the U.S. education system is primarily funded at the state level by local property taxes. Based on a recent report, state and local funding represents 90.4% of the total education revenue in the United States (Johnson, Zhou, & Nakamoto, 2011). This arrangement makes the United States, and the context for principal leadership, distinct from other nations that have more centralized direction and uniform funding systems (e.g., Sweden), and aligns the U.S. education system with other nations where education is primarily funded by local or regional governments (e.g., Canada, Spain, Germany, and Japan).

Local school districts, which are the equivalent of local education authorities elsewhere, play a significant role in public education and especially in regard to school resources. School districts serve as the fiscal agents for schools. As previous discussions about the configuration of U.S. education have noted, "state government defines the role of the local school board, establishes standards for delivering services, institutes teacher [and principal] certification provisions, and restricts the taxing and spending practices of school districts" (Wong, 1999, p. 6). School districts receive funds from the state and, in turn, reallocate funds to individual schools on the basis of allocation formulas. These formulas primarily allocate staffing positions and discretionary dollars to each school based on the number and characteristics of the enrolled students. Various school-level factors influence which resources are ultimately allocated to the school. These factors include total student enrollment, the characteristics of the student population, the socioeconomic status of the community, as well as the characteristics of the staff (Nakib, 1996; Roza, 2008, 2010).

Principals ultimately make resource decisions within the context of the district funding system. The extent to which they can make alternative use of resources is influenced by the administrative relationship between the district and the schools (Monk & Hussain, 2000; Tucker & Codding, 2002). Principals working in school districts with a highly-centralized administrative structure may have limited discretion in deciding how resources should be used. As noted in previous research, principals in these centralized systems often cannot select their teaching staff, award or withhold bonuses, determine what resources the school will receive or how federal funds are allocated, or decide which staff will be retained in the event of district staffing changes or budget cuts (Tucker & Codding, 2002). These limitations have led some in the school finance community to believe that principals rarely make significant changes in the way that resources are used (Rettig & Cannady, 1993). This assertion reflects a funding system wherein school resources are "trickling down" to schools, leaving principals to simply assign these resources to their stated purpose (Hill, Roza, & Harvey, 2008, p. 5).

However, in districts with a more decentralized administrative structure, like the one found in this study, principals may have significantly greater authority to make decisions about the use of school-level resources, but may have few resources available depending on the financial condition of the school district (Wohlsetter & Mohrman, 1993). As Roza (2010) noted:

> The logic behind devolving resource decisions to [schools] . . . reflects the notion that school personnel are better equipped than district administrators to use their [school's] resources efficiently and effectively to meet student needs. . . . When building leaders are able to make decisions . . . those decisions can be tailored to the needs of their students, thereby resulting in more efficient, effective, and possibly innovative use of resources. (p. 81)

As conceived in the United States, school-based management requires principals to assume new responsibilities for a variety of management roles. The school principals in decentralized districts have the flexibility to make budgetary decisions, hire and assign staff, structure program resources, and allocate time throughout the school day. Researchers have found that principals will often direct resources toward higher priority programs and instructional supports that improve the instructional program (Odden & Archibald, 2000; Klein, Medrich, & Perez-Ferreiro, 1996). Furthermore, these changes are thought to contribute to improving student achievement (Odden & Archibald, 2000). It bears noting that decentralized administrative structures of the kind found in this study are not unique to the United States. In fact, the education systems in a number of countries have adopted similar structures, such as England and Wales.

Education researchers have offered different assessments of the role that principals may assume in decentralized administrative systems, especially with respect to the allocation of resources. Looking at schools in England and Wales, Whitty, Power, and Halpin (1998) found that "the principal is often seen as the central figure in the self-managing school,"[3] as his or her role becomes increasingly focused on "responsibility for financial and administrative issues" (p. 12). Accordingly, Whitty and colleagues (1998) suggested that a principal leading a self-managing school may adopt responsibilities "which more closely resemble [a] corporate director, business executive and even entrepreneur" (p. 12) and thus shed some of his or her responsibilities as the academic or instructional leader of the school. Research from the United States does not support this view. Indeed, researchers in the U.S. suggest that principals often engage in academic or instructional leadership by making strategic resource decisions (Plecki et al., 2009). Portin, Schneider, DeArmond, and Gundlach (2003) found that effective principal leadership involves the simultaneous use of instructional, managerial, and human resources leadership. Finally, Grissom and Loeb (2011) asserted that how principals manage school resources is seen as an essential component of effective instructional leadership.

For the purposes of this study, I assume that principals may engage in both instructional leadership and managerial leadership in their schools, and that making strategic decisions about the use of resources is one of the ways that they accomplish this. As has been noted elsewhere, principals make resource decisions within "the broader and highly variable political, organizational, and values-based context in which school leadership occurs" (Plecki, 2000, p. 545). Moreover, "the process of school resource allocation takes place in an environment that expects school leaders to focus on excellence, promote equity and participation, reduce inefficiency, and respond appropriately to changing circumstances" (Plecki, 2000, p. 545). How principals navigate this context, what they do to manage tensions related to resources in their schools, and which actions are effective is an area of leadership practice about which limited empirical evidence exists.

Despite emphasizing the importance of principal leadership with regard to resources, it is important to note that previous research has suggested that U.S. school principals have few discretionary resources available to them, regardless of the administrative arrangement within their school districts. As a result, principals likely have limited flexibility to mitigate the impact of funding and staffing reductions (Guthrie, 1996; Hill, Roza, & Harvey, 2008; Roza, 2010). Compounding matters, principals must make resource decisions within the broad provisions of highly-qualified teacher requirements and stringent seniority provisions in teacher collective bargaining agreements. These requirements restrict a principal's opportunities to manage staffing reductions or to reassign staff in response to such reductions.[4] As some have argued, the current approach to reducing staff in schools during times of fiscal distress undermines student achievement by eliminating effective teachers who may be in the early stages of their careers and, thus, have less seniority (Goldhaber & Theobald, 2011; Sepe & Roza, 2010). Further, the current approach to school staffing disproportionately impacts students in schools located in poorer communities, which are staffed by many novice teachers (Sepe & Roza, 2010).

The existing research provides very few clues about the actions principals might take to prepare their schools for budget reductions or what decisions they may make. One common strategy that principals adopt is to convert staffing units allocated by the district for non-instructional positions into positions for certificated classroom teachers or instructional support positions to decrease class sizes and increase support for students (Miles & Darling-Hammond, 1998; Odden & Archibald, 2000; Walter, 2001). Additionally, Trimble (2002) disclosed that leaders can augment district funding by pursuing external funding, analyzing financial information to determine where and how resources might be used differently, and manage other school resources for greater efficiency. As Plecki and colleagues (2009) noted, the actions taken by leaders are "certainly influenced by the availability of resources . . . However, it would be a mistake to assume that investing in learning improvement can only be contemplated in times of fiscal plenty" (p. 97). Indeed, as Plecki and colleagues (2009) asserted, these fiscally challenging times "provide the opportunity for leaders to critically examine their investments in staffing resources and consider ways in which resources can be shifted, reallocated, or repurposed with a more strategic scope or focus" (p. 97). This view challenges the common perception that principals rarely engage in purposeful reallocation activities within their schools (Rettig & Canady, 1993). It also serves as the stimulus for this research, which seeks to understand the leadership actions taken by a school principal in a school facing district-imposed budget reductions.

RESEARCH DESIGN

To complete this research, I constructed a case study of the principal of a school in the United States. This school is located in a school district that was part of a large national study of educational leadership (Knapp, Copland, Honig, Plecki, & Portin, 2010; Plecki et al., 2009). For this case study, I selected one school and focused specifically on the principal's leadership actions in relation to school resources. I sought to understand how the principal engaged, informed, and ultimately led her staff in preparation for budget cuts and what specific leadership actions she took. A case study design was appropriate for this research, as the primary goal was to describe the principal's leadership actions in response to district-imposed staffing reductions (Merriam, 1998; Patton, 2002).

PARTICIPANTS

I purposefully selected the principal for this study on the basis of the recommendation of district administrators. The only criteria that I used for the district's recommendations was that the school principal had to have been in the same school for at least three years and that the school must serve a large number of low-income students and students of color. The district administrators recommended a principal who, in their view, was a savvy investor of school resources. They described her as a leader who understood and managed the tension between improving student learning and dealing with successive budget reductions. The district administrators noted that this principal would present an intriguing case, as she actively involved staff in making decisions about resources. They also highlighted her extended tenure (12 years) at the school.

In addition to the principal, I selected participants at the district office and school who were involved in making resource related decisions. At the district level, I selected participants on the basis of functional or organizational charts, job responsibilities, or departmental roles. At the school level, I selected participants on the basis of the principal's recommendation. I interviewed 12 respondents for this study, including the principal, resulting in a total of 23 individual interviews. The characteristics of the study participants, including their years of experience, number of interviews completed, and roles in the resource process, are shown in Table 7.1. The participants were predominately female, had between two and 22 years of experience, and were all engaged in various ways in the making of decisions about the use and allocation of resources in the school.

TABLE 7.1   Characteristics of the Participants Included in the Case Study

	Participant's Gender	Years of Experience	Number of Interviews	Role in Resource Process
Principal	Female	22	5	Primary decision-maker for the school regarding resources, staffing allocation, etc.
First Grade Teacher	Female	10	1	Serves as an advisor to the principal about resource matters.
Third Grade Teacher	Male	12	1	Serves as an advisor to the principal about resource matters.
Fifth Grade Teacher	Female	13	2	Serves as an advisor to the principal about resource matters.
Seventh Grade Teacher	Female	14	2	Serves as an advisor to the principal about resource matters.
Title I Director	Female	7	2	Determines financial allocation for schools based on the number of students living in poverty.
HR Director	Female	6	2	Determines staffing allocation for schools based on the total number of students enrolled in those schools.
Assistant HR Director	Female	4	2	Provides information to principals about excess or overstaffing, staffing reassignments, and transfers.
Finance Manager	Female	2	3	Provides information to principals about available financial resources.
School Director	Male	9	2	Advocates for school principal when additional resources are needed.
Superintendent	Female	2	1	Sets broad policy for resource allocation including how staffing will be allocated, on what basis, and for what purposes.

DATA COLLECTION

I collected data for this study over two consecutive school years beginning in 2007–2008 and concluding in 2008–2009. The data collection involved repeated interviews with school and district staff, observations of key meetings and interactions, and the collection of artifacts from the school and district. I made 11 visits to the district and 14 visits to the school. I coordinated my visits with the school principal to ensure that I had the opportunity to observe the principal, her leadership team, or district administrators discussing the school's resources. The visits often coincided with schoolwide staff meetings, grade-level team conferences, leadership team meetings, and meetings between the principal, her district supervisor, and staff in both the finance and human resources departments.

Semi-Structured Interviews

I developed protocols for the principal, teacher leaders, and central office administrators to guide the semi-structured interviews that I conducted as part of this research. For the principal, each interview protocol sought to generate an increasingly rich understanding of the school, its students and teachers, the resources available, and her leadership. For the classroom teachers, I conducted interviews before and after a spring staff meeting at which the principal presented to them the resources available for the coming school year. The initial interview aimed at understanding what the teachers were thinking about the upcoming meeting. The questions that I posed after the meeting sought to understand whether the teachers agreed or disagreed with the information and decisions, how they felt these decisions would unfold, and what impact they perceived these decisions may have. Finally, my interviews with the district leaders sought to understand how resources "flowed" to the school.

School and District-Based Observations

I also completed nearly 65 hours of observation at the school and nearly 40 hours of observation at the district office. I observed activities where the principal acted individually or collectively with members of the leadership team on matters related to the school's resources. This frequently involved leadership team meetings between the principal and teacher leaders. At the district level, my observations focused on meetings among the principal, her supervisor, and human resources and finance staff. The observations provided an opportunity to triangulate what the principal, classroom teachers, and other study participants reported in their interviews with me.

Artifacts Collected from the School and District

I triangulated my interview and observation data with documents obtained from the school and the school district. The documents provided additional information about the resources allocated to the school, the regulations governing how the resources at the school could be used, and the guidance provided from the district to the principal about the effective use of resources. At the school level, I collected staffing rosters, school improvement plans, and copies of the school's master schedule. Each of these documents provided valuable insight into the decisions made by the school about the use of resources. As such, the artifacts frequently confirmed or added depth to the statements that the school-level staff made during their interviews.

DATA ANALYSIS

I did not pre-define qualitative codes for this analysis; rather, I allowed the codes to emerge from the data, and then I grouped the codes into identifiable patterns related to the principal's leadership actions (Miles & Huberman, 1994; Patton, 2002). As I reviewed the data, I looked for passages of text related to the district and school resource contexts and the specific leadership actions taken by the principal, the teacher leaders at her school, or district administrators who worked with the school. I paid particular attention to the leadership actions that the principal carried out to mitigate the impact of the declining resources on her school. Consistent with previous research on the resources available to schools, the initial codes confirmed that the majority of the principal's actions were related to teacher assignment, developing the master schedule, providing professional development, and so on.

After applying codes to all of the data sources, I aggregated the codes into patterns. Consistent with Miles and Huberman's (1994) discussion on pattern coding, I grouped the initial open codes according to actions, statements, emergent themes, or constructs that reflected the principal's leadership practices related to her school's resources. After completing additional coding and further collapsing the codes into broad themes, the categories that emerged from the data were engaging and educating staff, developing scenarios, identifying non-negotiable investments, and anticipating resistance. Each of these categories became central to my discussion of the principal's leadership.

LEADING WITH LESS: AN ILLUSTRATIVE CASE FROM AN URBAN MIDDLE SCHOOL

The findings from this study indicate that the principal took specific leadership actions in order to prepare her school for the district-imposed budget reductions. The principal actively engaged in this preparatory effort, working both with her leadership team and the staff as a whole. The principal spent considerable time gathering information from the school's leadership team and teaching staff about the resource needs in the school. As part of this effort, she engaged her leadership team in developing scenarios that illustrated for the staff how different resource decisions would impact the school. Further, the principal used the scenarios to frame different resource choices for the staff and to educate the staff about the process of funding the school as well as the various restrictions placed on resources by the district, the state, and various program guidelines. One of the key strategies that she adopted was to clearly identify non-negotiable investments upfront. Woven together, these actions formed the basis for the principal's leadership. Before examining each of these actions, I will describe the contexts in which these actions were taken, including the characteristics of the students, staff, and the resources at the school.

School and Leadership Context

The school is located in a large urban school district and had an enrollment of 387 students in 2007–2008. The school served students who were between six and 13 years of age, who were enrolled in kindergarten through grade seven. Nearly three-quarters of the school's students were from low-income families. Given the ethnic diversity of the student body, one-quarter of the school's students qualified for bilingual education services, as Spanish and Mandarin were the native languages for most of its students. The school received approximately $230,000 in discretionary funds, with the largest proportion of these funds coming from the federally funded Title I program. Resources from this program could be used for supplemental education services as well as additional staffing.

The principal had worked in the school district for 22 years and had served as the administrator of this school for 12 years. She previously worked as a middle school assistant principal, instructional coach, curriculum developer, and language arts classroom teacher. The school employed a combination of 36 staff, including 27 classroom teachers. Most of the classroom teachers were veterans with an average of 11.4 years of experience. The principal had hired the majority of the teachers and instructional staff. According to the school's website, the school's primary goal is to "build a balanced, rigorous curriculum that supports and nurtures well-rounded citizens." The school staff had designed an instructional program that emphasized literacy for students ages six through 11 (or grades K–5) and mathematics for students ages 12 and 13 (grades six and seven). In the previous five years, student achievement had risen in reading, writing, and mathematics.

Much like other schools in this district, the school had experienced a significant decline in school staffing, program resources, and district support. Furthermore, the principal assumed a significant number of additional responsibilities, as the district had become increasingly decentralized. In one of my first interviews with the principal, she characterized the school in terms of "what it used to be" and noted the following:

> When I came here, we had a lot more to work with than we do today. I'd say the school looked how you would expect a normal school to look. It had small classes, pretty much two teachers for every grade, a library, music, art, and physical education. All that stuff. We had a pretty strong parent group, and we also had a pretty middle class student body... When you look at the school now... you see a lot less... We aren't providing what we used to provide, and that's hard for me to watch because the children we serve have much less. They have much, much less. I tell my staff that my passion is to provide anyone who walks through our door with an education. That's why I became an educator. But when I see what we have to cut or make do with... it breaks my heart.

The principal indicated that the school had lost some of its strongest classroom teachers, an innovative literacy program, and support that would have helped the school's increasingly diverse student population.

Defining the Principal's Leadership Actions

The principal's actions clearly defined how a school leader might prepare staff for budget reductions and what reaction the staff might have. One of the strongest points that emerged from this case study was that the principal sought to mitigate the potential "push back" or resistance from her staff by engaging them in the decision-making process. The principal began working to address these reductions soon after receiving word from the district. She attended grade level team meetings throughout the school, met with her leadership team, and discussed the potential cuts with the school's parent group. The purpose of her outreach was to gather information about the school's current needs as well as to identify the investments that could be used differently or more efficiently. The teachers commented on the principal's outreach in my interviews with them. As one classroom teacher noted, "I have worked for three principals, and this is the first one who has really asked me what I thought we should do with the resources." Another teacher, who also served on the school's leadership team, added "the principal does a lot of leg work to get information and ideas, but the decision comes back to us and we make it together." During an interview with the principal, she noted that "listening to the teachers talk about their students' needs is one of the few ways that I get to hear information about the impact that the resources have on students. So, it's really important for me as an instructional leader to hear that information and to base our decisions on that." These interviews revealed three overarching concerns for the school. First, the principal and the teachers expressed a strong desire to maintain on-site counseling support for students in the sixth and seventh grades. Second, the elementary level teachers were especially concerned with maintaining the school's strong focus on literacy, which they felt had achieved significant results. Third, the school staff felt compelled to do more to support the growing number of bilingual students, especially those who were transitioning into the school community.

Following her outreach with teachers throughout the school, the principal convened a meeting with her leadership team to discuss the reductions and to formulate a set of scenarios to lay out the choices available to the school. The meeting provided an opportunity for the principal to, as she described it, "report back what I heard from the staff." It also served as an opportunity to discuss various scenarios with her leadership team to address the reductions while also advancing the school's instructional goals. The principal shared with me that this meeting "served as a gut check for the school and the leadership team . . . I don't like to make decisions without input, and that is something that you have to be very upfront about when it comes to making decisions about resources and money and people." The teachers who had attended the meeting also reflected on the experience. One teacher, who had worked with the principal on previous budgets, noted, "I think this year is the hardest because we have so much going...We have so much work going, and having to stop any of it would just be really hard for us at this point." As reflected in my observation notes, the meeting between the principal and her leadership team was "tense" and "emotional." I observed that the teachers and the principal seemed to struggle with the decisions they had to make, in particular, how to sustain the school's focus on literacy while expanding support for bilingual students. The choices that the principal and the leadership team made in the meeting became the basis for a subsequent exchange with the entire school staff.

Framing the Choices Available and Educating the Staff

Following her initial meetings with classroom teachers and her leadership team, the principal presented two possible scenarios to the school staff for their consideration. The two scenarios, as depicted in Table 7.2, represented the agreements that the leadership team had reached and responded to the needs initially identified by the principal during her discussions with the grade level teams. Scenario A was characterized by the teacher leaders as the "literacy" scenario. It maintained much of the current school program while making reductions in instructional aides to offset the costs. Under the first scenario, the leadership team assumed that the staffing would be reduced, as would the school's discretionary funding. The leadership team identified support for kindergarten and the counselor as the non-negotiable items. They would also retain a full-time literacy coach and a full-time library aide. However, under this scenario, the leadership team would reduce the counselor to half-time and eliminate the technology teacher who had been hired on a temporary contract. They would also reassign a fourth grade teacher to kindergarten. As one of the teacher leaders who helped develop the scenarios noted, "I feel like this does the least to help us move our programs forward this next year . . . It really is the status quo, I guess, and that worries me. I'd say that it's more of a focus on literacy

TABLE 7.2   Scenarios Presented to the Staff by the Principal

	Current Year 2007–2008	Scenario A Literacy Focus	Scenario B ESL Focus
Assumptions		Part-time staffing reduced $25,000 reduction in discretionary funds	Part-time staffing reduced $25,000 reduction in discretionary funds
Non-negotiable	Kindergarten Counselor	Kindergarten Counselor	Kindergarten Half-Time Counselor
Additions	Literacy coach Library aide	Keep full-time literacy coach Keep full-time library aide	Add full-time ESL aide Add full-time ESL teacher
Cuts/Changes		Cut counselor to half-time Cut technology teacher Re-assign 4th grade teacher	Cut literacy coach Cut overtime and stipends Cut counselor to half-time Re-assign 4th grade teacher
Teacher stipends	~$10,000 stipends	~$10,000 stipends	~$7,500 stipends
Remaining funds	~$175 for supplies	~ $250 for supplies	~$500 for supplies

than we need." One limitation of the literacy scenario, however, was that it did little to support the school's growing bilingual student population.

Scenario B emphasized the needs of the school's increasing bilingual student population, but made significant changes to the existing resources. The scenario eliminated the school's literacy coach, technology teacher, and also reassigned a fourth grade teacher to teach kindergarten. The counselor was cut to half-time, and a part-time office clerk was eliminated. In exchange, the school gained two bilingual instructional support staff and a full-time bilingual teacher. As the principal commented, "This scenario does more to put support where it's needed, but it also makes a lot more changes that I am not sure the rest of the staff will support. It's sort of the unknown solution, I guess." One of the teacher leaders who helped craft this scenario added that the choice was "more difficult because some of the school's biggest gains have been made in literacy, and that's something that the staff has celebrated. It's been something that the staff has taken pride in despite all that we've had to change because of the budget." Taken together, the scenarios represent the two choices derived from the input of the staff.

After working with her leadership team to develop the two scenarios, the principal convened a meeting of the school staff. The purpose of the meeting was two-fold: a) it provided an opportunity to educate the staff about the funding process, and b) it served as a forum to discuss the scenarios with the staff. As the principal explained, "You really have to connect the dots between what we say we want to do and the money and people we have to do it ... You have to connect the dots in a way that people see it and understand what we mean." A teacher elaborated on this view by saying, "What [the principal] does is to keep us all focused on ... the challenge or the problem that we need to tackle." I observed the meeting at which these scenarios were presented to the staff and recorded the staff discussion of the scenarios in my observation notes. As reflected in the following passage, the meeting was a highly structured activity designed to bring the staff to an agreement about the appropriate use of resources. The principal took a leading role in guiding the discussion, but largely deferred to the staff to make the final decision.

> The staff assembled in the library after school had let out for the day. The teachers sat in grade level teams at round tables. The principal stood centered in front of the group near a board with chart paper. The meeting was scheduled for an hour-and-a-half. The first 30 minutes of the agenda were devoted to the principal's presentation. The principal began her presentation by explaining how the district determined which resources would be allocated to the school. After this, she presented the staff with the two scenarios developed by the leadership team. She explained the scenarios by writing the numbers by hand on the chart paper. She referred to this as a "math problem" that the staff would need to work on together. After presenting both scenarios, she

asked the staff to discuss the choices at their tables. After they discussed the options for 30 minutes, the principal reconvened the group. The principal acted as the facilitator of the discussion and helped move the conversation. She repeatedly asked the staff, 'What does this do to move us forward?' And, at times, she asked 'What does this do to hold us back?' The meeting concluded when the group had reached a decision.

Based my observations and the follow-up interviews with the principal and teachers, the tension in their discussion concerning the two scenarios was related to the value of continuing to have a full-time literacy coach versus a full-time bilingual education teacher. This was a tension that the principal had anticipated based on her outreach to the staff. As the principal reflected in a follow-up interview, "I think the staff was really torn today between the literacy coach and the bilingual teacher . . . I think their decision to go with the stronger bilingual program will allow us more flexibility as we move forward." A teacher who attended the meeting and endorsed the option of a stronger bilingual program offered a similar view: "I was torn with the choices until I realized that we could do more with our literacy program if we shifted toward more bilingual activities." The literacy coach, who under the scenarios selected by the staff was redeployed as a classroom teacher, echoed this view: "I have helped build a foundation, but now it's time to build on that, and that's where bilingual expertise is needed. Would I like to continue as the coach? Sure. But I am comfortable going back into a classroom." When asked why she felt the staff supported the decision, the principal expressed the belief that "staff see that I am not hiding anything from them, and that builds trust with them to know that we are doing something different here."

Identifying the Non-Negotiable Investments

Based on conversations with the staff and the principal, one of the most important actions that the principal took before laying out the scenarios with the staff was to identify the non-negotiable decisions. She identified these issues through her initial conversations with the staff and leadership team. These items were choices that the staff had previously agreed on and upon which other choices were made. Among the non-negotiable items, the principal noted that she would not give up the support of her assistant principal, as his support enabled her to get into classrooms. Further, the staff collectively agreed that keeping at least one half-time counselor was vital for the students in the sixth and seventh grades. As one of the classroom teachers commented, "I think we have a very clear sense of what we will not let go of under any circumstances. I think we have some commitments that we just won't sacrifice. For me, it's our commitment to language and literacy."

In reflecting on her presentation to the staff, the principal explained why she thought that it was important to identify the non-negotiable items before making decisions. She stated, "I think the staff needs to know what is off the table from the start. If you don't make that clear and manage those expectations, I think it leads to more frustration and worry and anger when they invest time in suggestions that don't have any chance." The staff generally acknowledged that some of the choices they would prefer to make were beyond the scope of their influence and could not be considered. For example, many of the non-negotiable items were related to compliance issues or contract matters over which the principal had no control, but for which the district and school were accountable. The district's human resources director offered some insight into the limitations imposed on principals using examples specifically related to human resources. The human resources director said, "I hear the most concerns from principals about the HQ [highly-qualified] teacher requirements and the hiring, assignment, and transfer process. Both of those requirements take away a lot of the flexibility we grant to principals for other decisions. There's not much we can do with either rule, though. It is what it is right now." As the principal explained, "The district allows us to make significant changes to the staffing allocation as long as we don't go over the projected staffing or fail to adhere to the HQ requirements and the contract with the teachers." This expectation restricted the scope of the actions the principal and her staff could take. As she later noted, "There are ways to use the resources we are given differently, but even with that flexibility, you still have to maintain some rules...at any point in time we have about three positions to work with...the rest is pretty much locked in."

DISCUSSION

This case study expands our current understanding of what it means for a principal to exercise academic leadership while dealing with a reduction in resources. This understanding is invaluable, as it is estimated that school districts throughout the United States will continue to deal with declining resources caused by the national recession for the foreseeable future (Ellerson, 2010a, 2010b). Understanding how principals, including the one in this study, respond to the fiscal challenges that impact their schools is essential if we are to know how to sustain critical improvements in teaching and learning. As this case demonstrates, principals can make resource decisions an important part of their instructional leadership by engaging and educating staff, and developing ways of communicating the choices available to the staff.

The findings from this research challenge our existing understandings of principal leadership related to school resources. For example, contrary to previous research about school-level resource allocation, which suggests that principals do not engage in systematic resource reallocation (Rettig & Cannady, 1993), the principal's leadership in the school in this case study clearly demonstrates that a principal may engage in resource reallocation more actively than previously thought. This point represents the view held by Plecki and colleagues (2009) that resource reallocation is a focal concern for principals who are focused on improving instruction in their schools. As illustrated by this case study, the principal sought to sustain improvements in student learning by bringing the staff to a consensus about the investments that were needed and those that were not needed.

Further, the case study demonstrates that the principal's role as a managerial leader cannot be separated from his or her role as an academic or instructional leader. Although some international scholars challenge this view (i.e., Whitty et al., 1998), the findings in this study are more consistent with previous research conducted in the United States (i.e., Grissom & Loeb, 2010; Plecki et al., 2009). The principal did not see a clear separation between leading her school's academic program and managing her school's operations. Instead, she saw these as two dimensions of her leadership practice that were integrally related to the improvement of teaching and learning in her school. This point is supported by previous research. For example, Grissom and Loeb (2011) suggested that schools with improved student learning outcomes often benefit from effective management demonstrated by the school principal, and school staff, parents, and other stakeholders identify managerial effectiveness as an important aspect of principal leadership. It also represents prior research on principal preparation that has asserted that principals should be prepared to understand the contested and frequently overlapping contexts surrounding resource decisions in their schools (Plecki, 2000).

The case study also illustrates that the burden of solving budget crises need not fall on the principal alone. This point is particularly illuminating because the principal is typically thought to be the sole leader of a school's resources. This study, however, revealed that a principal can successfully engage the school's staff in making difficult decisions about the use and potential reallocation of resources. This conception is supported by existing research that has suggested that principals often share leadership responsibilities with other formal and informal leaders in the school (Spillane & Healey, 2010). As this case study illustrates, under certain conditions, resource decisions may be a viable area for shared leadership or decision-making. Moreover, when staff is engaged in these decisions, there may be opportunities to clarify the school's learning improvement priorities and non-negotiable items that ultimately enhance the support provided to the students who attend the school.

Indeed, one of the unique elements of this case study is the degree to which the principal actively engaged staff in an open discussion about the use of resources in the school. Again, in contrast with previous research, the principal proved that decisions about resources need not be the sole responsibility of the principal. Rather, the principal demonstrated that leaders can work collaboratively with teachers and others to make resource decisions. The principal sought to draw from the expertise of the teachers in ways that invited them to join the decision-making process, while also educating staff about the funding process. Her use of scenarios translated abstract resource decisions into tangible choices about which the teachers could offer valuable input. Each of these actions proved critical to successfully identifying alternatives that, on one hand, responded to declining resources and, on the other hand, sustained investments in learning improvement and built upon previous learning improvement efforts. Indeed, the case study illustrates that engaging staff in the planning and decision-making processes may offset political tensions that might arise when principals opt to make decisions without such engagement.

PRACTICAL IMPLICATIONS AND DIRECTIONS FOR FUTURE RESEARCH

This case reiterates that principals can reallocate resources to support learning improvement, and that these decisions need not be made without engaging classroom teachers or other staff. The case clearly reflects that the reallocation of resources in support of learning improvement can become a powerful source of leverage for school leaders, both in terms of building relationships with staff and in providing resources to the students and teachers who need them. The findings from this research add credibility to those who argue that the allocations of fiscal resources and human resources are critical components of improvement efforts. The findings also have implications for the way that principals prepare for managerial practices as well as for future research related to school-level resource allocation.

On a practical level, this case study offers insight for practicing principals who are wondering how to approach reallocation decisions in these austere times. Given the declining resources available to schools and school districts, these decisions will likely become more common in schools throughout the United States. As the principal's leadership illustrates, these challenges need not circumvent conversations about improving classroom instruction or boosting student learning. Rather, these conversations can be woven into the larger discussion of how to improve the school's performance and service to its students. The principal's use of scenarios provides a compelling strategy for principals to engage their staff in resource planning. Moreover, the strategies discussed provide practical examples of allocation decisions that have been made in times of retrenchment. Assuming that other districts will face reductions of a similar magnitude, the actions taken by this principal demonstrate how reallocation can be linked to sustained improvement efforts. In this case study, the principal thoughtfully reconsidered previous investments in order to manage new reductions and mitigate the impact that they would have on the school. Counter-intuitively, the principal also became more engaged with her staff as reductions were required.

Further, the case challenges how the educational leadership field prepares aspiring principals for resource decisions. Consistent with an argument presented in a discussion related to teaching school finance in leadership development programs (Plecki, 2000), these findings indicate that the way principals are prepared to make difficult decisions about the use of school resources is as much a matter of preparing them to manage the resources themselves as it is to manage the political and ethical challenges that arise when one makes resource-related decisions. Too frequently, leadership preparation programs emphasize the technical aspects of school budgeting without considering the micro-political or cultural dimensions within the school that shape the way that resource decisions are interpreted and enacted. Principals who complete preparation programs are often prepared for the technical tasks, but do not make salient connections between these activities and the leadership actions necessary to link them to instructional improvement. As this case study illustrates, effective budget management and instructional leadership go hand-in-hand.

Finally, this case study presents viable avenues for future research. It clearly raises questions about the leadership actions that principals in various contexts might take to manage declining school resources. The study also raises potential questions about the politics of school-level resource allocation and the strategies that principals employ to mitigate these politics when faced with the prospect of eliminating positions, programs, or supports that the staff deems essential. Related to this, the study also offers an interesting opportunity to investigate how principals educate their staff about the resources available as well as what understanding classroom teachers and other non-administrative staff have about the resources available to schools. Each of these avenues provides opportunities to enhance our understanding of school-level resource allocation, principal leadership in relation to school resources, and the dynamic context in which principals exercise instructional leadership.

NOTES

1. Within the context of the United States education system, local education authorities are referred to as school districts. School districts serve as the fiscal agents for schools and define the context for the principal's leadership regarding the allocation and use of both fiscal and human resources.
2. The assistance was provided to states as part of the American Recovery & Reinvestment Act of 2009.
3. Whitty, Power, & Halpin (1998) use the term "self-managing schools" to collectively describe schools in England and Wales that function in a decentralized setting.
4. The 2001 re-authorization of the Elementary & Secondary Education Act, also referred to as No Child Left Behind, requires schools and school districts receiving federal education funding to employ classroom teachers who are endorsed or certificated in the content area to which they are assigned.

REFERENCES

Darling-Hammond, L., & Snyder, J. (2003). Organizing schools for student and teacher learning: An examination of resource allocation choices in reforming schools. In D. H. Monk & M. L. Plecki (Eds.), *School finance and teacher quality: Exploring the connection* (pp. 179–205). Larchmont, NY: Eye on Education.

Ellerson, N. M. (2009). *Schools and the stimulus: How America's public school districts are using ARRA funds.* Arlington, VA: American Association of School Administrators (AASA). Retrieved December 10, 2011, from http://www.aasa.org/research.aspx

Ellerson, N . M. (2010a). *Surviving a thousand cuts: America's public schools and the recession.* Arlington, VA: American Association of School Administrators (AASA). Retrieved December 10, 2011, from http://www.aasa.org/research.aspx

Ellerson, N. M. (2010b). *Projection of national education job cuts for the 2010–11 school year.* Arlington, VA: American Association of School Administrators (AASA). Retrieved December 10, 2011, from http://www.aasa.org/research.aspx

Fuller, B., Loeb, S., Arshan, N., Chen, A., & Yi, S. (2007). California principals' resources: Acquisition, deployment, and barriers. Stanford, CA: Policy Analysis for California Education (PACE). Retrieved December 10, 2011, from http://cepa.stanford.edu/content/california-principals'-resources-acquisition-deployment-and-barriers

Goldhaber, D., & Theobald, R. (2011). *Managing the teacher workforce in austere times: The implications of teacher layoffs* (CEDR Working Paper 2011-1.2). Bothell, WA: University of Washington. Retrieved December 10, 2011, from http://www.cedr.us/publications.html

Grissom, J. A., & Loeb, S. (2011). Triangulating principal effectiveness: How perspectives of parents, teachers, and assistant principals identify the central importance of managerial skills. *American Educational Research Journal, 48*(4), 1–33.

Guthrie, J. W. (1996). Implications for policy: What might happen in American education if we it were known how money is actually spent? In L. O. Picus & J.

L. Wattenbarger (Eds.), *Where does the money go? Resource allocation in elementary and secondary schools* (pp. 253–268). Thousand Oaks, CA: Sage Publications.

Guthrie, J. W., & Peng, A. (2011). A warning for all who would listen—America's public schools face a forthcoming fiscal tsunami. In F. M. Hess & E. Osberg (Eds.), *Stretching the school dollar: How schools can save money while serving students best* (pp. 19–44). Cambridge, MA: Harvard Education Press.

Hill, P., Roza, M., & Harvey, J. (2008). *Facing the future: Financing productive schools.* Seattle, WA: University of Washington. Retrieved December 10, 2011, from http://www.crpe.org/cs/crpe/view/csr_pubs/251

Johnson, F., Zhou, L., & Nakamoto, N. (2011). *Revenues and expenditures for public elementary and secondary education: School year 2008–09 (Fiscal Year 2009)* (NCES 2011-329). Washington, DC: U.S. Department of Education, National Center for Education Statistics.

Klein, S., Medrich, E., & Perez-Ferreiro, V. (1996). *Fitting the pieces: Education reform that works.* Washington, DC: U.S. Department of Education, Office of Educational Research and Improvement. Retrieved December 10, 2011, from http://www.ed.gov/pubs/SER/FTP

Knapp, M. S., Copland, M. A., Honig, M. I., Plecki, M. L., & Portin, B. S. (2010). *Learning-focused leadership and leadership support: Meaning and practice in urban systems.* Seattle, WA: University of Washington. Retrieved December 10, 2011, from http://depts.washington.edu/ctpmail/

Mead, S., Vaishnav, A., Porter, W., & Rotherham, A. J. (2010). *Conflicting missions and unclear results: Lessons from the education stimulus funds.* Washington, DC: Bellwether Education Partners. Retrieved December 10, 2011, from http://bellwethereducation.org/wp-content/uploads/2010/11/Bellwether_Conflicting-Missions-Unclear-Results.pdf

Merriam, S. B. (1998). *Qualitative research and case study applications in education.* San Francisco, CA: Jossey-Bass.

Miles, K. H., & Darling-Hammond, L. (1998). Rethinking the allocation of teaching resources: Some lessons from high-performing schools. *Educational Evaluation and Policy Analysis, 20*(1), 9–29.

Miles, M. B., & Huberman, A. M. (1994). *Qualitative data analysis: An expanded sourcebook* (2nd ed.). Thousand Oaks, CA: Sage Publications.

Monk, D. H., & Hussain, S. (2000). Structural influences on the internal allocation of school district resources: Evidence from New York State. *Educational Evaluation and Policy Analysis, 22*(1), 1–26.

Nakib, Y. A. (1996). Beyond district-level expenditures: Schooling resource allocation and use in Florida. In L. O. Picus & J. L. Wattenbarger (Eds.), *Where does the money go? Resource allocation in elementary and secondary schools* (pp. 85–105). Thousand Oaks, CA: Sage Publications.

Odden, A. R., & Archibald, S. (2000). Reallocating resources to support higher student achievement: An empirical look at five sites. *Journal of Education Finance, 25,* 545–564.

Patton, M. Q. (2002). *Qualitative research & evaluation methods* (3rd ed.). Thousand Oaks, CA: Sage Publications.

Plecki, M. L. (2000). Money isn't everything: Teaching school finance in a leadership development program. *Journal of School Leadership, 10*(XX), 542–560.

Plecki, M. L., Knapp, M. S., Casteñada, T., Halverson, T., La Sota, R., & Lochmiller, C. (2009). *How leaders invest staffing resources for learning improvement.* Seattle, WA: University of Washington.

Portin, B., Schneider, P., DeArmond, M., & Gundlach L. (2003). *Making sense of leading schools: A student of the school principalship.* Seattle, WA: University of Washington. Retrieved December 10, 2011, from //www.crpe.org/cs/crpe/view/csr_pubs/24

Rettig, M. D., & Canady, R. L. (1993). Unlocking the lockstep high school schedule. *Phi Delta Kappan, 7,* 310–314.

Roza, M. (2008). *Allocation anatomy: How district policies that deploy resources can support (or undermine) district reform strategies.* Seattle, WA: University of Washington. Retrieved December 10, 2011, from http://www.crpe.org/cs/crpe/view/csr_pubs/230

Roza, M. (2010). *Educational economics: Where do school funds go?* Washington, DC: The Urban Institute Press.

Rubenstein, R. (1998). Resource equity in Chicago public schools: A school-level approach. *Journal of Education Finance, 23*(4), 468–489.

Sepe, C., & Roza, M. (2010). *The disproportionate impact of seniority-based layoffs on poor, minority students.* Seattle, WA: University of Washington. Retrieved December 10, 2011, from http://www.crpe.org/cs/crpe/view/csr_pubs/340

Spillane, J. P., & Healey, K. (2010). Conceptualizing school leadership and management from a distributed perspective: An exploration of some study operations and measures. *The Elementary School Journal, 111*(2), 253–281.

Trimble, S. (2002). Common elements of high performing, high poverty middle schools. *Middle School Journal, 33*(4), 7–16.

Tucker, M. S., & Codding, J. B. (2002). *The principal challenge: Leading and managing schools in an era of accountability.* San Francisco, CA: Jossey-Bass.

Walter, F. (2001). *District leaders' guide to reallocating resources.* Portland, OR: Northwest Regional Educational Laboratory (NREL).

Whitty, G., Power, S., & Halpin, D. (1998). *Devolution & choice in education: The school, the state, and the market.* Buckingham, UK: Open University Press.

Wohlsetter, P., & Mohrman, S. A. (1993). *School-based management: Strategies for success.* New Brunswick, NJ: Consortium for Policy Research in Education.

Wong, K. K. (1999). *Funding public schools: Politics and policies.* Lawrence, KS: University Press of Kansas.

CHAPTER 8

SCHOOL-BASED INSTRUCTIONAL LEADERSHIP IN DEMANDING ENVIRONMENTS

New Challenges, New Practices

Michael S. Knapp, Simangele T. Mkhwanazi, and Bradley S. Portin

Instructional leadership has long been recognized and widely advocated as a central facet of school administrators' roles (e.g., Glickman, 2002; Hallinger, 2005; Leithwood & Duke, 1999; Smith & Andrews, 1989). The literature on school-based instructional leadership to date has tended to focus on school principals, detailing ways that people occupying this position exert direct and indirect influence on teaching and learning in the school (Reitzug & West, 2011), while also noting how easily the function gets crowded out of the principal's daily work by burgeoning management responsibilities (Portin, DeArmond, Gundlach, & Schneider, 2003). A parallel strand of research has brought recent scholarly attention to another position, that

The Changing Nature of Instructional Leadership in the 21st Century, pages 187–214
Copyright © 2012 by Information Age Publishing
187

of the school-based instructional coach or teacher leader (e.g., Mraz, Algozzine, & Watson, 2008; Taylor, 2008).

Yet, research is beginning to highlight different ways of construing instructional leadership work in the school (e.g., Hallinger & Heck, 2010; Halverson, Grigg, Prichett, & Thomas, 2007; Printy, Marks, & Bowers, 2009; Spillane, Diamond, & Jita, 2003) and acknowledging ways instructional leadership might be shaped by the context of high-stakes testing (Reitzug, West, & Angel, 2008). Recent research thus reflects several shifts in thinking about this aspect of school leadership, if not school leadership more generally. These developments shift focus from the individual to the team, from leaders' actions to interactions among leaders and followers, from person- and position-centered conceptions of leadership to more distributed conceptions, and from decontextualized ways of understanding leadership work to ways that situate leadership inextricably within particular organizational contexts.

These general shifts are occurring in a particular policy environment that is making unprecedented demands on schooling and school staff, as it ratchets up pressure to show progress in efforts to serve an increasingly diverse student population. And it does so with the admonition that schools ensure the success of all members of this population.

Understandably, given this policy environment as well as the demographic realities of schooling, teaching practice itself—the primary reference point for instructional leadership—is itself changing. Consider the words of this veteran teacher in a California high school during the 2007–2008 year:

> When I got into teaching, it was like you were your own little enterprise and you got to shut your door and manage your classroom the way you wanted and teach the way you wanted. As long as you did your work and didn't slide, nobody bothered you. Twice a year you'd have an evaluation or whatever, but it wasn't any big deal. But now times have changed. Anybody can come in at any time. Your classroom should be open, you should be in a fishbowl, basically, and showing what you're doing at all times. And kids should be monitored for whether or not they're actually getting the information. So I think it's just a different time. And I think accountability is—can be—a negative word. But we are accountable, just like somebody in an office... (Knapp & Feldman, 2011, p. 31)

Arguably, those school staff who are involved in guiding, directing, and supporting teachers in this new way of doing things are themselves likely to be challenged to re-envision their own practices.

This chapter presents a conceptual argument about this changing landscape of instructional leadership, rooted in findings from a recent national study of school leadership aimed at learning improvement (Knapp, Copland, Honig, Plecki, & Portin, 2010; Portin et al., 2009).[1] The chapter summarizes recent decades of literature that discusses and conceptualizes instructional leadership, often narrowly, as a central function of the school principalship. From this work, we derive several dimensions of instructional leadership, which we treat as the "core work" of the instructional leader. Then we describe four additional, interrelated dimensions, each with theoretical as well as empirical roots that have come into prominence in the past decade, in relation to a policy environment dominated by high-stakes standards-based reform. To elaborate and illustrate these dimensions—which we treat as the "new work" of instructional leadership—we draw selectively on the findings of our research, as well as other studies. The chapter concludes by reflecting on the extensions and further exploration of this new work in various national contexts and settings.

The empirically grounded, conceptual analysis in this chapter explores the following questions concerning each of the four new dimensions of instructional leadership work:

1. What is the nature of the leadership work and who carries it out?
2. In what senses is it "new" work—that is, departing from, and adding to, the work that instructional leaders might have done, or thought they needed to do, in prior years?
3. In what ways does the new work reflect and respond to the conditions of schooling set by a high-stakes, standards-based reform environment?

We confine our discussion to the exercise of instructional leadership in the school, by administrators or teachers who normally reside there. In so doing, we acknowledge that instructional leadership may be exercised by district/local educational authority staff, both from a distance and through visits to schools in coaching, mentoring, or professional development capacities. Similarly, staff from third-party organizations may strike a similar relationship with schools, directly or indirectly offering instructional leadership that is welcomed and even sought after by school staff. We leave a full exploration of such leadership sources and practices to other discussions, noting here that dynamics we describe may implicate external as well as internal sources of leadership.

LENSES FOR VIEWING INSTRUCTIONAL LEADERSHIP PRACTICE

We bring a particular set of lenses to this discussion. The first, which we call "learning-focused leadership," has grown across a decade now, through various scholars here and abroad (e.g., Copland & Knapp, 2006; MacBeath &

Dempster, 2009; Murphy, Elliott, Goldring, & Porter, 2006; Resnick & Glennan, 2002; Stoll, Fink, & Earl, 2003). In our formulations of these ideas (see Copland & Knapp, 2006; Knapp, Copland, Plecki, Portin, & Colleagues, 2006), learning, and especially professional learning, sits at the heart of leadership, as does student learning, and what we call "system learning." The three are inescapably linked to each other—each derives input from the others, while reciprocally informing them, as the arrows in Figure 8.1 schematically suggest. Each of the round discs in the figure positions the relevant learning in the center, surrounded by learning opportunities. They are all interconnected. Learning-focused leadership aims simultaneously at all three and presumes that failing to take all three into account makes it less likely that any one will be achieved.

This way of approaching school-based leadership treats leadership, whatever its focus, as the *shared work and commitments* that both shape the direction of the school and its learning improvement agenda, and also mobilize effort and energy to pursue that work. Drawing from a growing line of theory that treats leadership as a distributed, organization-wide phenomenon (Ogawa & Bossert, 2000; Spillane, 2006) reflecting school-wide leadership capacity (Lambert, 2003), we locate leadership inside the interactions among a variety of people occupying different kinds of positions within the

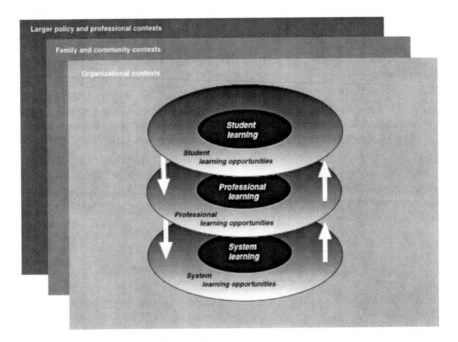

Figure 8.1 The lens of learning-focused leadership.

school, rather than concentrating on leadership as constituted in actions, utterances, or commitments of any individual.

Learning-focused leadership is all about trying to maximize learning for students, professionals, and the system within several contexts, represented schematically by rectangular frames in Figure 8.1—the organizational context of school or district, the students' community and family context, and the larger policy and professional context in which formal education takes place. The changing nature of these contexts, especially the larger policy environment, have much to do with leadership practices at the school level.

Our second lens concerns instruction, a main target of learning-focused leadership. Instruction can be viewed productively in interactional terms—as the interaction among learners, teacher, and content, in environments (City, Elmore, Fiarman, & Teitel, 2009; Cohen, Raudenbush, & Ball, 2003; Grossman, Stodolsky, & Knapp, 2004). The result of these interactions is the learning that students can demonstrate in various ways, as mastery of content, new forms of participation, and the exercise of new skills. By extension, professional learning presumes the interaction of adult learners (teachers or administrators) with other "teachers" (facilitators or instructional leaders), and professional content (problems of pedagogical practice and their potential solutions).

As in the framing of learning-focused leadership, this view of instruction emphasizes its context-embedded nature. There are many relevant contexts, as early work on the contexts of teaching has established (McLaughlin & Talbert, 1993)—especially those that project policy expectations, communicate professional norms, represent the community's character and goals for schooling, and embody basic ideas about subject matter. The subject matter context, for one thing, shapes basic assumptions about the content being taught, what constitutes "knowledge," and how it can be mastered (Grossman & Stodolsky, 1995). The local community context, defined by culture, language, and economic circumstances, has profound implications for learners' approach to schooling and, in turn, the school's approach to teaching them (e.g., Berliner, 2009; Valenzuela, 1999). And contemporary policy environments, dominated by a standards-based reform theory and associated accountability systems, project expectations for instructional practice and what it will produce, while tying results to consequences for students, teachers, schools, and school leaders (Knapp & Meadows, 2005). Each of these environments *permeate* instruction—they express themselves "inside" the act of classroom teaching and learning, at the same time that they sit "outside" the school.

Putting these conceptual anchors together gives a working notion of instructional leadership: *the shared work and commitments that provide direction for instructional improvement and that engage the efforts and energy of teachers and others in pursuit of powerful, equitable interactions among teachers, learners, and content, in response to environmental demands.* Such a definition departs in some respects from a decades-long tradition of research on effective schooling and the part that leadership plays in it (Lezotte, 1994). Therein, a broadly accepted three-part notion of "instructional leadership" has emphasized efforts, primarily by school principals, to define school mission, manage the instructional program, and promote positive school learning climates (Hallinger, 2005; Hallinger & Murphy, 1985). This line of thinking has undergirded an accumulation of evidence (see Hallinger, 2003, 2005; Hallinger & Heck, 1996; Leithwood, Louis, Anderson, & Wahlstrom, 2004; Robinson, Lloyd & Rowe, 2008; Southworth, 2002, for successive reviews of this evidence) concerning the nature and effects of instructional leadership, especially as practiced by principals, helps to establish the enduring "core work" of instructional leaders, whoever they may be, while stopping short of identifying those aspects of leadership work that respond to contemporary reform contexts, and how reform contexts *become part of* the school leader's work. The bulk of the accumulating evidence to date, however, has concentrated on the principal as *the* instructional leader, as recent meta-analyses note (e.g., Robinson et al., 2008), in keeping with the original preoccupations with the strong, directive, instructionally focused principal in early work on effective schools and school improvement processes (Hallinger, 2003).

More recent extensions of this line diversify understandings of instructional leadership in several respects and marry it to other images and models of school leadership. Some scholarship has identified intrinsic links between instructional leadership and the professional development function (e.g., Drago-Severson, 2007; Graczewski, Knudsen, & Holtzman, 2009), also elaborating the picture of the principal's direct supervisory work with teachers (Blase & Blase, 1999). Other research widens the view of instructional leadership as a function shared by teachers and principals, through collaborative inquiry and other means; here, the merging of transformational and instructional leadership into more "integrated" models are noteworthy (Marks & Printy, 2003), as are the extensions of this thinking to demonstrate the *shared* dimension of both transformational and instructional leadership (Printy et al., 2009). Related work rooted in longitudinal studies has highlighted the reciprocal, mutually reinforcing forms of *collaborative* leadership (Hallinger & Heck, 2010) and *collective* leadership (Leithwood & Jantzi, 2008; Leithwood & Mascall, 2008). Still other studies illuminate how instructional leadership entails shifting school practice to base instructional improvement around data (Halverson et al., 2007), and the development and use of tools and leadership practices that connect teachers with other communities of practice (Coldren & Spillane, 2007; Printy, 2008). Finally, other research distinguishes the mental maps of instructional leadership held by novice principals from those of more experienced counterparts (Ruff & Shoho, 2005).

Using these lenses, this chapter considers new priorities, practices, and facets of instructional leadership within an expanded, environmentally responsive vision of leadership practice. Then, leaning heavily on research we have been doing over the last three years, we examine productive ways to exercise leadership.

MODES OF INQUIRY AND DATA SOURCES

At the intersection of these framing ideas, this chapter connects pertinent literature to a recent investigation of learning-focused leadership in urban schools and school districts (Knapp et al., 2010; Portin et al., 2009). That study, operating within a qualitative case study tradition that generated "basic" interpretive research on the phenomenon (Merriam, 2009), collected data during 2007–2008 and the first part of the following year, through repeated visits to 15 schools in four urban districts (in different states). The timing of data collection, five years after a comprehensive standards-based reform policy was enacted at the federal level (the "No Child Left Behind" law of 2002), enabled the study to explore responses to a well established high-accountability environment, reinforced by federal, state, and local action. Data came from interviews with various school and district participants, shadowing of leaders' work and leadership events, and archival sources.[2]

Through these data sources, the study generated detailed portraits of school-based instructional leadership in the case study schools, as carried out by teams of staff (e.g., principals, instructional coaches, content specialists). Cross-case analysis in an inductive, theory-building process yielded strong claims and evidence from multiple contexts. The analysis in this chapter then connects these empirically derived patterns of instructional leadership work with the conceptual dimensions of instructional leadership apparent in the literature.

ENDURING FEATURES OF INSTRUCTIONAL LEADERSHIP

Before considering what is changing about instructional leadership work, it is important to establish what has not changed and is unlikely to change over time. Here, decades of research help to identify what could be construed as the "core work" of instructional leadership, and also the "groundwork" necessary to make the function a normal and expected part of daily educational practice in schools.

Traditional Views of Instructional Leadership: The Core Work

Traditional definitions of instructional leadership are bound up with notions of who does it. Two enduring images have been with us for a long time. For one, the idea of the principal as instructional leader has long dominated discourse about school-based instructional leadership, though it has gone through several cycles of attention and inattention since the early 1980s, when this aspect of school leadership first came into focus (Hallinger, 2005; Ylimaki, 2007). This leadership activity exists in tension with everything else principals do to manage a school, and in this tension, instructional leadership often gets short shrift (Hallinger, 2005; Portin et al., 2003). The principal's instructional leadership can even be argued, as some critics of early instructional leadership theories have done, to be unlikely to occur or be sustained, given the structural constraints on the principalship and the management demands of schooling (Hallinger, 2003). A second image of the instructional leader—the instructional coach and related roles such as embedded staff developers, content specialists, or data coaches, as well as other "teacher leadership" roles (e.g., Mraz et al., 2008; Neufeld & Roper, 2003; Taylor, 2008; York-Barr & Duke, 2004)—avoids this tension but encounters others. And the second image still concentrates on individuals in designated positions who engage in various practices that often entail face-to-face work with teachers.

These two images, of principal or coach as instructional leader, may obscure the full extent of instructional leadership practice, as recent work on shared, collaborative, and distributed images of instructional leadership have helped to point out (e.g., Bredeson, 2009; Hallinger & Heck, 2010; Printy et al., 2009). The dominant images tend to treat the individual as the vehicle for leadership, as in the instructional leadership exercised in the principal's engagement with teachers in the supervision cycle, or in the coaching relationship that a teacher leader may strike up with colleagues. In these images, much of the activity occurs as face-to-face interaction between a teacher and an individual in a formal instructional leadership role.

To be sure, direct interaction between a principal or coach and teachers for purposes of instructional improvement, either individually or in groups, embodies some enduring aspects of the instructional leadership terrain (and here, the principal's role may be either direct or indirect). For one thing, these leaders convene and engage conversations about more powerful instructional practice and how teachers might reach for it. For another, as they always have, individual instructional leaders in schools scaffold and motivate teachers' professional learning about content, pedagogical expertise, how they assess learning, and even how students learn. Finally, at the core of instructional leadership, the principal or coach prompt, introduce, and model changes in classroom practice that serve students better. These activities are inescapably part of instructional leadership, and they constitute the "core work" that instructional leaders have always done, and always will be doing. Put another way, instructional improvement will not happen absent conversation about teaching and learning among educational practitioners, scaffolding and motivation of professional learning, and exposure to improved forms of instructional practice. The instructional conversation may or may not reflect the efforts of a designated individual like a principal or coach in a formal instructional leadership role, but it is likely to be prompted and guided by some combination of administrative and teacher participants.

Paralleling these core dimensions of instructional leadership, the literature also establishes a broader terrain of activity, especially by the school principal, who holds bottom-line responsibility for what takes place in the school. As summarized by Hallinger (2005), the following aspects of instructional leadership practice in the school emerge from the past 25 years of research on this phenomenon:

- Creating a shared sense of purpose in the school, including clear goals focused on student learning.
- Fostering the continuous improvement of the school through cyclical school development planning that involves a wide range of stakeholders.
- Developing a climate of high expectations and a school culture aimed at innovation and improvement of teaching and learning.
- Coordinating the curriculum and monitoring student learning outcomes.
- Shaping the reward structure of the school to reflect the school's mission.
- Organizing and monitoring a wide range of activities aimed at the continuous development of staff.
- Being a visible presence in the school, modeling the desired values of the school's culture.

These dimensions of leadership practice, generally associated with the principal, have been growing through decades of work on school improvement, and find their expression most recently in comprehensive and empirically grounded models of school improvement (e.g., Bryk, Sebring, Allensworth, Luppescu, & Easton, 2010).

Groundwork: Positioning and Normalizing Instructional Leadership

Implied by the core functions identified above is a stage-setting function or "groundwork" (Portin et al., 2009), often carried out by the school principal, as well as others, including the school district central office leaders. These individuals lay the groundwork for instructional leadership by "normalizing" instructional leadership as a regular and ongoing activity in the school. This implies a cultural shift in getting staff used to the idea that continually improving practice is not an occasional concern but rather an everyday activity and an integral part of contemporary standards-based teaching practice. By laying this groundwork leaders legitimize the efforts of individuals who participate in instructional leadership work, full or part time, other than the principal, assistant principals, or department heads. Typically, these individuals are accomplished teachers, acting as teacher leaders, who guide and support their colleagues. Legitimizing their work means clarifying the often ambiguous nature of the instructional leadership role that these teacher leaders take on, work that staff would normally expect of an administrator, if they expected it at all.

A glimpse from our research on learning-focused leadership in urban schools gives clues about the groundwork that must be laid, as this teacher leader notes:

> We've already built that culture of intervisitation so we're accustomed to commenting on each other's practice and giving each other constructive feedback, suggestions—whatever. So we've kind of built that culture of being able to comment on each other's practice...

In this example, and many others from our research, the groundwork was laid by patiently establishing a culture that supported continuous reflection on practice, discussion among teachers about what was happening in classrooms, and a common sense of what might be expected in the actual practice of instructional leadership. Scholars have long noted the central role that principals especially can and must play in "developing...a school culture aimed at innovation and improvement of teaching and learning" (Hallinger, 2005, p. 233). This role has been especially emphasized in research and theory on transformational leadership in the school, which emphasizes the building of motivation, shared purpose, and ownership among staff, but which by itself may be a helpful precondition for, but not a guarantee of, effective instructional leadership (Robinson et al., 2008), and which may merge with instructional leadership to create more "integrated" forms of leadership practice (Printy et al., 2009).

NEW CHALLENGES, NEW PRACTICES
FOR INSTRUCTIONAL LEADERSHIP

The core work and groundwork we have just described stops short of recognizing or foregrounding the essential elements of instructional leadership that are increasingly evident in the repertoire of instructional leaders. These constitute the "new work" of instructional leadership—in particular, four other dimensions that reinforce and elaborate the core work of instructional leadership—as shown schematically in Figure 8.2 below.

The new work includes: 1) orienting instructional improvement activities to the growing diversity in classrooms, schools and communities; 2) using data and evidence in powerful ways to inform classroom teacher practice as well as the leadership work itself; 3) working within and through instructional leadership teams; and 4) engaging the demands of the environment not as a barrier but as a resource for instructional improvement work. Along with recent theory and evidence, which point in varying degrees towards all of these dimensions, the findings of our research on learning-focused leadership in urban schools shed light on the exercise of instructional leadership in relation to each dimension, and how it departs from earlier conceptions of instructional leadership, while reflecting the demands and conditions of contemporary reform contexts.

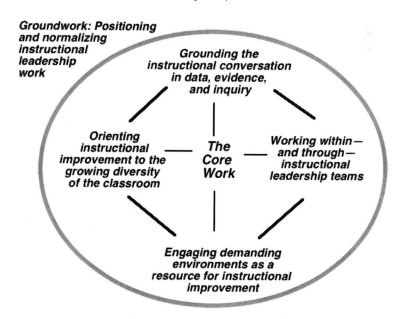

Figure 8.2 The new work of instructional leadership.

ADDRESSING THE GROWING DIVERSITY
OF THE CLASSROOM

As they build a school culture that expects and accepts instructional leadership work by various staff, school leaders take on particular challenges that contemporary schooling conditions present them. One such challenge lies at the intersection of an increasingly diverse student population and the moral imperative (rooted in state and local learning standards and accountability expectations) that *all* students will be helped to succeed (Louis, 2003).

The Nature of Diversity-Focused Instructional Leadership Work

In urban classrooms, where growing student diversity is keenly felt, instructional leaders find themselves helping teacher colleagues develop classroom practices that recognize diversity and help students succeed—students who bring different needs, prior learning, and backgrounds to school. This presents a different and inadequately understood challenge to instructional leadership, especially in schools with "histories of poor student achievement, and that are situated in communities with high levels of poverty, cultural diversity, and neighborhood crime" (Ylimaki, 2007, p. 11). In our own research, instructional leadership teams focused extensively on differentiating instruction to meet these needs and helping teachers visualize and assume culturally and linguistically responsive strategies adapted to the diverse learners they found in their classrooms. One principal described his approach in this way:

> Well, we started with a book club—actually we started with an idea of teachers trying to define what differentiated instruction really meant to them, and as I said, we came up with many different definitions, so then I introduced them to a book on differentiated learning, differentiated instructional strategies. And my challenge to everyone is to try at least one lesson a day so that as the year goes on, towards the end of this school year, most of our teachers will end up with 100 lessons that they've tried in a little toolbox going into next year.

This school leaders' work was in direct response to his teachers' recognition that they were facing a different student population. One teacher put it: "These students aren't the same as they used to be." A variety of responses to this situation were evident in the elementary, middle, and high schools we studied, among them:

- *Intensifying efforts to assess accurately and regularly what students know and are still struggling with,* and to help teachers use the results of these assessments in an immediate and flexible way to address students' learning needs (this approach relates closely to another dimension of instructional leadership discussed below).

- *Promoting cultural responsiveness,* by organizing the school to maximize its responsiveness to the full range of learners, and engaging teachers in conversation about cultural differences, multiple learning styles, and ways to build instruction around these differences.
- *Paying explicit attention to second language issues,* by highlighting the role that language backgrounds other than English might be playing in students' participation in schooling and classroom activity, and providing a support system for general education teachers who did not have specialized ESL or bilingual training.

These approaches do not exhaust the possibilities, but they capture a range of ways in which instructional leadership teams engaged questions of student diversity and learning needs, and helped teachers learn constructive approaches to addressing them. This view echoes a long established view that instructional leadership is likely to reflect the school's context, and, in fact, may be hard to understand absent a close examination of a variety of contextual conditions, as recently noted: "Effective leaders respond to the changing needs of their context. Indeed, in a very real sense, the leader's behaviors are shaped by the school context" (Hallinger, 2003, p. 346). In this spirit, instructional leadership in the diversifying context of contemporary schooling is adapting, and needs to adapt, if it is to offer meaningful guidance, direction, or support to classroom teachers.

What is New About an Instructional Leadership Focus on Diversity?

Classrooms in many parts of the United States have been racially, ethnically, and linguistically diverse for many decades, and the public educational system as a whole has long embraced enormous differences in students' social class and cultural backgrounds, though not always in close juxtaposition within the same classroom or school. But in urban schools or classrooms, if not in many settings, this diversity is increasing, especially in the growth of immigrant student populations who speak languages other than English at home—a group now representing 10% of the overall student population in this country (National Clearinghouse for English Language Acquisition, 2006) and growing more rapidly than any other segment of the U.S. student population (Freeman & Freeman, 2007). This fact and related conditions rooted in poverty, interracial conflict, and stressed communities confront the teachers and those who would support them with unprecedented challenges for which they are not generally well prepared. Add to that the contemporary imperative rooted in standards-based reform policy, which directs and compels schools to engage the growing diversity.

Clearly, the intensive focus on differentiation in response to student diversity stems from standards that insist that all students *will* learn to locally and state determined standards, the current embrace of mastery assumptions (all students *can* learn), and the series of incentives, sanctions, and practices that compel schools to take these commitments seriously (OECD, 2011). Prior case study research illustrates this idea at work in the principal's instructional leadership within an urban high-poverty elementary school (Ylimaki, 2007). There, the principal recognized the need for a more differentiated approach to her increasingly diverse student population and engaged others, including a group of teacher-run committees, in developing and promoting a more explicitly differentiated approach to teaching.

GROUNDING THE INSTRUCTIONAL CONVERSATION IN DATA AND EVIDENCE

As noted above, consideration of data (especially related to student performance) becomes a natural part of the response to student diversity and the desire to differentiate instruction. Various scholars have noted this aspect of certain forms of instructional leadership (e.g., Halverson et al., 2007; Reitzug et al., 2008; Ylimaki, 2007), extending the picture of related practices far beyond the traditional domain of principal supervision, in which summative and formative data have long been collected about teacher performance. Other studies, more directly focused on the use of data and evidence in schooling and school reform, have examined how school leadership, both individually exercised and in the collective context of collaborative data teams, brings data and evidence to bear on instructional improvement (e.g., Lachat & Smith, 2005; Wayman, Midgley, & Stringfield, 2007; Wayman & Stringfield, 2006). In the schools we studied, data and evidence played a prominent role, as in many aspects of the overall attempt to improve teaching practice and learning outcomes, and they figured prominently in the way learning-focused leadership was exercised.

The Nature of Evidence-Focused Instructional Leadership Work

As such, attempts to use data of various kinds quite naturally appeared in instructional leadership work, as the following principal explained about work done with school staff about common assessment:

...The teachers record those scores on grade level sheets that we then use. Just before you came, I met with the math instructional leadership specialist and we kind of went over some of the general trends that we saw in the September results, and she's got some sense of where she needs to be next. I don't know if the kids pointed it out to you, but we actually post the results. We have a data board that's very public, which has been great, because the kids are kind of involved in it, and it gets parents involved and we do that graphically. We break it down both by content area and by kind of question, so we report out the open response and multiple choice differently.

In this instance, data had become a medium of instructional leadership work on several levels: as a basis for principal and math instructional leadership specialist to identify what to focus improvement efforts on, as a tool for breaking down areas of strength and weakness in teaching and learning, and as a means of communicating progress (and areas for improvement) to students, staff, and parents. The visible data record of school performance in this instance can also be understood as a public device for underscoring areas of emphasis in the school's continuing efforts to get better.

The pervasive attention to the use of data in the sites we studied involved more than just a careful look at annual test scores and a resulting priority setting process. Instructional leadership teams were engaged in at least these other activities (see Portin et al., 2009):

- *Multiplying the forms of data that would be regularly considered by school staff in seeking to understand their practice.* Instructional leaders were helping teachers pay close attention to student work products, interviewing students and teachers, and surveying staff and parent perceptions of the school learning environment, alongside several forms of interim assessments.
- *Developing in-school "data systems."* Some were more elaborate than others, offering teachers immediate, cumulative access to information about each of their students, and about trends over time. (One school's solution was maintaining a "data binder" on each student, that centralized all relevant information about the student's progress.) Others were more "quick and dirty," offering a reference point for thinking more specifically about what was being taught, and how, to a particular student or group of students.
- *Enhancing the staff's data expertise.* Instructional leaders were helping to connect teachers' questions to challenges identified as part of the school's learning improvement agenda, as well as using data to initiate difficult conversations about what was working and what was not, which students were succeeding and which were not.
- *Creating regular occasions for data-informed conversations about instructional practices, and how they could be improved.* In some instances, this

conversation happened through ongoing structures, such as weekly grade-level or departmental planning meetings, and in others, through regular professional development or other interactions.

- *Promoting and modeling an inquiry culture.* School leaders sought to develop such cultures by posing questions and seeking to answer them through activities that approximated action research or less formal inquiry cycles. In the most elaborate forms of this practice, schools created inquiry teams, which carried out year-long inquiry activities targeted at the needs and possibilities for improving teaching and learning for designated segments of the student population. Less formally, instructional leaders made question asking a public habit.

What is New About Evidence-Focused Instructional Leadership

Ever since a wave of interest in diagnostic-prescriptive teaching in the 1970s (Arter & Jenkins, 1979) and debates over measurement-driven instruction in the 1980s (e.g., Bracey, 1987; Popham, 1987), school leaders and educational reformers have considered anchoring schooling to some measures of student performance and student learning needs. But the convergence of high-stakes accountability demands and the technological means for easy access and manipulation of data has created a working environment that presses for data-based practice in a more far-reaching and compelling way, as well as a huge opportunity for instructional leadership (Wayman, 2005). A broader context for evidence-based practice resides in the push over the last decade by the federal government to renew and strengthen the connections between educational practice and the findings of strong educational research. Paralleling this has been a noticeable increase in participatory research, teacher research (Cochran-Smith & Lytle, 1993), action research (e.g., Reason & Bradbury, 2001), the application of inquiry cycles to educational reform (e.g., Copland, 2003), and the development of various data-based practices in schools (e.g., Boudett, City, & Murnane, 2006). These developments all have set the stage for greater attention to evidence in many kinds of daily practice within schools. In particular, recent work on collaborative data use in schools underscores key roles for leadership in helping staff "calibrate" their respective understanding of data, developing a common focus tied to student learning, engaging teachers in instructional improvement, and creating technological supports for data-based inquiry (Wayman et al., 2007).

This emerging research and others have begun to recognize the impact on instructional leadership, as one research team observed:

> The press for data-driven decision making, then, is not a call for schools to begin to use data, but a challenge for leaders to reshape the central practices and cultures of their schools to react intentionally to the new kinds of data provided by external accountability systems. (Halverson et al., 2007, p. 161)

Related analyses of school leadership response to accountability pressures, including our own, position school leaders, especially the principal, as someone who can make strategic use of the data generated for accountability purposes to focus the instructional improvement conversation in the school (e.g., Knapp & Feldman, 2011).

WORKING WITHIN AND THROUGH INSTRUCTIONAL LEADERSHIP TEAMS

There is growing recognition in the literature on school-based instructional leadership that its long preoccupation with the school principal as the school's instructional leader has obscured the potential for *shared* instructional leadership, exercised through collaborative inquiry with teachers or other means, to more fully meet the school's improvement needs (Hallinger, 2003; Printy et al., 2009; Ylimaki, 2007). Related work on the nature of leadership practice as a more distributed phenomenon or "school capacity" (Coldren & Spillane, 2007; Heck & Hallinger, 2009; Lambert, 2003; Spillane, 2006) has helped to draw attention to the way multiple people in the school, working in concert (though not necessarily in explicit or close coordination) can and do contribute to the leadership of instructional improvement activities.

The Nature of Team-Based Instructional Leadership

As this emerging research and our own (Portin et al., 2009) suggests, instructional leadership is shared work. All of the schools we studied had more than one instructional leader, and they worked together in one or more team configurations to coordinate their practice, consider what they would do to help teachers improve their teaching, and problem solve the many issues that arose along the way. Teams included individuals occupying different full or part-time roles (some in administrative positions, others in teaching positions or instructional support roles of several kinds). In one large elementary school, we found the principal working with—and working through—a group that included assistant principals, content coaches, and teacher leaders in both formal and informal roles with a variety of different titles (assessment coordinators, inquiry team members). The challenge, then, for all those engaged in instructional leadership work within the school was to find sufficient common ground, joint understanding of where and how they wanted teachers to improve, and how to take advantage of their differing strengths in a common effort.

These developments have meant role changes for principals and teacher leaders alike. While they often still worked directly with some teachers in the building, principals more often found themselves leveraging their influence *through* the work of this instructional team, whose members offered teachers the more direct forms of support, guidance, and direction related to classroom improvement practices. On their part, the teacher leaders or other staff on the team formed a bridge between classroom and supervisory leaders, and between current instructional practice and the school or district learning improvement agenda. Together, the team members:

- *Worked on working as a team,* by making the idea of teamwork and a "team culture" a norm for their professional work, and even beyond them, a norm for the school as a whole.
- *Recognized and utilized the distribution of instructional and related expertise among team members,* who possessed differing knowledge and skills in content areas, grade levels, assessment, and data use.
- *Engaged in dialogue with each other about teaching and learning,* and in this "microcosm" developed approaches to, and occasions for, engaging teaching staff in the same or similar conversations.
- *Provided a support system for each others' efforts as instructional leaders*— as team members encountered challenges in their work (e.g., resistance from teachers, logistical complications, problems of instructional leadership practice) and as they experienced success.

What is New About Team-Based Instructional Leadership

Schools have long featured teams and team structures, and as such, a central concern of leadership has always been to maximize team functioning; a well-developed set of generic principles has evolved to characterize "the team leadership model" and associated practices (see Hill, 2007). But the proliferation and clustering of roles with specific school-wide *instructional* improvement responsibility does not have such a long history and is traceable to the increased press for demonstrable improvements in teaching practice, on the one hand, and a growing understanding of the potential power of professional communities as vehicles for new professional learning, on the other. Add to that increasing recognition of the school principal's limits as a singular instructional leader (Hallinger, 2003, 2005), coupled with the growing capacity of teacher leadership (Marks & Printy, 2003; Taylor, 2008), and the stage is set for a cadre of individuals within the school to take on the instructional leadership function. But to do so effectively creates new kinds of work for participants, who come to the instructional leadership team with relatively little experience in such an endeavor, differing expertise, and varied positions within the school. Studies have begun to recognize the "new demands" that principals face leading through other instructional leaders, and have begun to show in certain cases how school leaders might achieve the "synergistic interdependencies" and institutional support that an effective leadership distribution entails (Printy et al., 2009).

ENGAGING DEMANDING ENVIRONMENTS AS A RESOURCE

The final dimension of the new instructional leadership work in schools concerns the environment in which it takes place. Schools and classrooms exist in a particular policy context: a school district or local educational authority that is exerting its own pressures on schools to be better, within a state that creates standards and clear expectations for performance and improvement, and within a federal standards-based reform system that is pressuring schools year by year to show continuous improvement. And the communities served by schools offer their own unique configurations of resources and constraints that condition what school leaders feel compelled to do and able to accomplish. Each of these features of the school's context influence the district learning improvement agenda, how it instructionally guides the teaching and learning in schools, the kinds of assessment and accountability systems that pertain to schools, and the data practices that are encouraged or required. In short, school-based instructional leaders work within a demanding environment. It is a fact of their working lives that they must contend with, as noted in some research, a driving force for changes within their leadership practice:

> Accountability systems provide standards and incentives for schools to develop the instructional and assessment practices necessary to reach achievement standards. The new instructional leadership is a direct response to the demands of new accountability systems. (Halverson et al., 2007, p. 161)

The Nature of Instructional Leadership that Engages Demanding Environments

In responding to these environmental demands, school leaders are always tempted by several obvious default responses: treat the environment as an obstruction and look for ways to get around it or treat whatever cannot be avoided as a set of requirements and simply comply with them, as best one can. But beyond avoidance or compliance, school leaders can see the environment as a resource, a prompt for improvement activity, an occasion for getting things to happen in the school, and a source of tools for undertaking this work. In most of the schools we studied, instructional leaders took the latter course, leveraging environmental demands to further improvement work within the school.

They did so in several ways:

- *Internalizing external expectations for teaching and learning.* By embracing the districts' expectations for raising achievement, addressing equity issues, and teaching in more powerful ways, instructional leaders created school-based learning improvement agendas that melded what the outside world wanted of the school with what school staff felt most committed to. As one principal said, "The district's expectation is my expectation . . . and that's going to be a concerted effort by all of my administrative staff."
- *Taking advantage of discretion (where it was granted) and whatever assistance or resources were offered by district leaders* who were in a position to support them in their professional learning as instructional leaders or to help them access the kind of expertise that was needed.
- *Building and exploiting peer networks.* Instructional leadership team members were often accessing peer networks and job-alike colleagues across the district, as a source of ideas, moral support, and guidance. District central office staff and new structures within the district sometimes facilitated these peer-to-peer connections (see Honig, Copland, Rainey, Lorton, & Newton, 2010).
- *Treating accountability requirements and associated data and tools as occasions for conversation and focused improvement work.* The most obvious demands of the outside world, embodied in measures of students and school performance, offered instructional leadership teams numerous occasions for focusing teachers on particular areas and aspects of teaching practice, where improvements were needed.
- *Leveraging external expectations in support of their own commitments to serve students.* Finally, they used demands of the environment as support for the moral argument that the school needed to serve schools better.

A school in New York City illustrates the dynamic at work. This small high school serving a linguistically diverse student population found a number of issues in their bilingual curriculum and a lack of connection across grades and with both state standards and district assessments. The principal took advantage of the autonomy granted her by the district to contract with a third-party organization to help them in a curriculum mapping exercise to link subject areas with a broader articulated picture of the school's mission, the district and the state standards. The principal said,

> With the differentiated instruction and the curriculum mapping, teachers are now talking, teachers are meeting more to see how they can do more of an integrated curriculum, but also they are able to have conversations about kids. If I tell you, 'Okay, John is really struggling in ESL,' and you are the Native Language Arts teacher and I found out he's really struggling in native language too, then we know that it's not just because he's not ready to move forward.

At the hands of this instructional leader, the state and district requirements became an occasion for engaging and advancing the instructional conversation among teachers, and for moving toward a more functionally integrated set of practices within and across classrooms.

What is New About Instructional Leadership that Engages Demanding Environments

As the high-stakes accountability environment has grown and intensified across the last decade following the passage of *No Child Left Behind* legislation, the environment of schooling has become more demanding, and its demands are frequently criticized for making education more limited and limiting for students who have been historically underserved (e.g., Darling-Hammond, 2007; Sunderman, Kim, & Orfield, 2005). School leaders working at the intersection of the school's teaching and the expectations of the larger system surrounding the school—both principals and other members of instructional leadership teams—can manage this intersection in various ways. In our research, teacher leaders, for example, acted as a conduit between system expectations and the classroom and provided a two-way flow of information between classrooms and supervisory leaders, while helping teachers visualize ways to make their practice more standards-based (Portin et al., 2009). As they did so, they took advantage of accountability demands as an occasion for prompting teachers to consider new possibilities for their practice. Their work gives new meaning to research that has established important links between the way leaders lead and contextual demands and conditions (Hallinger, 2003), only here a broader point is being established than a "contingent" understanding of leadership as adapted to its immediate circumstances: rather, the emerging image of instructional leadership underscores its nature as accountable practice, and the opportunity that accountability demands may offer to the exercise to instructional leadership (see Knapp & Feldman, 2011).

HOW THE FOUR DIMENSIONS
OF THE NEW WORK CONNECT

As the above discussion has already suggested, the new work of instructional leadership is interconnected in many ways. The growing diversity of the classroom, for example, sets the stage for a more differentiated approach to teaching practice and the instructional leadership practices that can support teaching practice. This situation prompts the use of data and evidence in new ways, as do specific requirements of the demanding environment. These demands—along with the tools and the data that accompany them—create opportunities to reflect on practice, reconsider teaching and curriculum, and reflect on ways to improve the school experience for a range of students. The situation also offers more concrete ways to examine the progress and needs of individual children. These opportunities lend themselves to consideration in teams, starting with whatever instructional leadership teams are established within the school and including other teams in which teaching staff participate (among them, data or inquiry teams, grade/year-level teams or department-based teams, school planning teams). Those who exercise instructional leadership—and do so collaboratively—are in position to energize, focus, support, and otherwise guide the interconnections between these dimensions of leadership.

CONCLUDING REFLECTIONS

We offer these assertions about the new work of instructional leadership fully recognizing that they grow out of our own and others' study of leadership work in United States schools. But a burgeoning literature on "leadership for learning" around the world (see Townsend & MacBeath, 2011 for a wide-ranging compilation of this work) as well as work specifically focused on instructional leadership (e.g., Higgins & Bonne, 2011; Southworth, 2002) would suggest that many, if not most, of the dynamics we have described are manifesting themselves to some degree in other national contexts. In many countries, for example, the policy environment is demanding greater evidence of accountable practice, and those who support teachers' work and who assume overall leadership responsibility in the school are searching for ways to respond to these demands. Similarly, as the ongoing work of the Program for International Student Assessment (PISA) has focused on international differences, it has also illustrated that differential achievement influenced by cultural factors and social conditions is a shared challenge around the world. In the U.S. context, these differences are spoken of as the "achievement gap," but conditions that differentiate student learning outcomes are common in many countries. In each, the work that leaders and systems do to support improved pedagogical practice addresses this challenge. As we have illustrated in this chapter in the U.S. context, a key lever for change has been the reorientation of leadership activity that brings particular concerns and tools to the improvement of instruction.

We also acknowledge that our own work has investigated instructional leadership dynamics in urban school systems, under conditions that may be causing or accentuating the four dimensions we have described. Related findings from other studies, however, which have been carried out in a wider range of settings, suggest wider applicability for these ideas. For example, in one study that offered clear indications of two of the four dimensions at work (Halverson et al., 2007), the four study sites were selected to include a rural and suburban school as well as two urban schools, and not all of these schools served a high-poverty clientele.

In all these settings, the four new dimensions of instructional leadership can express themselves in a wide variety of ways. Instructional leaders can thus focus on diversity, work through data and evidence, operate within and through instructional leadership teams, and take advantage of environmental demands and resources in both direct and indirect ways, emphasizing "linear," "organic," or other styles of instructional leadership (Rietzug & West, 2011), with various mental maps (Ruff & Shoho, 2005), and integrating transformational leadership with more classically defined instructional leadership functions (Printy et al., 2009). The key idea is that the range and complexity of this work has grown, and leaders are finding ways to do it with each other and in closer relation to their evolving context for schooling.

It remains an open question how, and how successfully, school-based instructional leadership will continue to be exercised in an era of extreme fiscal austerity, such as the one currently facing schools in many national contexts. Only time will tell. But the evolution of leadership practice is already well under way, with a great deal of new learning about this work by many school-based staff, not just school principals. As such, the expansion of leadership practice we and others have been documenting is likely to continue.

NOTES

1. This chapter derives, in part, from *The Study of Leadership For Learning Improvement*, a multiple-strand investigation carried out by the Center for the Study of Teaching & Policy at the University of Washington, with support from The Wallace Foundation. We acknowledge the contributions of other research team members to the analyses and conclusions reported here, which reflect

those of the authors and not necessarily The Foundation. We are particularly indebted to other members of the study team whose efforts contributed to the insights reported here—in particular, Scott Dareff, Sue Feldman, Felice Russell, Catherine Samuelson, and Theresa Ling Yeh. For an overview of the full multi-strand investigation, see Knapp et al. (2010), *Learning-focused leadership and leadership support: Meaning and practice in urban systems.* Seattle WA: Center of the Study of Teaching & Policy, University of Washington. This document and final reports for each study strand appear on the Center website (www.ctpweb.org) and the Wallace Foundation Knowledge Center (www.wallacefoundation.org).

2. See Portin et al., 2009, pp. 110–120 for a more detailed description of the study's design and methods.

REFERENCES

Arter, J. A. & Jenkins, J. R. (1979). Differential diagnostic-prescriptive teaching: A critical appraisal. *Review of Educational Research, 49,* 517–555.

Berliner, D. C. (2009, March). *Poverty and potential: Out-of-school factors and school success.* Policy brief. East Lansing, MI: The Great Lakes Center for Education Research & Practice.

Blase, J. & Blase, J. (1999). Principals' instructional leadership and teacher development: Teachers' perspectives. *Educational Administration Quarterly, 35*(3), 349–378.

Boudett, K. P., City, E. A., & Murnane, R. J. (2006). *Data-wise: A step-by-step guide to using assessment results to improve teaching and learning.* Cambridge, MA: Harvard Education Press.

Bracey, G. W. (1987). Measurement-driven instruction: Catchy phrase, dangerous practice. *Phi Delta Kappa, 68,* 683–686.

Bredeson, P. (2009, November). Distributed instructional leadership in urban high schools: Transforming the work of principals and department chairs through professional development. Presented at the annual meeting of the University Council on Educational Administration. Anaheim, CA.

Bryk, A. S., Sebring, P. B., Allensworth, E., Luppescu, S., & Easton, J. Q. (2010). *Organizing schools for improvement: Lessons from Chicago.* Chicago and London: University of Chicago press.

City, E. A., Elmore, R. F., Fiarman, S. E., & Teitel, L. (2009). *Instructional rounds in education.* Cambridge, MA: Harvard Education Press.

Cochran-Smith, M. & Lytle, S. (1993). *Inside/outside: Teacher research and knowledge.* New York, NY: Teachers College Press.

Cohen, D. K., Raudenbush, S. H., & Ball, D. (2003). Resources, instruction, and research. *Educational Evaluation & Policy Analysis, 25*(2), 119–142.

Coldren, A. M. & Spillane, J. P. (2007). Making connections to teaching practice: The role of boundary practices in instructional leadership. *Educational Policy, 21*(2), 369–396.

Copland, M. (2003). Leadership of inquiry: Building and sustaining capacity for school improvement. *Educational Evaluation and Policy Analysis, 25*(4), 375–396.

Copland, M. A. & Knapp, M. S. (2006). *Connecting leadership with learning: A framework for reflection, action, and planning.* Alexandria, VA: Association for Supervision and Curriculum Development.

Darling-Hammond, L. (2007). Race, inequality and educational accountability: The irony of "No Child Left Behind." *Race, Ethnicity and Education, 10*(3), 245–260.

Drago-Severson, E. (2007). Helping teachers learn: Principals as professional development leaders. *Teachers College Record, 109*(1), 70–125.

Freeman, Y. & Freeman, D. (2007). Four keys for school success for elementary English learners. In J. Cummins & C. Davison (Eds.), *International Handbook of English Language Teaching* (Vol. 1, pp. 349–364). New York: Springer

Glickman, C. (2002). *Leadership for learning.* Alexandria VA: Association for Supervision and Curriculum Development.

Graczewski, G., Knudsen, J., & Holtzman, D. J. (2009). Instructional leadership in practice: What does it look like, and what influence does it have? *Journal of Education for Students Placed at Risk, 14,* 72–96.

Grossman, P., Stodolsky, S. S., & Knapp, M. S. (2004). *Making subject matter part of the equation: The intersection of policy and content—An Occasional Paper.* Seattle, WA: Center for the Study of Teaching & Policy, University of Washington.

Grossman, P. & Stodolsky, S. S. (1995). Content as context: The role of school subjects in secondary school teaching. *Educational Researcher, 24*(8), 5–11.

Hallinger, P. (2003). Leading educational change: Reflections on the practice of instructional and transformational leadership. *Cambridge Journal of Education, 33*(3), 329–352.

Hallinger, P. (2005). Instructional leadership and the school principal: A passing fancy that refuses to fade away. *Leadership & Policy in Schools, 4*(3), 221–239.

Hallinger, P. & Heck, R. (1996). Reassessing the principal's role in school effectiveness: A review of empirical evidence. *Educational Administration Quarterly, 32*(1), 5–44.

Hallinger, P. & Heck, R. (2010). Collaborative leadership and school improvement: Understanding the impact on school capacity and student learning. *School Leadership & Management, 30*(2), 95–110.

Hallinger, P. & Murphy, J. (1985). Assessing the instructional leadership behavior of principals. *Elementary School Journal, 86*(2), 217–248.

Halverson, R., Grigg, J., Prichett, R., & Thomas, C. (2007). The new instructional leadership: Creating data-driven instructional systems in school. *Journal of School Leadership, 17*(2), 159–194.

Heck, R. & Hallinger, P. (2009). Assessing the contribution of distributed leadership to school improvement and growth in math achievement. *American Educational Research Journal, 46*(3), 659–689.

Higgins, J. & Bonne, L. (2011). Configurations of instructional leadership enactments that promote the teaching and learning of mathematics in a New Zealand Elementary School. *Educational Administration Quarterly, 47*(5), 794–825.

Hill, S. E. K. (2007). Team leadership. In P. G. Northouse, *Leadership: Theory and practice* (4th ed., pp. 207–236). Thousand Oaks, CA: SAGE.

Honig, M., Copland, M., Rainey, L., Lorton, J. A., & Newton, M. (2010). *Central office transformation for district-wide teaching and learning improvement.* Seattle, WA: Center for the Study of Teaching & Policy, University of Washington.

Knapp, M. S. & Feldman, S. (2011). *Internal response to external accountability: The role of leadership in urban schools.* Paper presented at the annual meeting of the American Educational Research Association. New Orleans, LA: April 7–12, 2011.

Knapp, M. S. & Meadows, J. L. (2005). Policy-practice connections in state standards-based reform. In A. Datnow, K. Leithwood, & N. Bascia (Eds.), *International handbook of educational policy* (pp. 133–152). Dordrecht, The Netherlands: Kluwer Press.

Knapp, M. S., Copland, M. A., Honig, M. I., Plecki, M. L., & Portin, B. S. (2010). *Learning-focused leadership and leadership support: Meaning and practice in urban systems.* Seattle, WA: Center for the Study of Teaching & Policy, University of Washington.

Knapp, M. S., Copland, M. A., Plecki, M. L., Portin, B. S., & Colleagues. (2006). *Leading, learning, and leadership support.* Seattle, WA: Center for the Study of Teaching & Policy, University of Washington.

Lachat, M. A. & Smith, S. (2005). Practices that support data use in urban high schools. *Journal of Education for Students Placed at Risk, 10*(3), 333–349.

Lambert, L. (2003). *Leadership capacity for lasting school improvement.* Alexandria VA: Association for Supervision and Curriculum Development.

Leithwood, K. & Duke, D. L. (1999). A century's quest to understand school leadership. In J. Murphy & K. S. Louis (Eds.), *Handbook of Research on Educational Administration* (pp. 45–72). San Francisco, CA: Jossey-Bass.

Leithwood, K. & Jantzi, D. (2008). Linking leadership to student learning: The contributions of leader efficacy. *Educational Administration Quarterly, 44*(4), 496–528.

Leithwood, K. & Mascall, B. (2008). Collective leadership effects on student achievement. *Educational Administration Quarterly, 44*(4), 529–561.

Leithwood, K., Louis, K. S., Anderson, S., & Wahlstrom, K. (2004). *How leadership influences student learning.* New York: The Wallace Foundation.

Lezotte, L. W. (1994). The nexus of instructional leadership and effective schools. *The School Administrator, 51*(6), 20–23.

Louis, K. S. (2003). School leaders facing real change: Shifting geography, uncertain paths. *Cambridge Journal of Education, 33*(3), 371–382.

MacBeath, J. & Dempster, N. (Eds.). (2009). *Connecting leadership and learning: Principles for practice.* London and New York: Routledge.

Marks, H. M. & Printy, S. M. (2003). Principal leadership and school performance: An integration of transformational and instructional leadership. *Education Administration Quarterly, 39*(3), 370–397.

McLaughlin, M. W. & Talbert, J. E. (1993). Contexts that matter for teaching and learning. Stanford, CA: Center for Research on the Context of Secondary School Teaching, Stanford University.

Merriam, S. B. (2009). *Qualitative research: A guide to design and implementation.* San Francisco, CA: Jossey-Bass.

Mraz, M., Algozzine, B., & Watson, P. (2008). Perceptions and expectations of roles and responsibilities of literacy coaching. *Literacy Research and Instruction, 47,* 141–157.

Murphy, J., Elliott, S. N., Goldring, E., & Porter, A. (2006). *Learning-centered leadership: A conceptual foundation.* New York; The Wallace Foundation.

National Clearinghouse for English Language Acquisition. (2006). *The growing numbers of limited English proficient students: 1993/94–2003/04.* Washington, DC: Office of English Language Acquisition, U.S. Department of Education.

Neufeld, B. & Roper, D. (2003). *Coaching: A strategy for developing instructional capacity.* Washington DC: Aspen Institute Program on Education and the Annenberg Institute for School Reform.

OECD (Organisation for Economic Cooperation and Development). (2011). Against the Odds: Disadvantaged Students Who Succeed in School. Paris, France: Author.

Ogawa, R. & Bossert. S. (2000). Leadership as an organizational quality. In M. Fullan (Ed.), *The Jossey-Bass reader on educational leadership* (pp. 38–58). San Francisco: Jossey-Bass.

Popham, W. J. (1987). The merits of measurement-driven instruction. *Phi Delta Kappan, 68,* 679–682.

Portin, B. S., DeArmond, M., Gundlach, L., & Schneider, P. (2003). *Making sense of leading schools: A national study of the principalship.* Seattle, WA: Center on Reinventing Public Education, University of Washington.

Portin, B. S., Knapp, M. S., Dareff, S., Feldman, S., Russell, F., Samuelson, C., & Yeh, T. L.. (2009). *Leadership for learning improvement in urban schools.* Seattle, WA: Center for the Study of Teaching & Policy, University of Washington.

Printy, S. (2008). Leadership for learning: A community of practice perspective. *Education Administration Quarterly, 44*(2), 187–226.

Printy, S., Marks, H., & Bowers, A. (2009). Integrated leadership: How principals and teachers share transformational and instructional influence. *Journal of School Leadership, 19*(5), 504–532.

Reason, P. & Bradbury, H. (Eds.). (2001). *Handbook of action research: Participative inquiry and practice.* Thousand Oaks, CA: SAGE.

Reitzug, U. C. & West, D. L. (2011). A developmental framework for instructional leadership. In T. Townsend & J. MacBeath (Eds.), *International handbook of leadership for learning* (pp. 165–185). Dordrecht, The Netherlands: Springer.

Reitzug, U. C., West, D. L., & Angel, R. (2008). Conceptualizing instructional leadership: The voices of principals. *Education & Urban Society, 40,* 694–714.

Resnick, L. & Glennan, T. (2002). Leadership for learning: A theory of action for urban school districts. In A. Hightower, M. S. Knapp, J. Marsh, & M. W. McLaughlin (Eds.), *School districts and instructional renewal* (pp. 160–172). New York: Teachers College Press.

Robinson, V. M. J., Lloyd, C. A., & Rowe, K. J. (2008). The impact of student leadership on student outcomes: An analysis of the differential effects of leadership types. *Educational Administration Quarterly, 44,* 635–674.

Ruff, W. G. & Shoho, A. R. (2005). Understanding instructional leadership through mental models of three elementary school principals. *Educational Administration Quarterly, 41,* 554–577.

Smith, W. F. & Andrews, R. L. (1989). *Instructional leadership: How principals make a difference.* Alexandria, VA: Association for Supervision and Curriculum Development.

Southworth, G. (2002). Instructional leadership in schools: Reflections and empirical evidence. *School Leadership and Management, 22*(1), 73–91.

Spillane, J. (2006). *Distributed leadership.* San Francisco: Jossey-Bass.

Spillane, J., Diamond, J., & Jita, L. (2003). Leading instruction: The distribution of leadership for instruction. *Journal of Curriculum Studies, 35*(5), 533–543.

Stoll, L., Fink, D., & Earl, L. (2003). *It's about learning (and it's about time): What's in it for schools?* London & New York: Routledge Falmer.

Sunderman, G., Kim, J., & Orfield, G. (2005). *NCLB meets school realities.* Thousand Oaks, CA: Corwin Press.

Taylor, J. E. (2008). Instructional coaching: The state of the art. In M. M. Mangin & S. R. Stoelinga (Eds.), *Effective teacher leadership: Using research to inform and reform* (pp. 10–35). New York: Teachers College Press.

Townsend, T. & MacBeath, J. (2011). *International handbook of leadership for learning.* Dordrecht, The Netherlands: Springer.

Valenzuela, A. (1999). *Subtractive schooling: U.S.-Mexican youth and the politics of caring.* Albany, NY: State University of New York Press.

Wayman, J. C. (2005). Involving teachers in data-driven decision-making: Using computer data systems to support teacher inquiry and reflection. *Journal of Education for Students Placed at Risk, 10*(3), 295–308.

Wayman, J. C. & Stringfield, S. (2006). Technology-supported involvement of entire faculties in examination of student data for instructional improvement. *American Journal of Education, 112*(4), 549–571.

Wayman, J. C., Midgley, S., & Stringfield, S. (2007). Leadership for data-based decision-making: Collaborative educator teams. In A. B. Danzig, K. M. Borman, B. A. Jones, & W. F. Wright (Eds.), *Learner-centered leadership: Research, policy, & practice* (pp. 189–206). Mahwah, NJ: Lawrence Erlbaum Associates.

Ylimaki, R. (2007). Instructional leadership in challenging U. S. schools. *International Studies in Educational Administration, 35*(3), 11–19.

York-Barr, J. & Duke, K. (2004). What do we know about teacher leadership? Findings from two decades of scholarship. *Review of Educational Research, 74*(3), 255–316.

ABOUT THE CONTRIBUTORS

Bruce G. Barnett is a professor in the Educational Leadership and Policy Studies Department at the University of Texas at San Antonio, having entered the professorate in 1987. Besides developing and delivering master's, certification, and doctoral programs, his professional interests include: educational leadership preparation programs, particularly cohort-based learning and school–university partnerships; mentoring and coaching; reflective practice; leadership for school improvement; and the realities of beginning principals and assistant principals. Recently, he has become involved in international research and program development, co-authoring books on school improvement; researching mentoring and coaching programs operating around the world; and presenting workshops in Australia, New Zealand, England, Ireland, Hong Kong, and Canada. Bruce was appointed as the Associate Director of International Affairs for the University Council for Educational Administration. His role is to increase international cooperation and partnerships, encourage international memberships in UCEA, and develop international research and learning opportunities.

Jennifer Crawford is an assistant professor of Clinical Education in the Rossier School of Education at the University of Southern California. Crawford's long-term research agenda centers on how teachers navigate institutionally inscribed challenges to provide all students with opportunities to learn and develop in classrooms, schools, communities, and society. Her research interests include social and cultural analysis of schools, equity pedagogy, and bridging critical social science theory to teacher practice in the Americas.

The Changing Nature of Instructional Leadership in the 21st Century, pages 215–219
Copyright © 2012 by Information Age Publishing
215

Daniel L. Duke is a professor of Educational Leadership and Policy Studies at the University of Virginia. After teaching high school social studies and serving as a secondary school administrator, he embarked on a career in higher education. For over three decades he has taught courses on educational leadership, organizational change, and school reform as well as conducting research on various aspects of public schools. After serving on the faculties of Lewis and Clark College and Stanford University, he came to the University of Virginia as chair of Educational Leadership and Policy Studies. Duke founded and directed the Thomas Jefferson Center for Educational Design and helped establish the Darden-Curry Partnership for Leaders in Education (PLE), a unique enterprise involving the Curry School of Education and the Darden Graduate School of Business Administration. He serves as research director for the PLE. A prolific writer, Dan has authored or co-authored 27 books and several hundred scholarly articles, monographs, chapters, and reports. His most recent books include *The Challenges of Educational Change* (2004), *Education Empire: The Evolution of an Excellent Suburban School System* (2005), *Teachers' Guide to School Turnarounds* (2007), and *The Little School System that Could: Transforming a City School District* (2008). A highly regarded consultant, Dan has worked with over 150 school systems, state agencies, foundations, and governments across the United States and abroad. He has served as president of the University Council for Educational Administration and was chosen as Professor of the Year at the Curry School of Education.

Erica Hamilton is a practitioner-researcher with an interest in school-site leadership, particularly within schools that are attempting to provide equitable access for all students to an education that prepares them for both college and career. In 2011, she completed her doctorate at the UCLA Graduate School of Information Studies and Education. Her research and dissertation focused on leadership in linked learning schools (schools that prepare students for both college and career). After graduation, Erica returned to south Los Angeles to work as a linked learning coach, supporting high school leaders and teachers in the implementation of linked learning.

Ronald H. Heck is a professor of Educational Administration at the University of Hawaii at Manoa. He received his doctorate in organizations and policy from the University of California at Santa Barbara. Previously, he was an elementary, middle, and high school teacher, as well as a curriculum coordinator in Ventura County, California. He also was a professor at California State University, Long Beach. Besides working in the Educational Administration master's and doctoral programs at the University of Hawaii, his professional interests include leadership and school improvement, assessment of administrator and teacher performance, educational policy, and quantitative modeling. Ron's research has appeared in *Educational Admin-*

*istration Quarterly, Journal of Educational Administration, Educational Evalua-
tion and Policy Analysis, School Effectiveness and School Improvement, Educational
Management and Leadership, American Journal of Education, American Educational Research Journal, Organization Science,* and *The Leadership Quarterly.* He
has also co-authored several books on multilevel modeling.

Khairan Indriani is a program development advisor with experiences in
education capacity building, monitoring, and evaluation, mostly in Indonesia. She holds a B.A. in economics from Syiah Kuala University, Indonesia, and received her M.Ed. in education administration from Texas A&M
University. Her work is focused on the development of education quality,
policies, and accountability system initiatives in developing countries. She
also serves as a teacher trainer and education specialist within Indonesian
communities.

Michael S. Knapp is a professor of Educational Leadership and Policy Studies and director of the Center for the Study of Teaching and Policy in the
University of Washington College of Education. He focuses his teaching
and research on educational leadership and policymaking, school and
school system reform, the professional learning of teachers and administrators, and methods of inquiry and policy analysis. In recent years, Michael's
work has probed the meaning and forms of "learning-focused leadership"
in schools, districts, and state systems of education. While considering various settings and applications, his work pays special attention to the education of disenfranchised populations, mathematics and science education,
and the professional development of educators. He has written extensively
about his research, including eight books. Some of these are *School Districts
and Instructional Renewal* (2002), *Self-Reflective Renewal in Schools* (2003), and
*Connecting Leadership with Learning: A Framework for Reflection, Planning, and
Action* (2006).

Chad R. Lochmiller is an assistant professor in the College of Education at
Washington State University. His research and teaching interests relate to
the fields of educational leadership, education policy, and school finance.
Chad's research primarily focuses on federal, state, district, and university
efforts to develop educational leaders' capacity for instructional leadership.

Simangele T. Mkhwanazi is a doctoral student in Educational Leadership
and Policy Studies in the University of Washington College of Education,
with a research focus on teacher professional development in education
reform context, especially within developing nations. Specifically, she is in-
terested in issues that arise in teachers' professional learning as they try to
improve their quality of learning and classroom practice. Having worked
as a teacher in impoverished settings, she seeks to understand the profes-

sional development challenges that teachers encounter in such settings, and the ways that leadership, policy, and support strategies may address these challenges.

Gary R. O'Mahony is formerly a project director at the Australian Principals Centre where he was instrumental in implementing a range of professional career development programs for novice and experienced principals. His doctoral research centered on adult learning and socialization of Victorian beginning principals, and his research has been used in school systems in the U.S. and UK. He also has been a primary school principal, a state government senior project manager for principal professional development, and a consultant with a range of professional education consultancy groups. Gary is the director of his own consultancy company, O'Mahony & Associates Consulting, which provides state-based and regional programs in leadership for aspirant leaders, principals, and school teams. He has conducted international research and program development; co-authored books on school improvement; published articles on mentoring and coaching programs operating around the world; and presented workshops in Australia, the United States, New Zealand, and Canada. He presently facilitates the Bastow Leadership Program in training teachers in numeracy coaching and works with Hawker Brownlow Professional Learning Solutions in assisting schools to become professional learning communities.

Bradley S. Portin is the director of the Education Program and professor at the University of Washington, Bothell. A former public school principal, he has spent the last decade focusing on current roles of school principals and teacher leaders, and how roles are changing to meet learning needs for all students. In addition, he has been co-principal investigator for two Wallace Foundation-funded studies and has co-authored a number of monographs, including Portin, Knapp, Dareff, Feldman, Russell, Samuelson, & Yeh (2009), *Leadership or Learning Improvement in Urban Schools*. Bradley maintains extensive links with researchers internationally in their efforts to expand preparation, support, and research for school leaders.

Steven Rose is an international development advisor with extensive experience in educational leadership capacity building and monitoring and evaluation in the Pacific and South-East Asian regions. The focus of his work is on the development and implementation of school improvement and accountability policies, practices, and initiatives within developing countries. He also has extensive experience in working with indigenous Aboriginal communities in remote central and northern Australia and has over 30 years experience as a teacher, administrator, capacity builder and evaluator of education and community leadership and management programs.

Alan R. Shoho is a professor of Educational Leadership and Policy Studies at the University of Texas at San Antonio, where he has been for the past 18 years. He has been a provost fellow at UTSA. His research focuses on aspiring principals and assistant principals, high school social processes, and organizational cultures. Alan has published in a variety of venues including *Leadership and Policy in Schools, Educational Administration Quarterly, Journal of School Leadership, Journal of Educational Administration, The High School Journal,* and *The International Journal of Educational Management.* His recent publications include a comprehensive literature review on assistant principals and research on the challenges and experiences of new principals. In 2010, he served as the president for the University Council for Educational Administration. He earned his Ed.D. at Arizona State University, M.Ed. at the University of Hawaii, and B.S. in Electrical Engineering at California State University at Fullerton, whereupon he worked as an electrical engineer at Rockwell International designing gyroscope guidance systems for intercontinental ballistic missiles (ICBMs). Alan subsequently taught high school mathematics in Hawaii before moving into higher education. He teaches graduate courses in educational leadership including introduction to school administration, instructional supervision, principal internship, principles of ethical leadership, and a doctoral proseminar.

Autumn Tooms Cyprès is the director of the Center for Educational Leadership at the University of Tennessee. She began her career as a biology/chemistry teacher and school administrator at the elementary, middle, and high school levels in Phoenix, Arizona. She is the past president of the University Council for Educational Administration, and her research has centered on the politics of school leadership and school reform with an area of emphasis on the principalship. Autumn's primary area of interest is centered on building bridges between schools, those who lead schools, and those who prepare aspiring leaders. In addition to her books, Autumn's work can be found in journals such as *Educational Administration Quarterly, Kappan, Educational Leadership, The Journal of Cases in Educational Leadership, Education Policy, School Leadership and Management,* and *The Journal of School Leadership.*

Luana Zellner is an assistant professor in the Department of Educational Leadership and Counseling at Sam Houston State University, Huntsville, Texas. She holds a Ph.D. in curriculum and instruction from Texas A&M University. Her research and publications focus on administration of change in educational settings, transformational school leadership, and effective leadership training. She has over 30 years of experience as a special education teacher, program evaluator, and professor in leadership studies.

CPSIA information can be obtained at www.ICGtesting.com
Printed in the USA
BVOW042028091212

307689BV00004B/95/P

9 781617 359385